THE VARIETIES OF
NEW TESTAMENT RELIGION

The Varieties of New Testament Religion

By

ERNEST F. SCOTT, D.D.

NEW YORK

CHARLES SCRIBNER'S SONS

1944

PREFACE

THE NEW TESTAMENT has commonly been regarded as a uniform book, made up of a number of writings which are yet in
full agreement. For many centuries this was never questioned,
and texts were collected from all the writings without distinction
in support of every approved doctrine. Any suggestion that there
might be inconsistencies and contradictions in this fundamental
book was construed as an attack on the Christian faith. This attitude has now been abandoned. It is freely acknowledged by all
modern scholars that various types of teaching are represented in
the New Testament, but the idea still persists that they are closely
related, and attempts are constantly made to fit them together
into a single pattern. In the view of the present author this is
a mistaken effort and cannot but lead to many false judgments.
It is unjust to the New Testament writers, who are measured by
an arbitrary standard, and are condemned when they adopt some
other. It is unjust to the later Christian development, which is
conceived in many of the histories as a gradual departure from
the original faith, although the chief endeavour, in orthodoxy and
heresy alike, was to lay fuller emphasis on genuine New Testament ideas. Above all, the effort to harmonise New Testament
teaching does an injustice to Christianity itself, which is identified
with one given form of belief, while it embraces many. Freedom
of thought belongs to its very substance, and has done so from the
beginning. We have been fighting a great war in order to ensure
that various types of culture should have room to exist within the
same civilisation. It is at least equally important that different

v

modes of thinking should have the right to maintain themselves in the one religion. They are all legitimate and, if Christianity is fully to unfold its message, they are all necessary. This, in the author's view, was the position of the primitive church, as we know it from the New Testament. He has tried to show how each of the writers has made his own approach to the gospel, and has understood it differently from the others. All these interpretations have found their place, side by side, in the New Testament. It is the authoritative book of our religion, not because it lays down a fixed doctrine to which all must conform, but because it allows for a wide diversity of opinion. There are many signs today of a growing movement towards church unity, and with this movement the author is in the fullest sympathy. He cannot but feel, however, that in the desire for unity things that are more important may be sacrificed. Liberty is inherent in the Christian faith, and liberty always makes for difference. If the church is ever to be truly united, it must leave men free to differ. It must take its stand on no formal creed but on the New Testament, which lends its sanction impartially to many varieties of thought.

E. F. SCOTT.

August, 1943.

CONTENTS

THE VARIETIES OF
NEW TESTAMENT RELIGION

CHAPTER I

DIFFERENCE AND UNITY IN THE NEW TESTAMENT

THE CHURCH has always looked to the New Testament as its final court of appeal. Differences arise on almost every question of doctrine and practice, and cannot be settled by any process of argument. But behind the conflicting judgments there is always the word of the New Testament. For all sects and creeds this book is authoritative. It comes to us from the first age when Jesus was still a living memory, and the men who wrote it were endued with the Spirit. The aim of every controversy is to discover the verdict of the New Testament, which expresses the mind of Christ.

This verdict, however, has always proved indecisive. Christians have indeed been conscious that amidst all their differences they have the same religion, "one Lord, one faith, one baptism," and it is the New Testament which keeps them mindful of their brotherhood. But in their understanding of the common religion they are widely at variance. The history of the church in the early centuries is one of incessant conflict, in which all parties relied on the New Testament but were never able to reach agreement. In our own day the church is divided into hundreds of communities, opposed to one another but all professing the faith of the New Testament. This division may be due to many causes, but the ultimate one is the New Testament itself. The book which unites all Christians has also done more than anything else to

I

separate them. It is full of inconsistencies, and lends its support to almost every variety of opinion. There has never yet been a heretic who could not take his stand on some text of the New Testament; his opponents might answer him by others of a very different tenor, but they could not deny that on his own ground he was right.

No book, indeed, could be less fitted to serve as a touch-stone for orthodox belief. We possess it, thanks to modern printing, in a compact volume of no great size, with a title which covers all its contents. The illusion is thus created that while it falls into a number of sections it is a single work, and that each part of it must have a close relation to the whole. It is assumed that in this book the early church addresses us with a common voice, and declares, by the inspiration of the Spirit, what all Christians must believe. Such a view, however, is manifestly out of keeping with the facts. The New Testament is not a single book but a miscellany. It is made up of a number of writings which, for the most part, have nothing to do with each other. The writers were men of different minds and interests; they were scattered over a period of about a century, during which all conditions were changing; they wrote for various circles of readers, and adapted their teaching to the special needs and problems which happened at the time to be most urgent. In a work of this kind it is vain to look for any uniformity. The New Testament doctrines have become blended in our minds, so that they all seem to hang together; but the unity we find in them is that of a composite photograph, which does not correspond, when taken as a whole, with any definite object. Our religion is derived from the New Testament, but the elements of it have been combined by an artificial process. No New Testament writer thought of Christianity in just the way that we do now.

It has often been argued that the differences in the books are

merely on the surface, and are due to nothing else than diversity
of authorship. When a dozen people look at the same thing, each
from his own point of view, they will describe it differently but
their accounts can all be harmonised. They are obviously speaking of the same house or mountain, and each of them adds some
necessary detail which the others have missed. It may be argued,
too, that in a diversity of opinions there may still be essential
agreement. Writers of a given period may vary widely from one
another, but they all move within the same circle of ideas, and
their differences only bring home to us more forcibly the general
identity of outlook in that age. The New Testament thus speaks,
in a number of voices, for the common mind of the early church.
But the differences in the various books cannot be disposed of so
easily. When the Epistle to Romans is compared with the Epistle
of James or the book of Revelation it cannot be said that the
ideas are substantially the same and are merely expressed with
some change of emphasis. We cannot but feel that the writers are
at variance in their whole conception of the Christian message.
We have to deal, not with modes of presentation, but with distinct types of teaching. The teachers are all Christian, and are
equally sincere and fervent, but they have understood the gospel in different ways. How can we account for this disagreement,
almost from the first, as to the meaning of the new religion?
Nothing, one might think, could be more explicit than the teaching of Jesus. He expressed himself in the simplest terms and took
pains, by parable and illustration, to make his thought still
clearer. Why was it that his followers, some of whom had actually listened to him, were all divided as to the purport of his
message? However we regard it this must always be the outstanding problem of early Christianity.

The divisions are commonly attributed to the peculiar conditions under which the message was first proclaimed. Originally,

we are told, there was little to distinguish the new religion from
ordinary Judaism. Jesus himself had declared that he had not
come to destroy the Law; his object was only to enforce the principles which lay at the heart of it. He shifted the emphasis from
the ritual to the ethical. He reduced the countless separate rules
to the few which were essential. He restored to their rightful
place some demands of the Law which had been unduly neglected. Like John the Baptist, his predecessor, he accepted the
apocalyptic hopes which had found their way, apparently
through Persian influences, into traditional Judaism. The Kingdom of God was at hand. A day was approaching when all men
would be called to judgment, and would be excluded from the
Kingdom unless they had proved faithful to the will of God. They
must, therefore, repent and so order their lives in the present that
they might be ready for the Kingdom when it came. It is thus
contended that Jesus did little more than clarify the existing religion. In ordinary course his teaching would have been forgotten,
or would have been absorbed into a larger Judaism. His group of
followers had little to distinguish them from the mass of their
countrymen, and could not long have maintained themselves as
a separate sect. But the life of Jesus had fallen in a remarkable
age, when thinkers were everywhere breaking away from conventional beliefs and feeling out in new directions. It was so even in
Palestine, despite the efforts to keep men confined within the fence
of the Law. The Jewish mind in the first century was exceedingly
active, and was striving for a liberty which was denied it in the
official religion. Jesus had taught how the Law might be obeyed
in the spirit rather than the letter, and there were many who welcomed him as a deliverer. Liberal Jews attached themselves to
the church and, while calling themselves followers of Jesus,
allowed free play to their own thinking. Christianity was thus
from the outset highly diversified, and became far more so when

it was carried by Paul and other missionaries into the Gentile world. All races had now been fused in the Roman empire and, in every great city, were busily exchanging their ideas and traditions. Luke, in the book of Acts, describes the people of Athens as occupied with nothing else than in telling or hearing some new thing; and the same was true, in a less marked degree, of all the cities of that age. There has never been a time, except perhaps our own, which has been so full of intellectual ferment. By contact with other types of culture men had been shaken out of their accustomed grooves. They had become critical of everything that had been taken for granted; they experimented freely with new theories, from whatever quarter they might come. This spirit of enquiry was especially active in religion. Civil liberty had been suppressed under the all-powerful Roman order, and with the closing of all previous outlets the minds of men were driven inward. If there was little vital religion there was an endless curiosity about religion. Every new gospel was assured of a hearing and found at least some who were willing to accept it seriously as their rule of life.

In this manner, it is held, the rapid extension of Christianity in the first century has to be explained; and it cannot be denied that the explanation, up to a certain point, is a just one. The missionaries did not require to force their message on an indifferent world. They found men ready and even eager to listen to it, and there was the possibility everywhere that the seed might fall on good ground. It is also held that here we have the true explanation of those divisions which arose so quickly in the Gentile church. Many types of religion had already won their adherents, but it was felt that in each of them an element was lacking. Christianity seemed to supply the want. It might not be acceptable as a whole and its intolerance of every other form of belief was repellent to the ancient mind. But it was always possible to retain some existing cult and hold, in conjunction with it, what appeared most valuable in the Christian faith. Thus there arose a variety of sects, diverging widely from each other, but all with some claim to call themselves Christian. Every spiritual movement of the time sought to avail itself of the new teaching, which manifestly had much to offer. Philosophical, ethical, social, and mystical beliefs were found to become living and effectual when they allied themselves with Christianity. Even popular superstitions took on a new character if they made Jesus a central figure. It can thus be understood how the many divisions in the church came into being. They were not so much new varieties of the Christian faith as old types of religion disguised in a Christian form. After the earliest period Christianity ceased to be a single religion and broke into a cluster of religions which ought to be viewed separately although they are vaguely classed together as Christian.

Now it may be granted that in this reading of the early history there is much that answers to the facts. The chief danger to the new religion was that it might be assimilated by those around it, and its escape from this danger is the most striking proof of its intrinsic power and originality. It did not, indeed, escape quite scatheless. The foreign beliefs undoubtedly affected the Christian teaching, not so much in any direct manner as through the general atmosphere they created. They formed the medium which could not but colour men's vision when they tried to understand Christianity. We are learning, in these days, that the physical world must be explained in the light of conceptions which had no place in the older science and mathematics, but we have not yet adjusted ourselves to the new assumptions. We can make nothing of them unless we envisage them, as best we can, in terms of our previous thinking. The Gentile Christian in the first century was in much the same position. The new message was entirely strange to him. He believed that it was true, but before he could apprehend it he had to interpret it through ideas which properly belonged to one or another of the older religions. Hence in the Gentile world Christianity took many forms, according to the alien type of belief which was used for explaining it. There may have been no conscious assimilation, and probably with the majority of earnest Christians there was not. They honestly believed that the faith they now professed was the Christian one, and resented any suggestion that it was mixed with baser material. But, as we can now see, the prevailing cults still held their own, although they were so modified as to bring them into line with the gospel.

This account of the history cannot, then, be set aside. Christianity was influenced, to a greater extent than we care to acknowledge, by the foreign religions, and our churches today are still divided by controversies which had their real origin in pagan beliefs of the first century. But the early development cannot be explained wholly from the action of external forces. The growth of a plant certainly depends on soil and climate and weather, but something is also due to the nature of the seed. Whatever may be the outward conditions, figs do not grow from thistles. One cannot but feel that in much of the modern discussion this simple fact is forgotten. It is believed that the Christian message in itself was negligible. What Jesus may have given we cannot determine, and it does not greatly matter, for at most he only supplied a nucleus which gathered around it, by a series of happy accidents, all that was valuable in ancient thought. Christianity became a religion for mankind in virtue of those accretions, not from anything that was inherent in itself. But a theory of this kind will explain nothing. It makes all the problems more difficult, since it requires us to look through the telescope from the wrong end.

Two things are evident as we study the New Testament writings. On the one hand those early teachers are not primarily concerned with ideas. They are not philosophical thinkers who start with a given conception and elucidate and enlarge it with the aid of other conceptions, taken over from thinkers before them. They set out from religious facts. Christ appeared on earth and died and rose again; those who believe in him have entered into a new relation to God, and possess a higher and more satisfying life. No doubt ideas play a great part, and are borrowed from many sources; but they are always secondary. The one object is to affirm the Christian facts, and ideas are employed for no other purpose than to make them surer and more intelligible. One might infer from some modern commentators that Paul was little more than a man of multifarious and ill-digested learning. Every verse is illustrated by parallels from ancient authors, Jewish and Hellenistic, and the impression is left on us that he merely turned over his note-books and so patched up his Epistles to the Romans and the Corinthians. This was certainly not his method. His whole interest was in the Christian message and what it meant to him. The ideas are all subordinate, and he knew and cared little where they came from, so long as they helped him to proclaim the gospel. So in the New Testament generally, the message itself is the one thing that matters, and we must consider the writings with this fact in mind. As you look at a building you do not think of the individual stones. Without them there could be no building, and they have all come from some quarry, and it needed time and skill to put them together. But your mind is on the building, and it was the same with the architect when he designed it.

On the other hand it is evident that the New Testament writers express their own passionate convictions. They do not merely take up a tradition where some other man left off, and try to carry it a little further. They speak out of a knowledge and experience which are entirely their own. The modern enquiry is based, for the most part, on the so-called "historical method," which is now dominant in almost every field of study. It is assumed that everything has come about by a progress from small beginnings, and the aim is to trace the stages in this gradual advance. How is the work of Shakespeare to be explained? You must go back to Anglo-Saxon literature and mark how it developed, and how new influences crept in from time to time, and enriched and broadened the original stream until at last you have *Hamlet* and *Othello*. No one can be quite satisfied with this account. There was something in Shakespeare himself which created his poetry, and when this is left out all other enquiry will help us little. The historical method is nowhere so sterile and misleading as when it is applied in the field of religion. It requires us to think of Christianity as wholly the product of external forces. Jesus appeared inevitably in the onward march of Judaism. There is nothing in his teaching which cannot be fully accounted for by the work of prophets, scribes, apocalyptists. As he was himself the outcome of his time so his religion owed everything to things which happened afterwards. New elements were continually gathered into it, and it thus grew like a snowball from tiny beginnings into a faith for all mankind. Now a view like this rests on a complete misconception of the nature of religion. No one can deny that in religion, as in everything else, the law of progress is operative, but it only affects the forms and vehicles, not the substance. It cannot be said that faith in God has now grown stronger than in the early centuries. All that has happened is that with wider knowledge we are able to express our faith in new and perhaps more adequate terms, and to apply it in larger spheres of action. All the time we are conscious that our faith itself is poorer than that of the old saints and martyrs. The very fact that they did not possess our science and culture gave them an actual advantage. They could feel nearer to God, they could apprehend him with a directness and intensity to which we cannot now attain. The historical method had indeed proved wonderfully fruitful, but where it helps us is only in the understanding of Christian doctrines and customs and institutions. About Christianity itself it can tell us little, and tends to confuse our thought of the religion with that of its forms and vestures. A history of costumes may be interesting and instructive, but as a history of the human race it has very minor value. Before it means anything we must study the race, and discover the needs and impulses which have caused it from time to time to adopt those different modes. So to understand the history of our religion we must begin with its nature as a religion. It is futile to reverse the process and examine the historical changes, in the hope that we shall thus explain Christianity, or explain it away.

The key to the later development must therefore be sought in the character of the Christian message. Many interpretations have been placed on it, but this is not due merely to later circumstances, forcing into it a variety of meanings which were not originally there. All that came out of the religion as time went on was already in some manner present in it, along with much else that was afterwards obscured. Nothing, indeed, is more misleading than the conception often held of the gospel as something little, which was gradually magnified by the efforts of later teachers. We picture to ourselves the astonishment of Jesus if he could have foreseen the world-wide church, the theological systems, the vast Christian enterprises, the whole life of humanity transformed by his modest work in Galilee. Could he have believed that such a tremendous outcome was possible? But his feeling, we can hardly doubt, would have been one of bitter disappointment. The outward magnitude of the results would not have impressed him. He would have realised that out of all he had given them men would only preserve a few fragments, and would distort and narrow even these.

The truth is that the original message was not something meagre but was rich and many-sided, so much so that it eluded all efforts to grasp it as a whole. This is apparent from one plain fact which cannot be controverted. The teaching of Jesus all centred on his proclamation of the Kingdom of God, and Christian thinkers have been trying ever since to explain what he meant by the Kingdom. He had in his mind the new age of apocalyptic prophecy, the inner fellowship of the soul with God, the future life of the blessed, the church on earth or the church invisible, the brotherhood of man which will some day replace our social disorder. Every theology has suggested some new interpretation, and the strange thing is that every interpretation is right. Jesus was thinking of all those aspects of the higher life with which his message has been identified; only with him they were all blended together and were merged in a greater conception. To understand the later history of Christianity we must allow for this comprehensive quality in Jesus' own teaching. It was not confined to some rudimentary idea, which contained in it just enough substance to give the initial impulse to a new religious movement. It was itself far larger and deeper than anything which has proceeded from it. The later teachers did not expand and enrich it but sought only to unfold some portion of what Jesus had given.

This does not mean that his thought was complex, like that of Origen or Augustine or Thomas Aquinas. One of his chief aims was to speak simply and directly, and to clear the great truths of religion from the theological tangle which had obscured them. Neither does it mean that his principles were novel and startling, and continued to puzzle his interpreters long after his death. There was little in his teaching that was strictly new. It had been assumed in almost every previous religion that men ought to be just and merciful, that they should be helpful to their fellowmen, that they should serve God willingly and set their hearts on spiritual ends. Modern enquirers have set themselves to prove that Jesus had been anticipated, and that hardly one of his maxims was entirely his own. Endless labour has been devoted to this task, which was not worth undertaking. It was inevitable that Jesus should repeat much that had been said already. For ages men had been engaged in the business of living, and had arrived at a number of principles which they knew by long experience to be true. When Jesus impressed on them that they ought to be truthful, compassionate, high-minded, he was saying again what wise men had said before him, and if he had spoken differently he would have been a false prophet. Yet there was one thing in his teaching which was altogether new. He took those principles which men knew already, and made them real and effectual. He so proclaimed the will of God that his followers could live by it, as if it were their own. This, it was soon perceived, was the distinctive thing about Jesus' message; what was its secret? At first sight it appears very strange that so little is made in the New Testament of the actual sayings of Jesus. Outside of the Gospels they are rarely quoted, and from this it has been inferred that Jesus' religion was displaced after his death by one that was alien to it. But the seeming forgetfulness of his message was due to nothing else than a true insight into its purpose. The disciples were conscious that behind the teaching there was something further, and that here they must discover the meaning of their religion. The word was with power; what was the nature of this power?

It was seen from the first to be inseparable from the personality of Jesus. The religion took its name from its Founder, and from him also it takes all its significance. Other religions go back to individual prophets, Moses, Buddha, Zoroaster, Mohammed; but they would be little affected if nothing were known of these founders, or if it could be proved that they never existed. The men are only the symbols of ideas and beliefs which would remain the same however they had originated. In Christianity the religion is one with its Founder. "I determined," says Paul, "to know nothing but Jesus Christ and him crucified"; and this has been the position of every Christian teacher who has had a vital message. It is sometimes said that in the hands of his disciples the religion of Jesus became a religion about Jesus, and thereby changed its character. But the supposed distinction is an unreal one. In his own teaching Jesus had indeed said little about himself, but his personality had been the vitalising element in all that he taught. The disciples rightly felt that they must put him at the centre if they would preserve the meaning of his message. There have been men in history who stand out as great personalities. We recognise that there was a peculiar force in them, and that something tremendous would never have happened if these men had not appeared. We think of them, however, only in relation to the work they accomplished. Of some of the greatest of them we have little biographical knowledge, and this is no matter for regret. It was the work that mattered, and the men must be judged by that, and an intimate record of their personal lives would be only a distraction. But with Jesus the personality was everything. He brought a revelation, but he was himself the revelation, and the chief aim of his followers was to know him, and in some measure to explain him. They often did so in terms of a metaphysic which has ceased to be acceptable, but this does not affect the truth of the fundamental idea. By what he was in himself Jesus revealed God. "In him," says the Fourth Evangelist, "was life." What he gave was not a creed or a philosophy or an ethic but a new life, which had its source in himself.

Christianity was thus in its nature manifold. It grew out of the personality of Jesus, and represented that attitude of mind which he had first made possible. As men acquired this new outlook they could not but feel that all things became different. The Christian message, the more it was understood, was found to have infinite meanings and applications. Men were renewed in their own minds, and this involved a renewal in all the interests of their lives. Something of this kind may be observed in every message that carries with it a sense of liberation. It has consequences which far outrun what may seem to be its immediate object, and effects a change in everything. Take, for instance, the French Revolution. It turned on a new political idea, but we can now see that the whole achievement of the nineteenth century, in art, literature, and social endeavour, proceeded from that movement. It transformed men's ways of thinking, so that henceforth they could think of nothing without seeing it in a new light. This was true in far greater measure of the work of Jesus. It did not take the form of a violent commotion, and when it is dismissed by many modern writers as itself unimportant they are influenced unconsciously by this fact. They cannot get away from the vulgar judgment that events are great in proportion to the noise they make, and since Jesus passed his life in a remote province and was hardly heard of until after his death they cannot believe that he was himself responsible for the vast movement which is called by his name. His own work can have contributed very little, and was only the accident which gave a final impulse to mighty forces, as the touch of a child's finger will launch a battleship. He taught, however, that the greatness of human actions is not to be measured by the tumult which accompanies them, and this truth applies, in a supreme degree, to himself. He was the sovereign power in history. He not merely took the initial step towards the new religion but he created it, and all that it afterwards became was involved in his own work. Unless we allow for this significance of Jesus we can make nothing of the Christian religion.

It is from this point of view that we have to consider that diversity of teaching which meets us in the New Testament. The message, as Jesus himself gave it, was inherently a many-sided one, and when it was taken up by men of various temperaments, when it was brought to bear on all the complex interests of that extraordinary age, its manifold character at once revealed itself. It was not changed into something different by the surrounding influences. They served only to accentuate one element and another that it possessed already. Many types of doctrine came into being, and took on the character of the beliefs and philosophies which were current in that time. They sometimes appear to have more in common with alien religions than with Christianity, but they were all its genuine offspring. As we examine them we never fail to see that they have their roots in something that was actually present in the mind of Jesus. These varying interpretations all find their place in the New Testament, which is indeed our authoritative book, although the nature of its authority has been sorely misunderstood by many who have most honoured it. They assume that these inspired teachers were all in strict agreement and prescribed for us a system of doctrine to which Christian thinking must always conform. This, in their view, is the chief value of the New Testament, that amidst the flux of opinion it stands guardian over a type of belief which is the only one that can be recognised as truly Christian. Such a view, however, is contrary to the facts. The New Testament is not a uniform book, composed by men who were all of one mind and were closely collaborating with one another. It presents Christianity under a great variety of forms, and for this very reason presents it truly. For the Christian religion is many-sided, and appeals to men differently according as they approach it with their different minds. Freedom of interpretation is not an abuse, due to error or waywardness and calling for stern repression. It belongs to the nature of Christianity, which is no longer itself when this freedom is withdrawn. The New Testament, so far from imposing one rigid doctrine, is the Magna Charta of Christian liberty. In those early days, when men most fervently believed in the new message, they claimed the right of interpreting it, each in his own way, and this right is still valid, and whenever it is challenged an appeal can be made to the New Testament. In this sense the book is authoritative.

It is hard for us now to realise that in the first age of the church the idea of orthodoxy did not exist. We have grown accustomed to think of it as inseparable from the Christian faith, so that for many people faith and orthodoxy mean the same thing. The Christian, as they conceive him, is one who accepts a number of given beliefs and holds to them unswervingly in the approved form. To the early church this idea was quite foreign, and its place was taken by the conception of the Spirit. It was believed that Christ, on his departure, had bestowed on his people a divine power, which would lead them to all truth. They were no longer to be bound by old traditions or by judgments imposed on them from without. Each Christian was to hold himself accountable to Christ alone, and to keep the faith as the Lord revealed it to him by the Spirit. Paul condemns all dependence on human leaders as a kind of apostasy. Those who see the truth only through the eyes of other men, however gifted and revered, are not truly Christian, for the Christian is guided solely by the Spirit, which is the Spirit of liberty. In the early days there was little danger that this freedom might be abused. The current of Christian faith was running so strongly that no one was likely to drift out of it into some perilous course. At a later time the channel had to be marked out and guarded. Especially when the church was opened to Gentile converts, bringing with them their strange opinions, faith could not be left wholly to the direction of the Spirit. Yet this was undoubtedly the principle which was accepted by the early teachers, and it was involved in the very idea of Christianity. Through Christ men had become children of God; they had made their wills one with his will; they could believe that he was inwardly controlling them, and they were free to understand his gospel in the manner that was most real to themselves. The result was a large diversity of interpretations, each of them one-sided, but within its own compass true. In the New Testament we have a number of those early types of teaching, brought together in a single book. The church holds that the book was given by inspiration, and this is no mere dogma but an accurate definition of how it came into being. Its authors believed that they possessed the Spirit. They gave utterance to those conceptions of the truth to which the Spirit had guided them. They were at no pains to agree with one another, or to follow some beaten track of thought, but listened only to the inner voice as it spoke to each one of them. Inspiration could not but mean diversity, and it cannot be denied that this has proved confusing. If the Christian doctrines had been logically thought out, and presented in a book which had all its parts harmoniously fitted together, the later ages would have been spared infinite trouble. There would have been no place for the quarrels and controversies which have brought reproach on our religion. The church might have moved forward as a united body, with no dissipation of its energy. But if the New Testament had been a perfectly consistent book we should never have known the full scope and meaning of our religion. All the witnesses would have agreed in their evidence because they were all looking at a few selected facts from the same point of view. It is the differences in the New Testament which enable us to comprehend its message, in all its length and breadth. The very fact that they exist brings home to us an essential part of the message, for

Christianity is the religion of freedom. It secures to every believer the right to draw near to God and to know the revelation for himself. The whole meaning of the New Testament is bound up with its inconsistencies.

The character of the book is thus due, in the last resort, to the nature of the gospel itself. It was inherently many-sided. It had its roots not in some particular doctrine but in a new attitude to God, a new perception of the meaning of life. Such a gospel was capable of many interpretations. No one could take in the whole of it and each believer was drawn to that aspect of it which had most significance for his own mind. The early teachers were satisfied that this had been the intention of Jesus. They were not disturbed when they found themselves differing from each other, but were convinced by this that they had rightly understood the gospel. It required that each thinker should follow his own path, trusting in the guidance of the Spirit. One of Paul's favourite phrases is "freedom of speech," and the idea expressed by it is never absent from his mind. He saw that diversities of opinion were implicit in Christian faith, and this was impressed on him more and more by his experience as a missionary. Jesus had himself suggested, in his parable of the Sower, that the seed would grow differently according to the nature of the soil, and after his death the parable had found its wider application. The seed was now falling on minds of the most diverse character. Its growth was affected by every phase of the varied intellectual life of that age. It was scattered over many lands and cities, and was influenced by the local peculiarities. Under these conditions "freedom of speech" was necessary. When the Christian tried to express his faith he could not do so in some one approved fashion. His faith was that which the word of Christ had produced in his own soul, placed as he was in a given environment, with the powers and limitations which were inherent in himself. Papias, the earliest of the Fathers, says of Matthew's Gospel: "It was written in the Hebrew tongue, and each man interpreted it as he thought best." This may refer to translations or paraphrases which were made of a primitive Gospel, but something more is probably intended. The record of Jesus was adapted to many different types of mind. A religion which had arisen in Palestine was now offered to the world at large, and everywhere men responded to it and made it their own possession by explaining it in their own manner. The one gospel, before a generation was over, had branched out into many.

Nevertheless, with all its diversities, the gospel remained one. This was never doubtful to any Christian. Paul puts away from him with horror the very thought that Christ can be divided.* He declares that all believers, whatever leaders they may choose to follow, are members of the one Body of Christ. This sense of unity was, indeed, the characteristic mark of Christians. The name by which they called themselves was "the brethren," and amidst all differences they were ever conscious that they were one family, bound in love and service to one another. This unity was apparent even to the outside world, which knew nothing about the new religion except that those who professed it were brought into intimate union. Other religious societies were on friendly terms and a man might belong to several of them at the same time. Christianity stood by itself. It united its own people in the closest bonds, and then divided them as by a wall from the rest of mankind. This constituted its danger, and was felt to justify the persecutions. Rome had set itself to weld the separate nations into one, and Christianity was defeating this noble aim. Its object was to gather converts out of those races which Rome was uniting, and knit them together in a rival brotherhood.

*I Cor. 1:13.

The New Testament, while it reflects the many divisions within the church, is also our best evidence of its essential unity. Writings of the most diverse character are yet collected in one book. They were all employed in the common worship, although their first readers must have perceived, much more clearly than we can do, that at many points they were at variance. The voices were different but it was felt that they were all in harmony and must be heard together. What was the nature of this harmony?

It has been argued in recent years that at some very early time the church had agreed on certain articles of faith which were to underlie all its teaching.[†] They were drawn up in a brief formal summary, of much the same character as the Apostles' Creed which emerged at a later date. All the missionaries were furnished with this outline of the faith, either in written form or as a piece committed to memory. They were free to expand and elucidate it as they thought fit, but were expected to preach the gospel on this basis and no other. In proof of this theory it is pointed out that a number of phrases are repeated in different books, as if the writers were falling back on certain formulae which every one would recognize. It is claimed that when these are collected and put together we can in some measure reconstruct the primitive creed which gave direction to all Christian thinking.

The theory may be valid in so far as some beliefs were so generally held that the terms in which they were expressed had become more or less stereotyped. This was only natural in a time when all teaching was by word of mouth. Everything had to be carried in the memory, and important facts and ideas were thrown as far as possible into concise statements which were passed on from one teacher to another. Not a few peculiarities in the New

† Very able discussions will be found in C. H. Dodd, *The Apostolic Preaching and its Development*; and P. Carrington, *The Primitive Christian Catechism*.

Testament may be thus explained. Again and again we have the impression that the writer is reciting a formula, much as a modern author may quote a familiar proverb or line of poetry. It does not follow that his thought is derived from this quotation or seriously influenced by it. He introduces it merely because it gives forcible expression to his own general idea.

It is impossible to believe that there was ever an apostolic message in the sense that the approved Christian teaching was set forth in a definite form of words. If this was done it must have been in the very earliest days, and from all we know of the primitive church it was not in a position to draw up a set statement of what must be taught and believed. The disciples were in no mood of calm theological reflection. Their faith was given them through ecstatic experiences, and they could not have defined it, even if they had wished to, in any rigid terms. Moreover they did not constitute an official body with power to impose its own convictions on the whole mass of believers. They were indeed the foremost teachers of the church and their opinions carried weight; but the Spirit had been bestowed on all Christians alike. Paul tells us that at the Council of Jerusalem he did not allow himself to be overborne by those "who seemed to be pillars." ‡ When it came to matters of faith his own judgment was no less valid than that of Peter and John. This attitude, we may be sure, was not peculiar to himself. All who called themselves Christians had the same confidence that they knew the mind of Christ through the Spirit, and would have resented any attempt to dictate to them what they must believe. And for that part the disciples were not in full agreement among themselves. It becomes evident, as we examine the Gospels, that they represent different conceptions of the work of Christ, suggesting that from the very first the church was divided.¶

‡ Gal. 2:9.
¶ This is worked out in detail by F. C. Grant, *The Kingdom of God.*

If the disciples were thus unable to convince each other they could not have decided on a form of belief which should be imposed on the whole church.

Much has been made of the use in the New Testament of a specific word, the "announcement" or "preaching" (*kerygma*), to denote the substance of what was taught by the Apostles. Does not this imply that they were the bearers of a clear-cut message, summarizing the new beliefs? It may be observed, however, that the word is applied to Christian teaching generally, without regard to its precise nature and content. If the literal meaning of the word is to be pressed, it refers to the function of a herald (*keryx*) who proclaims an event which has happened or is going to happen. A herald announced the outbreak of war, the result of a battle, the accession of a king, or the calling of an assembly. His task was not that of arguing or persuading, but simply that of making a fact known. This, in its essence, was the work of the Christian preacher. He announced certain facts of supreme importance—that the end of the world was near, that all men will be brought to judgment, that Christ had died and risen again for men's salvation. To be sure the bare announcement was not enough, and it was necessary to explain who Christ had been, and why his work had a surpassing value, and how men should believe in him and serve him. All this, however, was apart from the immediate task of making the announcement. Paul describes himself as not merely a herald but an "ambassador of Christ." * The duty laid upon him was to "persuade men" †—to convince them of the truth of his message. But the message and the exposition of it were two different things, and had not to be confused together. The message consisted in the fundamental Christian facts which might be interpreted in various ways, and no one interpretation was considered binding. All Christians, as a matter of course, accepted

* II Cor. 5:20.   † II Cor. 5:11.

the facts. That Jesus had lived and died and risen again, that he had proclaimed the Kingdom of God and offered himself as the Messiah, these things were matters of history, and men only needed to be made aware of them. In stating them the missionary might employ his own words or adopt formulae which had passed into general use; this could make little difference. It is, indeed, hard to see why the question of "forms" has engrossed so much attention in recent study of the New Testament. Great issues are supposed to depend on whether the Christian teaching was transmitted freely or in terms which had acquired a certain fixity. But if the facts were the same the modes of stating them did not greatly matter. I may employ the usual formula and say "all men are mortal," or vary it by saying "death is the appointed end of all human existence." A sensible man prefers the ordinary form, but however you choose to express it the fact is the same.

The unity which runs through the New Testament must not be sought in some formal creed to which all teachers were obliged to adhere. They were indeed in agreement on those facts which had given rise to the new religion, and concerning which there could be no doubt in any Christian mind. They could not but announce the facts in much the same terms, and to that extent we may speak of an apostolic message. But the facts themselves offered no guarantee that they would have just the same significance to all who believed them. On the contrary, they at once raised problems which were capable of many solutions. That all men are mortal is a fact, however you please to state it, but on the ground of it you may hold a purely animal view of life, or determine to use well the little span allotted to you, or reason that since this life is fragmentary there must be another beyond it. So in Christianity the real task of the teacher began when the facts were admitted. Jesus was the Messiah, but what did this involve? He had proclaimed the Kingdom of God, but what was it and how were men to attain to it? On every point of the message there was room for the widest divergence, and this became ever more evident. From the outset Christians differed in their understanding of that gospel on which they were all agreed. The writer to the Hebrews compares it to a two-edged sword, quick and powerful, which divides the joints and the marrow, and so it has always proved itself. It not only divides those who accept from those who refuse it, but among Christians themselves it makes sharp divisions. The mere fact that all professed the same beliefs in much the same words was not enough by itself to create the sense of brotherhood.

Nevertheless the church felt itself one, and the New Testament with all its diversities of teaching, bears witness to this unity, which may be ascribed in some measure to external causes. The various communities, although each of them preserved its independence, were closely associated. Missionaries were itinerant and as they travelled from place to place diffused the same ideas and customs. In course of time this work of the Apostles was reinforced by a growing literature. Paul's Epistles were circulated in all the scattered churches. The Gospels were used everywhere as handbooks of instruction, and by means of them the minds of Christians were insensibly moulded in the same pattern. And nothing, perhaps, contributed so much to the union of the church as the persecutions which were intended to destroy it. Not only did they bring Christians together under pressure of a common danger, but they forced attention on things that were essential. When the faith was something which a man might be required to die for, he became aware of what it meant to him. The minor issues on which he might dispute with his fellow-Christians fell out of sight, and he thought only of the vital truths which were the same to all.

It was these central elements in the religion which formed the true bond of union. The Fourth Evangelist, with a profound discernment, conceives of the Cross as a magnet, which attracts the people of Christ out of the world and holds them together. "I, if I am lifted up will draw all men unto me." [‡] A like thought finds expression in the book of Revelation,[¶] and it was by no accident that the Cross became the Christian symbol, the eternal reminder that all Christians, however they differ, are to feel themselves one. It stood for the ultimate meaning of the new religion, transcending everything that might confuse and divide.

This sense of what Christ had done for his people was inseparable from a devotion to Christ himself. If the church possessed any formal statement of its faith, it was contained in the simple affirmation, "Jesus is Lord," which occurs three times in Paul's Epistles, and always in such a context as to show that it was the regular church confession.[§] Apparently it was made by every convert on the occasion of his baptism. The author of I Peter declares that the rite becomes effectual by "the answer of a good conscience towards God," [*] and almost certainly the reference is to the solemn confession in virtue of which the convert was received into the church. It has been held that this declaration at baptism was the original Christian creed, which was gradually amplified and defined until it assumed the later forms. Superficially this may be true, but the confession "Jesus is Lord" was not a creed, and to place it on such a footing is to obscure its whole character and purpose. It was not a statement of doctrine but an affirmation of loyalty. In the act of baptism the believer took his oath of allegiance, accepting Jesus as the Master, to whose will he now surrendered himself. To understand the confession we have to turn, not to the argumentative chapters of Romans and Galatians, but to those passages where Paul speaks of Christ in terms of passionate devotion. It is noteworthy that the convert was not required

‡ Jn. 12:32.   § Rom. 10:9; I Cor. 12:3; Phil. 2:11.
¶ Rev. 5:9.   * I Pet. 3:21.

to say "Jesus is the Messiah." That would have been a statement of doctrine. It would have bound the person who uttered it to a particular interpretation of the nature and work of Christ. But with a sure instinct the church avoided any sharp definition even of its primary belief. All that it demanded was a personal loyalty. The believer was left to form his own conception of what Christ had been, so long as he recognized his supreme claim to obedience. This was the bond which united all Christians, however they might be outwardly divided. A good citizen may be fervently devoted to his party, made up of people who hold his own views on one disputed question and another. He is also devoted to his country, and this loyalty is of an altogether different kind. It is grounded not in his opinions but in his affections, and unites him with those who at almost every point may be violently opposed to him. The unity of the early church was of this character, and found its expression not in any theological statement but in a common promise of obedience to Christ.

The Christian faith was thus inseparable from the Christian ethic. Jesus in his teaching had laid down a new rule of life, and had himself given the example of how it should be put into action. "If ye love me, ye will keep my commandments" ; [†] there could be no devotion to Christ without the effort to follow his way of living. In all times the Christian ethic has been the constant factor in the Christian religion. Doctrines and modes of worship have been constantly changing, but the idea of how the Christian man should act has never varied. The mediaeval saints thought differently from ourselves on almost every subject ; there are sects today with whose ideas we find it impossible to have any sympathy. Yet when it comes to action all Christians feel alike ; the moral standards which held good a thousand years ago are valid today and

† Jn. 14:15.

always will be. This was recognized from the very beginning. Again and again it is impressed on us in the New Testament that the real test of a man's faith is his practice; his actions are the "fruits of the Spirit," and "by their fruits ye shall know them." As we now see it the Christian ethic is self-evidently the highest, but we must never forget that in the early centuries it was new and strange, and was not generally admired. To the pagan mind such qualities as pity, humility, patience under injuries were the marks of a weak, low-spirited man. Christians were persecuted not so much for what they believed as for the way they acted. Yet they followed the rule which Jesus had taught, and in so doing felt themselves to be at one, over against the unbelieving world. Then as now, the plain man cared little about theological subtleties. He might be warned against certain teachers as dangerous heretics, but it is doubtful whether this had much effect on his judgment. He recognized as his fellow-Christian one who was living, as he tried himself to live, in the Christian way. This was the obvious bond which held all sections of the church together.

There is no need, therefore, to look for any formal creed in order to explain why the New Testament teaching although so diversified is yet so much of a unity. In its inner life the church was united in the same manner as in its outward constitution. As yet there was no ecclesiastical system. A great number of separate communities had come into being, up and down the empire, all of them self-governing and with no visible relation to each other, and yet conscious that they were bound together as the body of Christ. They also held their faith in so many different forms that the one religion might seem to have broken into many, and yet it never ceased to be one. The unity consisted in nothing clearly definable but in a frame of mind which was common to all Christians. They realized that as the people of Christ they had entered on a citizenship which made them members of one another. In that ancient world the grand distinction was that of free men and slaves, and it may be said that this distinction was now asserted on a higher plane. Christians were aware that while others were still in bondage to the powers of this world they had obtained their freedom. They might have differences among themselves, as in a city there may be dissensions, but they were members of the one free community, and in the hour of crisis they stood together. It is vain to seek in the New Testament for any other kind of unity than this one of a common devotion, and without this all attempts to create a harmony would have defeated their purpose. An island may show a wide variety in soil and vegetation, but it remains one, and stands firm in mid-ocean, because underneath there is the same rock basis. So the new religion in all its manifold forms had the same foundation, and its essential unity was never in doubt.

This was not fully apparent at the time. Christians were indeed conscious that they held the same faith and formed a single brotherhood. The New Testament writers are careful to lay stress on this unity and to indicate its nature. They address themselves to "those who call on the name of the Lord," "those who are in Christ," "those who are called to be saints," "all who love the Lord Jesus." It was taken for granted that nothing more was necessary for membership in the church than the confession "Jesus is Lord." We hear repeatedly in the book of Acts of converts who knew nothing in detail of the Christian beliefs but who professed faith in Christ and on the ground of that faith were baptised. Instruction was given to them later, but their response to the simple call was enough to make them Christians. The very reason why definite creeds came into being was that many believers, perhaps the greater number, had only the vaguest knowledge of any doctrines. Their religion was genuine but it was necessary to "edify" them—to build up into something stable and concrete the faith which they could not explain. But while it was realized that the gospel did not consist of doctrines, the growing variety of doctrine caused serious misgiving. There was a sense that the brotherhood of the church was in danger. Christians must be persuaded to believe and think the same things, or they would presently drift apart. The later New Testament books are full of appeals for unity. It was felt that if the church was to survive and accomplish its task in the world it must close its ranks. There must be one type of teaching for the one body of Christ.

These fears were natural, and have continued to distress the church ever since. We can now see, however, that they were largely groundless, and that the divisions were preparing the way for a fuller unity. Paul has a premonition of this truth, although like the others he deplores the growth of parties which seemed to be breaking up the church. He was the first of all thinkers to discern the great principle of unity through difference. Again and again he declares that the one Spirit must operate through diversities of gifts, and as the highest example of perfect unity he takes the human body, which is made up of countless parts, all differing in function and yet acting together under one will and in the service of one life. This, as we are learning to see, is indeed the principle on which nature works. It feels its way towards ever higher types of unity by first disintegrating—setting various elements against each other until they combine for some larger purpose which would otherwise be out of reach. This physical law holds equally true in human society. In our own time we have been engaged in a life and death struggle against the idea of a uniform state. We rightly see that if there were no division, if every one were compelled to think like his neighbor and merge his will and action in those of the mass, there would be no progress, no fulfilment of the true ends for which the state exists. No unity is worth having unless it has grown out of differences, and allows room for the widest difference. This is true most of all in the church, which claims to pattern itself on that higher order which will be realized in the Kingdom of God. It rests on the principle that men are free personalities, who of their own accord submit their wills to the divine will. Separate from each other they yet love the same things and look to the same ends, and the more individual they can make their service the closer will be their union.

It is not difficult to see that a premature agreement among Christian teachers would have been disastrous. There would indeed have been an undivided church, but it would not have grown out of the free activity of the Christian mind. At best it would have represented one type of opinion, which to many would have been unnatural, and which, in course of time, would have become ever more narrow and rigid. As it was, the church accepted no control but that of the Spirit, and encouraged all varieties of thought. The gospel seemed to be disintegrating but all the time it was unfolding itself, and was moulding the church with its many members into a unified body of Christ.

CHAPTER II

THE PRIMITIVE TEACHING

THE SEER of Revelation beheld a city with twelve foundations, on which were inscribed the names of the twelve Apostles of the Lamb. Christians in all times have looked back in reverence to those Apostles. They were indeed the foundations. The world-wide church which arose afterwards was built on that first community which was formed under their leadership at Jerusalem. It was not merely the beginning of the church but was the primary force in its development. Missionaries went forth from it, carrying to all nations the message proclaimed by the Apostles.

All historians of the church have set themselves to determine the nature of the earliest message. The task is a difficult one, for the period in which Christianity was just emerging and was not yet fully conscious of itself is wrapt in darkness. Some light is thrown on it in the opening chapters of Acts and by occasional references in Paul's Epistles, and the attempt is made to piece out from these notices some kind of crude theology which is attributed to the first teachers. The method, however, is a fallacious one. Great movements have never started with formal doctrines. They have their source in passionate convictions, which tended only to weaken through the later efforts to explain and define them. We learn little about the Reformation from a study of the various Confessions in which its principles were formulated in set terms. When we think of the great upheaval and then turn to those dull, precise statements, we feel disillusioned. If men were only fighting over certain theological subtleties was the struggle worth while?

We need to remind ourselves that by means of doctrine the Reformers were seeking to affirm a new aspiration towards freedom and pure religion. These were the real issues, and we only lose sight of them when they are confused with the doctrinal formulae. This is pre-eminently true of the beginnings of Christianity itself. Without much difficulty we may collect a number of ideas which apparently found a place in the early teaching, and call these the primitive beliefs, out of which everything else was gradually evolved. Thus it can be argued, and this has often been done, that the church was nothing at the outset but an obscure Jewish sect, distinguished from the others by a few peculiar beliefs. No one can rest satisfied with such an explanation. If Christianity set out with nothing of its own but those few additions to Jewish doctrine, how did it come to reveal itself, within a single generation, as a new religion capable of transforming the world? The ideas, when formally stated, do not tell us anything. Behind them were burning convictions which could not be put into words, and in these the power of the message consisted. They had not been arrived at by any rational process, for all this was to come later; and to begin with there was only the overwhelming sense of a new world of truth which had been disclosed through Christ. It is profoundly significant that the earliest mode of Christian thinking was not reflection but vision. The opening chapters of Acts are full of miraculous happenings—voices and appearances of angels, revelations made in dream and ecstasy. All this is often dismissed as the accretion of legend, and the inference is drawn that since nothing was definitely known about the first days the blank was filled in by imagination. As in the early history of nations so in that of the church there was a mythological period which may be left out of account. But the truth is that our best knowledge of Christian origins is given us in those legends. Whatever may be their historical value they correspond to realities which could not be otherwise described. Paul thinks of his visions and revelations as the great events of his missionary career, far more remarkable than any of his labors. He had been caught up to the third heaven. He had listened to unspeakable words, which it was forbidden him to repeat. The early disciples lived amidst such experiences. It may be doubted whether any of them would have been able to state clearly what he thought and believed. He could only have said, "I saw the Lord," "I heard a voice speaking to me," "It was revealed to me by the Spirit." The writer of Acts is aware that everything in the early days must be explained from that ecstatic mood which was then the normal one. We are not to think of the disciples as forming some elementary doctrines which they proceeded to expand and demonstrate. They were conscious rather of an inrush of divine power and certainty. They lived in a world in which old things had passed away and all things had become new. The formation of doctrine marked the ebb of that first exultant period in which the truth was given immediately by way of revelation.

Christianity, then, did not grow out of a few ideas, at the outset vague and tentative but apprehended more and more clearly in the light of reflection. It is true that the disciples called themselves "the believers," in the sense that they accepted the claim of Jesus to be the Messiah, which the body of their countrymen denied. This in itself was an intellectual judgment, and we conceive of them as making it deliberately, after due consideration of the evidence. In later times the church has been satisfied with this kind of belief. It has required the assent of the mind to certain propositions, such as that the scriptures are inspired, that Christ fulfilled the prophecies, that he stood in a given relation to God. To hold the right view on these matters is all that is necessary to make a believer. It is evident, however, that much more is implied in the term as we find it used in the New Testament. The believers were those who confessed Jesus as Lord, and thereby surrendered themselves to his will. Paul declares that faith is the one means of salvation, and it is often assumed that he put some new, mystical construction on that mere assent which was demanded by the primitive church. But faith had always the value attributed to it by Paul. The act of believing involved a new attitude to God, a new kind of life, the sense of a divine energy bestowed by Christ on his people. To be sure there were certain ideas to which the "believers" assented, but these served only to mark out that new condition of a man's whole being which constituted his faith.

The church, then, did not set out from some articles of belief, which at first were very simple but were gradually elaborated. It took its stand on an experience which lay behind the beliefs, and out of which they grew. Men were conscious that through Christ they had entered on a new life. Who was he that he should produce this change in them? What had he done? We can make nothing of Christian thought until we realise that it is concerned, not with arbitrary dogma, but with fact. The astronomer has to examine the various theories which have been put forward to account for the motions of the stars, and may find them all mistaken and suggest a new one. But whatever the theory, he is trying to explain the fact that the stars move. The Christian thinker likewise has to deal with a fact. Something takes place in the human soul under the influence of Christ. All the doctrines which are supposed to account for it may be wrong and may call for refutation; but all this is incidental and the fact is still there to be explained. It was in this way that the New Testament teachers understood their task. They were conscious of a new life imparted through the Christian message, and offered one doctrine and another which appeared to throw some light on the mystery. But they did not regard the doctrines as in themselves binding and necessary. At best they were only imperfect efforts to interpret that living experience which was the substance of the Christian faith.

There never was a time when the believers were all agreed on their interpretation. The minds of men are different, and cannot but respond differently to the same impulse. That this law held good even in the earliest Christianity is apparent from our Gospels, which preserve the first reflections of the church on the work of Jesus. It used to be taken for granted that while the Fourth Gospel is theological in character the Synoptic Gospels are plain narratives of fact; but this now appears doubtful. There are signs that even Mark, our oldest Gospel, has a theological as well as an historical aim.* The author has his own conception of Jesus' Messiahship, and is guided by it in his record of the events. Not only in the Gospels but in the primitive documents which lie behind them there seem to be traces of different forms of teaching. The Kingdom of God is represented sometimes as national, sometimes as universal; it is described now as a better earthly order, now as the heavenly order which cannot be realized until the earthly one is destroyed. So there are marked differences in the conception of Jesus himself. He is regarded as the national deliverer foretold by the prophets, as an angelic being, manifest for a time on earth, as the divine Wisdom who instructs men in the true way of life. Imbedded in the Gospels we seem to have the fossil remains of various theologies which divided the church even in its earliest days.

This view of the records is sometimes based on an analysis which is too subtle to be convincing, and which involves a straining of isolated words and phrases. A whole theology is extracted from a single verse, and is labelled, by some process of divination, with the name of Peter or James or Stephen. One cannot but feel at times that Gospel criticism, instead of advancing, has now yielded its harvest and is running to seed. In so far as real differences can be traced in the records they do not necessarily point to controversy, but only serve to remind us that in the first age every-

---

* *Cf.* R. H. Lightfoot, *History and Interpretation in the Gospels.*

thing was still fluid. The church had not yet decided on any creed. All teachers were free to offer their own opinions, and the same teacher could pass, when he thought fit, from one opinion to another. This is what always happens when a new principle has come to light but cannot yet be definitely formulated. We can see it happening at the present time in the field of physical enquiry. The experts as yet are all at variance, and are willing to acknowledge that their findings are only provisional. Each honest investigator leaves the door open for at least two or three hypotheses, any one of which may prove true. It must have been the same in the early days of Christianity. The idea of a number of groups, bitterly opposed to one another, is wholly misleading. All teachers were assured that God had spoken to men through Christ, and that the Kingdom was near. What it was and in what form it would come no one could tell for certain, and all were at liberty to guess. Peter, we may be sure, would never have claimed some type of thought as peculiar to himself, as opposed to James or John. At most he would have said "I incline to this interpretation, but the other may be nearer the mark, or perhaps both should be taken together." This was indeed his attitude with regard to Paul. There was much in Paul's thinking with which he was not wholly satisfied, and in matters of practice he frankly differed from Paul. Yet he took no exception to Paul's version of the gospel. He admitted that God, who wrought mightily in himself, was mighty also in this mission to the Gentiles, and he gave Paul the right hand of fellowship.†

It need not be denied that in our Gospels, and in the previous documents out of which they are compiled, there are many discrepancies, and the criticism which has detected them has thrown a useful light on the religion of the primitive church. Even in

† Gal. 2 : 7–9.

those first days the teachers differed in their interpretation of the message. Nevertheless Luke can truly say "they were all of one heart and one mind." As he contrasts the primitive age with his own he can see that in the Christianity of that time there was a full agreement on essential things, in spite of any minor differences. It is customary to speak of the primitive teaching as Jewish, and this is no doubt correct in so far as it belonged to Palestine, and was moulded by the traditional Jewish beliefs. Yet the term "Jewish Christianity" is misleading. It suggests that the religion taught was not fully Christian, and that the early believers had not yet realized that the message of Jesus was new and distinctive. This is to do them an injustice. The one thing which they apprehended with an intense conviction was the newness of the message. Through Christ they had received a new vision of God, a new conception of life. Luke dwells repeatedly on the joy and wonder which possessed them, as if they felt themselves to be mariners gazing on an unknown country for the first time. They may not have fully comprehended that the Law was now done away, but they were passionately aware that the new faith was different from the old. The very condition of their discipleship was to forsake father and mother, to break completely with all their most cherished traditions. That they made this break is the fact which stands out most clearly in the early record.

The idea of the primitive church as more Jewish than Christian is due to nothing else than a false perspective. We look on the early disciples from the Gentile point of view, and see that they practised Jewish customs and lived within the Jewish world of thought. Since they held so much in common with Judaism we conclude that this was the preponderant element in their religion. But a similar judgment might equally well be applied to Christians brought up under any particular culture, Indian or Chinese or Anglo-Saxon. They combine their faith with their own mode of

living and habits of thought, but it does not follow that their
Christianity is to that extent imperfect. The early disciples were
Jews, to whom the observance of the Law was a second nature.
They found it hard to conceive that a civilized life was possible
without the Law; but their adherence to Jewish practices in no
way affected their faith as Christians.

The truth is that between the Law and the gospel there was no
inherent conflict. Jesus himself observed the Law, and never felt
that it obstructed him in his fellowship with God. He recognised
that it was only concerned with external things—meats and
drinks, daily habits and the keeping of holy seasons—and within
this frame-work the purest religion was able to maintain itself.
The Law, in fact, was little more than a kind of national costume.
A traditional form of dress is in some countries associated with
religion, and tends at times to take the place of it; and when this
is so it may become a grave spiritual danger. Yet the rule holds
good that all races, however they choose to clothe themselves, can
pursue the same higher ends, and there was no reason why the
Jews, with their peculiar Law, should not also be devoted Christians. As Paul himself observes, in the very Epistle in which he
vehemently attacks the Law, "circumcision is nothing, and uncircumcision is nothing; all that matters is the new creation." ‡

The question of the Law only became a serious one when the
Gentiles began to enter the church. These aliens knew nothing of
the Law, and saw in it an encumbrance which was better thrown
away. For the Jews it was inseparable from the very idea of religion, and were they now to acknowledge that after all it was
unnecessary? Hitherto the believers had adhered to the Law without ever thinking about it. Their Christianity was quite apart
from those ordinances which belonged to the routine of life and
which all their countrymen took for granted. Now they were

‡ Gal. 6 : 15.

called on to decide whether the new religion could be liberated from the Law.

To many Jewish Christians this appeared to be impossible. Not only so, but when the Law was challenged they were inclined to make it more important than anything else. This is what always happens when some outward distinction has been called in question. It may be so trivial that hitherto it has hardly been noticed, but now when it is threatened it becomes the one thing that seems essential. Nations go to war over some point of precedence which makes no difference to anybody. Churches divide on some paltry rule of order or ritual, perhaps some mere phrase which at the outset had no significance. So when Christianity passed into the Gentile world the problem of the Law began to bulk ever more largely. For the primitive church this problem had hardly existed, but now it occupied men's minds almost to the exclusion of everything else. The term "Jewish Christianity" thus took on a very definite meaning. A party arose in the church which made the Jewish element in Christian teaching the fundamental one. Faith in Christ was regarded as secondary. The chief requirement was the keeping of holy days and the maintenance of all the rites and customs enjoined in the Jewish code. At this point the gospel and the Law plainly became incompatible. Paul could truly say, "If any man insists on the Law, he has fallen away from Christ." ¶

We must not, however, confound this attitude with that of Jewish Christians in the earlier years. There was no thought then of discarding the Law, but it was in no way an impediment to faith. Even at a later day, when the legal controversy had fairly begun, there was not the sharp distinction which is often assumed between Jewish and Gentile believers. As we study that period in which Paul was the central figure our sympathies are naturally with Paul. He was bent on carrying his message to the whole

¶ Gal. 5:4.

world, while the older Apostles confined themselves to their own country. He apprehended the gospel in its larger and deeper aspects, while they were fettered by racial prejudices and traditions. They not only held aloof from Paul but put difficulties in his way, and while we acknowledge their sincerity we cannot but think of them as short-sighted and narrow-minded. At this distance of time it appears self-evident that Paul was right. He stood for true Christianity while the religion of the others was a mixture or a compromise. This is what we imply when we describe their type of teaching as Jewish Christianity.

It cannot, however, be urged too strongly that a grave injustice is thus done to the older Apostles who, when all is said, were the original missionaries, without whom the world would never have known the gospel. Their position, if we try to understand it, was a perfectly valid one, and had nothing to do with mere prejudice or bigotry. Like Paul they believed that the message was intended for all men, but they held to the Old Testament idea that God would fulfill his purpose for the world through a holy nation. They made it their task, therefore, to convert Israel, the people which God himself had chosen; and they could not but feel that Paul was following a mistaken course. He was working at random, going here and there among the Gentiles and forming little isolated groups which did not represent any larger whole. Such a mission, as they saw it, was bound to be ineffectual. There needed to be a solid foundation before the building could stand securely. The new religion must have behind it the authority of a nation if it was to make any impression on the world. In such an attitude there was nothing that can be called narrow and unreasonable. It might well be argued that the weakness of the Christian mission has always been that, since the time of Paul and owing largely to his example, it has been left so much to private enterprise. There has never yet been a whole nation devoted to the Christian cause, working for it with the same combined energy which it throws into commerce or war. The efforts of saintly individuals are constantly thwarted by the indifference of their country, which acts on principles quite divorced from its religion. The aim of the Apostles was first of all to create a Christian nation. A mission to the world at large would come afterwards, but it could only fulfill its purpose through a regenerated Israel.

If the Apostles failed in their endeavor it was from causes for which they cannot be held accountable. For one thing, they could not have foreseen the growing obduracy of the Jewish people. It may be that Luke exaggerates the welcome which was given at first to the new message, but there can be little question that it met with an eager response. At the outset the people were open-minded; they recognized in the gospel something they had been seeking for; left to themselves they might have acknowledged in Jesus the true Messiah. But the same religious leaders who had attacked Jesus in his lifetime were now hostile to the church. They did not resort to open persecution but sought, in insidious ways, to undermine the new movement. A prejudice against it was fostered in the popular mind. Israel, in the words of Paul, was "hardened"—made callous and insensitive. After the first generation it became evident that the people as a whole would not receive the message and the idea of a Christian nation must be abandoned.

It must also be remembered that while the mission in Palestine was still in progress the great conflict with Rome was growing to a head. Religion was identified with national passions, and it was difficult for the Christian message, which rose above them, to obtain a hearing. The revolt had its final issue in the fall of Jerusalem and the ruin of the Jewish state. Israel had now ceased to be a nation, and the aim which the Apostles had set before them ceased to have any meaning. This was a disaster they had never foreseen, and if they failed in their enterprise they were not themselves to blame. There could be no thought now of making a Christian Israel, and the Jewish church had to content itself, as Paul had done, with a mission to individuals.

It is easy, therefore, to do injustice to Jewish Christianity, all the more so as we chiefly know it through those writings of Paul which were thrown out in the heat of the legal controversy. Paul is careful to discriminate between the Apostles themselves and the clique of extremists who falsely pretended to represent them, but he naturally speaks with bitterness, and leaves us with the impression that all Jewish Christians were blind to the true interests of the gospel. They were concerned only with trivial matters of ritual; they were animated by unworthy motives; they thought of salvation as coming by the Law and not through faith in Christ. It is unfortunate that we know so little of the Jewish church apart from Paul's account of it. If some record by one of its own leaders had been preserved we might have formed a very different conception. Much more if we had some means of looking at a Jewish community in being—not occupied with questions of controversy but quietly following the Christian life in its own way—we should have known better how to judge. We should probably cease to speak of Jewish Christianity at all, and think only of companies of people who happened to be of Jewish race but who made it their one endeavour simply to live as Christians.

In the book of Acts we do occasionally have glimpses of such communities. It may be that Luke idealises the primitive church in Palestine, but even so he must have drawn his picture on the ground of facts which were well remembered. He says nothing at all about observance of the Law, for in this respect the disciples behaved like all other pious Jews. He dwells only on the things which made them different. They were steadfast in their obedience to the Apostle's teaching. They held meetings for prayer and the common meal. No one had anything that he called his own, and each one willingly shared his possessions with others. They spoke boldly in the name of Jesus, and while exposed to ill-treatment and dislike were patient under suffering. Their mood was one of gladness as they waited daily together for the Kingdom of God. Luke has occasion to tell how Peter visited the little group at Joppa, and found it in mourning for Dorcas, who had devoted herself to making garments for the poor.[§] This was her idea of the Christian life, and not a bad one; and she was typical of the ordinary members of those Jewish churches. They did not spend their time, as we are often given to suppose, in arid disputation over questions of the Law. They were occupied, as Christians always have been, in acts of kindness, in the practical effort to make the new life a reality, and this was the distinctive thing about their religion.

It is true that the Jewish church has left us no writing by which we may check the evidence of Paul's Epistles. Yet we still have a document, or a series of documents, which cannot be neglected in any judgment of its character. The Synoptic Gospels are our record of the life of Jesus, but the traditions out of which they arose were those of the Palestinian church, and everywhere bear its impress. The mere fact that they were preserved is highly significant. It reminds us that the people to whom we owe them were interested, above all else, in Jesus' life and teaching. Their religious literature, if it may be so called, did not consist of theological pamphlets but of those concrete records of Jesus, which were recited week by week in their meetings for worship. It is significant too, that the records are selected with a marvellous instinct for what is essential in Jesus' religion. The incidents are those which bring him before us in his characteristic moments. The sayings are all such as have some bearing on his central message. In the sur-

§ Acts 9:39.

viving memories of him there must have been much that had no
particular import for Christian faith, but this secondary material
has nearly all been omitted. The record has been sifted, in the
Palestinian church, by minds which had a real understanding of
the thought of Jesus. In this connection we cannot but observe
the exquisite forms in which the traditions have been preserved.
In many instances the words attributed to Jesus cannot correspond
exactly to those which he uttered, for the same saying is reported
in two or three different versions. His idea has been reproduced
in language supplied by the early disciples, and they could not
have chosen such language unless they had been in perfect sympathy with the thought. Their memory of it has been of no
mechanical kind. They have so absorbed it into their own thinking
that they could repeat it in new words, such as Jesus himself
might have spoken.

The Gospels have a still further value as illuminating the character of the early church. They came into being for a practical
purpose. The disciples were no doubt interested in the life of
Jesus for its own sake, but they did not collect those narratives out
of mere curiosity about an extraordinary man. They did not preserve the teaching because it was striking and original and the
world's store of wisdom would be poorer if it were lost. They put
it on record because they desired to live by it. Judaism had its
Law, which every good Jew was required to know, so that he
might order his life according to the will of God. The Christians
also had their way of life prescribed for them, and it was given
them in the example of Jesus and the words he had spoken. It was
this need for practical guidance which brought the Gospels into
existence, and there can be no question that the church was indeed guided by them. To follow out literally those lofty demands
was indeed impossible, but they represented the kind of life to
which the Christian felt himself committed when he made the
confession "Jesus is Lord."

From the Gospels, therefore, we can learn what the church desired to be, and in some measure must have been, in the time when its membership was wholly Jewish. Judged by this testimony, which is the best we have, it was little affected by racial limitations. It was made up of Jews who remained faithful to the Law, but they were not legalists after the Pharisaic pattern. Their standards were those of the Sermon on the Mount. Their chief representative was Peter who comes before us always as a lovable, broad-minded man, passionately loyal to Jesus after the Crucifixion as he had been before. He was estranged from Paul over the unfortunate question of the Law, but Paul resented his action because he knew that Peter, in his heart, was no more fettered by the Law than he was himself.

So it is wrong to think of Jewish Christianity as little more than a new form of Judaism, in which the faith in Christ had only an incidental place. Its whole basis was purely Christian, and had it not been for the Gentile mission the problem of the Law would never have been raised, or would have gradually solved itself. Even when the Gentile mission had fairly begun the difficulty of the Law was not felt to be serious. Gentiles continued to enter the church, and no questions were asked about their legal credentials. The episode of Cornelius in the book of Acts is no doubt typical of what was constantly happening.* Here was a Gentile who manifestly had the true faith in Christ, and this was regarded as a sufficient pass-port, on the ground of which he was admitted to baptism. But when once the question of the Law had been formally raised it thrust itself into the foreground, and everything was made to turn on this disputed issue. The Jewish section of the church now ranged itself under the banner of the Law. It declared "except ye be circumcised after the manner of Moses, ye cannot be saved," † and from the time that it thus identified itself

* Acts 10: 1 ff.   † Acts 15: 1.

with the keeping of the Law it lost its vitality. Not because it maintained the Law, for it had always done so, but because it now based everything on a side-issue and neglected the essential message.

The error of the Jewish Christians was one which is only too familiar in the history of religion, and which has always proved fatal. It may be described as placing the whole emphasis on a negative. Jews and Gentiles alike believed in the gospel but while the Gentiles dispensed with the Law the Jews did not, and they staked everything on the mere denial of a position held by others. Nothing can ever come out of bare negation, and there is always the danger that it may take the place of what you positively believe. There are sects today whose opinions have long been untenable for any enlightened man, and which yet can produce some of the finest types of Christian character. The reason is that with all their narrowness they hold fast to some positive truths; but too often they are not content with that and take to denouncing all views that differ from their own. In course of time this mere antagonism becomes their religion, and then they merely cumber the ground. The principle holds good in the case of other sects which pride themselves on their liberalism. They have broken away from an outworn mode of thought, and this is well; but in their emancipation they contrast themselves with those who are not so favoured. They cease to have much interest in what they do believe, and are satisfied with not believing what other people do. The real argument against most forms of scepticism is not that they are false but that they are empty. It can matter little to anybody what you do not believe. The question always arises when you have condemned the errors of other men, what truth can you put in their place? The mere negation is only a beating of the air.

This, then, was the weakness of Jewish Christianity, and it is ultimately on this ground that Paul assails it. He shows that the teachers from Jerusalem are bent wholly on opposition. They are hostile to his person, to his methods, to his conception of the gospel. They wish to deprive his converts of everything he has given them, and have nothing to offer instead. Wherever he went they followed with the one announcement that what he had taught was wrong. Their Christianity was wholly negative, with the result that it ceased to count, and the movement went forward without it. One of the tragedies of Christian history was this disappearance, before the first century was over, of the Jewish church. It had given the new religion to the world, and seemed destined to mould and direct it, but it fell by the wayside. The church of Pentecost found its later representatives in those wretched Judaists who dogged the footsteps of Paul and made it their one object to thwart his splendid mission. It is a tragedy which has many parallels in religious history, and in history generally. Movements which began gloriously and brought liberty and new life have died out as mere obstructions, not because they had outlived their usefulness but because they allowed themselves to drift into mere negation. The thing they stood for was forgotten in the effort to hinder some other movement which was working for the same object in a different way. What the world demands is always the positive thing, however it may be presented, and those who do nothing to advance it are ruthlessly pushed aside.

It was by no accident, therefore, that the New Testament writings were the product of the Gentile church, and occupied themselves with the Gentile mission. This was the channel in which all Christian interests were now flowing, and the older channel was manifestly running dry. From the time that Paul appears on the scene we have only occasional glimpses of the church at Jerusalem. We almost forget that alongside of the Gentile communities there still existed the mother church, directed by men who had been the Lord's personal disciples. Thus we are apt to conclude that it was wholly negligible, and had exhausted itself, like the queen bee, in the one act of producing the active hive. This, however, is a mistaken judgment. Throughout the whole New Testament period the Jewish church continued to be a powerful influence. The history even of the Gentile communities is not intelligible unless we keep in mind the church in Palestine which lay always in the background.

For one thing, it was the connecting link between later Christianity and Jesus himself. It might do little in the way of direct missionary work, but by its very existence it kept the Christian movement in contact with the ultimate source of its vitality. This relation to Jesus which it preserved was no mere sentimental one, for we must never forget that it was the Palestinian church that collected those records which finally took shape in our Gospels. This, when all is said, was its supreme service. The mind of the Gentile church was progressive, and was intent on discovering ever new meanings in the Christian message, and applying it to needs and conditions which Jesus himself had not foreseen. The Jewish mind, trained in the discipline of the Law, was conservative. It turned to the past rather than to the future, and failed to discern those many things which were involved in the teaching of Jesus, although he had not expressly spoken of them. For this reason, however, the Jewish disciples were peculiarly fitted for remembering and transmitting what he had actually taught. If they contributed little to the advancement of Christian thinking they did a work of inestimable value by preserving what had been originally given. We owe far more to those reporters of Jesus than to the gifted theologians who discovered so much that was new and wonderful in his message. The later speculations have in great part lost their meaning; we have passed beyond them, and associate them with a bygone age. The Gospel record is the enduring treasure of Christianity. It bears witness amidst all changes to the authentic work of Jesus, and it comes to us from those disciples in Palestine who seemed a generation afterwards to be mere voices of the past.

Again, while it ceased to lead the Christian movement the mother church continued to exercise a supervision. Luke plans his history in Acts on the assumption that everything was centred in Jerusalem. The missionaries were sent out from Jerusalem, and returned from time to time that they might report on their work and have their mandates renewed. It has been contended that this picture is not in keeping with the facts, and that the Gentile churches, almost from the outset, went their own way, with little regard to what was done or thought at Jerusalem. But while he exaggerates, Luke is correct in his main idea. We can gather from Paul's own testimony that the church at Jerusalem was vested with a real authority, all the more powerful because it was undefined. In any disputed matters the mother church was the natural court of appeal. It was Paul's chief difficulty all through his mission that this revered church was supposed to be against him. The hostile emissaries found entrance into his communities because they came armed with letters of commendation from Jerusalem. This was what made them dangerous. They claimed to speak for the church to which Christians everywhere looked up with confidence as the acknowledged guardian of the faith. In this instance, as in many others, the influence of Jerusalem was harmful, but there can be little question that it made, in the main, for stability. The chief weakness of the church in the early period was its lack of any central control. It consisted of a great number of small communities, all standing apart and jealous of their independence. As yet there could be no thought of an official authority, for the church by its very idea was different from all earthly societies, and was subject only to the Spirit, which was equally present in all its members. But it meant much that there was one community which at least held precedence over the others. No church could feel that it lost any of its freedom or dignity by modelling itself on Jerusalem and seeking counsel from those elder brethren who had been the Lord's personal companions. Had it not been for this deference paid to Jerusalem the church would have had no common standards and might easily have fallen into chaos. In a larger sense also the primitive community kept the various churches together. As their mother it was the object of their reverence and affection. Apart from anything it might do by way of leadership it served a great purpose by its mere existence. It was like an actual mother whose family is widely scattered, brothers and sisters absorbed in their own interests and little concerned with one another. Yet while she survives, unable to do much more than sit by the fire, she is the bond of union, and all discords are kept in check. It is highly significant that when Paul sought to unite his churches by setting them to work on a common enterprise the scheme he devised was that of a collection for the poor at Jerusalem. This, he knew, was a cause in which all Christians would be willing to cooperate. Whatever might be their mutual differences they were all at one in their sentiment towards the mother church. There was a magic in the very name of the holy city.

In these ways the church in Palestine continued to exert an influence, although it refused to join actively in the onward movement. But there was value also in the fact that it was conservative and even reactionary. The Gentile church from the first was inclined to proceed too fast, and this was its principal danger. The Christian idea of liberty was intoxicating to those whose previous religion had been a bondage of routine. Conscious that they had left the past behind them and that all things had become new, they were easily swept off their feet by any novel doctrine. We hear constantly in the later books of "false teachers" who were everywhere at work, and shortly afterwards the church was struggling for its life with the Gnostic heresy. Throughout this chase after doubtful lights Jewish conservatism was of priceless value. It acted as a brake on forces which might have wrecked Christianity if they had been left to themselves. No one can study the writings of Paul without observing a change which gradually comes over his attitude. The Epistles of his earlier period are full of bitter attacks on his Jewish opponents. He is irritated, with good reason, by their refusal to move forward, and in this stubborn adherence to old traditions he sees the great obstacle to the Christian enterprise. In his later Epistles he is afraid of too much emancipation on the part of his Gentile converts. He draws closer to the Jewish section of the church, and thinks of it not as a drag but as an anchor. The question has often been raised in modern enquiry whether Paul was not far more of a Jew than we are wont to suppose, or than he himself suspected. It is argued that with all his insistence on the new Christian principles he had never really weaned himself from the prejudices of his early training, and remained to the end a Jewish rabbi. This, however, is to misunderstand his position. He had indeed attained to a full inward freedom. He was conscious, as no other man has ever been, that through Christ the believer enters on a new life in which the constraints that have hitherto bound him have ceased to exist. But this very sense of freedom which possesses the mind of Paul makes him anxious for himself and for the church. The old leading-strings have been cast aside, and men have now the full control of their own lives; but who is sufficient for these things? Paul was not displeased to know that while he proclaimed his gospel of liberty there were other teachers who still held fast to the Law. His position may in some degree be compared to that of the modern radical, who demands a new social system, and even a violent revolution, but is glad in his heart that there are forces working against him, and that his full programme will not be carried into effect. His misgiving is due, not to any insincerity, but to a well-grounded fear that human nature will not prove equal to the high privilege which the abstract thinker may justly claim for it. Paul had broken with the Law but did not care to discard it altogether. He allows it some place even when he protests most vehemently that Christ has made us free. More than ever when he saw that liberty in his Gentile churches was running to extremes, he grew in sympathy with those Jewish Christians who still held fast to the Law.

One thing becomes evident when we review the history of Jewish Christianity in the light of the New Testament record. There never was a type of teaching which can be set by itself and described as Jewish, in contrast to another type which was peculiar to the Gentiles. At the outset all Christians were of Jewish race and were simply "the believers," as opposed to the mass of their countrymen who did not believe. Their religion was not some mixture of the old and the new beliefs, but in all essentials was Christian. With the rise of the Gentile mission the Jewish Christians became conscious of their nationality. They were led to regard their Gentile brethren as aliens, and magnified their Jewish devotion to the Law. But even in this legal Christianity we can distinguish many gradations. There were Jewish believers who came very near to Paul's own position. While they still observed the Law they did not consider it indispensable. Some of them, apparently without much difficulty, came over to Paul, and assisted him in his mission. Peter himself was friendly to Paul, and was willing, in a Gentile city like Antioch, to fall in with Paul's conception of a Christian brotherhood in which the Law might be disregarded. It would seem, however, that Paul mistook the nature and extent of Peter's acquiescence. When Peter ceased to eat with the Gentiles he accused him of "hypocrisy," as if he were now pretending to a zeal for the Law, while in his heart he had disowned it. But Peter was not pretending. He was content to make the Law secondary, throwing it off when it interfered with the higher Christian obligations, but he was not prepared to abjure it. It might be binding only on Jews, but he was himself a Jew, and his religion had always been inseparable from it, and when he had once made his gesture of conciliation he fell back on his normal practice. A liberal Catholic may join in the worship of Protestants when he is their guest. He does this, not merely as an act of courtesy, but as an expression of his real belief that all Christians have a common faith which transcends their differences. None the less he remains a Catholic, and is guilty of no hypocrisy when he returns to mass and confession. The attitude of Peter, in fact, was in keeping with that of Jesus himself, when he declared that legal observances must not be set before the weightier matters, justice, mercy and faith, but took care to add "these ought ye to have done, without leaving the others undone."

There was another type of Jewish Christianity which assigned a positive value to the Law. It had its chief representative in James, who stood apparently in a certain opposition to Peter, and came to displace him in the leadership of the church at Jerusalem. From all that we learn about him, in the New Testament and in early tradition, he was strict in his observance of the Law, and earned the title, even among pious Jews, of "the Just"—the man pre-eminent in legal righteousness. On this account he has been hardly dealt with in many histories of the early church, as the chief adversary of Paul and of the higher interests of the gospel. This condemnation of James is, to say the least, ungrateful, for it was probably his fidelity to the Law which enabled the church to survive. The Jewish authorities were suspicious of the new movement and might have strangled it in its cradle, but they could do nothing while it was led by James, to whose orthodoxy not even the most critical Pharisee could object. On other grounds the ordinary judgment on James must be qualified. He was no mere reactionary, who held fast to the Law and tried to keep back the Christian mission. It must never be forgotten that at the Council, when the general feeling was hostile to Paul, James gave him the hand of fellowship and so ensured him freedom for his work among the Gentiles. This was not the act of a Jewish bigot, who had no interest in the gospel for its own sake. In the years that followed, James never withdrew his support from Paul, and offered him a cordial welcome when he paid his final visit to Jerusalem. It is true that he held to the Law, and would make no concessions as Peter was willing to do. If it had been James who came to Antioch he would have refused from the first, as a matter of conscience, to eat with the Gentiles, and Paul could never have accused him of inconsistency. Yet he was able to recognize that others might have principles which differed from his own, and which had still to be respected. It was on his proposal that the Council arrived at its decision, "Let Paul preach the gospel in his own way to the Gentiles, while we confine ourselves to the Jews." ‡ This was not a compromise, vainly attempting to combine two positions which in their nature were incompatible. We can see in it rather the attitude of a fair-minded man, who was anxious that all parties should be true to their own convictions. We can see in it too, a clear recognition that the gospel was something more than any one mode of interpreting it. James had found his way, from the opposite side, to the same conclusion as Paul: "Neither circumcision nor uncircumcision availeth anything."

Peter and James may be taken as representative of two forms of Jewish Christianity. There was a third form, which must be care-

‡ Gal. 2:9; *cf.* Acts 15:13 ff.

fully distinguished from both of them. For the strict Jewish party Christianity was nothing more than a new variation of Judaism, and the Law belonged therefore to its very substance. Jesus was indeed the Messiah, but his Messianic work consisted in his full assertion of what was given in Judaism. A religion in which the Law was abandoned, or was reduced to a secondary place, had no right to call itself Christianity. This party seems to have included a large proportion of the Christians in Palestine. When Paul arrived in Jerusalem on his last visit he was warned by James and the elders that their church as a whole was zealous for the Law and must be given some assurance that it was in no danger.¶ From another notice we learn that among the new converts were many Pharisees, and that they took a prominent part in the church meetings.§ An influence of this kind would inevitably have a powerful influence in the moulding of Christian opinion. But even within this strictly Jewish party there would be differences of attitude. It was possible to believe that the gospel was vitally bound up with Judaism and yet to think of it as a new revelation. This, indeed, is the position reflected in the speech of Stephen, and more fully set forth in the Epistle to the Hebrews. It finds its justification in Jesus' own saying; "Think not that I have come to destroy the Law; I came not to destroy but to fulfil." * The whole stress is laid on the idea of fulfilment. Christ had disclosed what had hitherto been hidden in the Law—the deeper truth concerning God and man's relation to him which it had only foreshadowed. His message, therefore, although inseparable from the Law and involved in it, was essentially new. It taught men to understand the Law in a manner which entirely changed its character. This was no doubt the attitude of many of those Jewish Christians whose religion, to all appearance, differed little from Judaism. They clung to the Law, and felt they would be lost without it, but

¶ Acts 21 : 18–22.   § Acts 15 : 5.   * Matt. 5 : 17.

what they now found in the Law was the new revelation of God's will which they had learned through Christ. They observed the Law with their minds set on its Christian fulfilment. There were others, however, for whom the Law itself was the thing that mattered. Christ had fulfilled it in the sense that he had given it a final sanction, and in their Christianity the Law obscured everything else. Probably they were a small minority, for there was so little to distinguish them from ordinary Jews that it was hardly worth their while to become Christians at all. But it is usually the minority which is most vociferous, and those half-converts were able to disturb the peace of the whole church. It was they who made it their business to attack the mission of Paul, and who succeeded, for a time, in thwarting it. Their sinister activities have confused our whole impression of the early church, and have brought a reproach on Jewish Christianity which it does not properly deserve.

There was, in fact, no radical difference between the Jewish type of Christianity and that which prevailed among the Gentiles. In so far as a conflict existed it turned on matters of custom which in the last resort were irrelevant to the genuine Christian message. This was realized in the generation after Paul, when the question of the Law dropped quietly out of sight. It was never settled, but the church ceased to be concerned with it. With their growing insight into the larger meanings of the gospel, men lost all interest in that legal controversy which at one time had clouded the whole horizon. This does not mean, however, that the controversy had been merely futile. It had served its purpose by making possible the final discovery that the issue in dispute was of no real consequence. Christianity had originated on Jewish soil, and had been entangled at the outset with Jewish practices and traditions; but it was now perceived that all this was only a wrapping which needed to be removed and thrown aside. Through the conflict with the Law our religion became conscious of itself. From the outset faith had attached itself to the essential things, but so long as the Law maintained its claim there was a confusion between the substance and the form. Christianity at last broke free from the Law. It left behind it the land-locked waters, and ventured with full sail into the open sea.

CHAPTER III

HELLENISTIC CHRISTIANITY

IT WAS never doubted by the early disciples that Christianity was a Jewish religion. Jesus had been born a Jew, and had worked solely among his countrymen. He had submitted to the Law, and had based his teaching on the Old Testament. In his own Person he had brought to fulfilment the hopes which had sustained the Jewish people through the long course of their troubled history. They had looked forward to the Messiah whom God would send for the deliverance of Israel; and Jesus was that Messiah.

Within a generation, however, this religion which was so intimately bound up with Judaism had been transplanted to the Gentile world. It had thrown off the yoke of the Law, and had found its centres in cities remote from Palestine. Among those who now professed it there were many who were hardly aware of its Jewish origin, and its future, as all thoughtful men could see, lay with the Gentiles. This surprising change has often been set down to historical accident. Palestine, it is pointed out, was a subdivision of the province of Syria and an integral part of the Roman empire. Not only so, but the Jews were a migratory people and had formed settlements in every region of the West. Through these Jews of the Dispersion the movement which had at first been local rapidly diffused itself. Above all, it was hardly started when it won a convert of towering gifts and unbounded energy. Paul was himself a Hellenistic Jew and made it his life-work to impart the new message to the Gentiles. By his deliberate effort it threw off its Jewish character and offered itself to the wider world.

This is all true, but serves only to explain the methods by which Christianity spread to the Gentiles, and does not account for the fact itself. Why was it that a religion sprung from Judaism so quickly made its way among races which knew nothing of Jewish history and tradition? Whatever may have been the contributory causes there must have been something in the religion itself which led to its expansion. It is wrong to assume, as we commonly do, that Christianity was in some manner forced on the alien peoples, and that the whole problem is to discover how it overcame their resistance. The fact is that the Gentiles themselves took the initiative. It is told in the book of Acts that Paul crossed into Europe in consequence of a dream in which a Macedonian called to him, "Come over and help us." This may be taken as a parable of what actually happened. The Gentiles were evangelised in answer to their own invitation. For the first disciples the gospel was a Jewish possession, and they wished to preserve it for the Jews. So far from pressing it on the Gentiles they put every difficulty in the way of Gentile converts, and Paul had to spend half his effort in the removal of those difficulties. It was the Gentiles who wanted Christianity, and who insisted on finding an entrance while the door was still closed on them. Much was due to the labours of the missionaries and to influences and conditions which assisted them, often without their knowledge; but all the rest would have gone for little had there not been something in the message itself which was like a loadstone to the Gentile mind.

The truth is that Christianity had never, in its essence, been a Jewish religion. Jesus had indeed worked among the Jews, and had employed their modes of thought; but he had addressed them not as Jews but simply as men. He had conceived of God not as a national divinity but as Father of all. He had affirmed the value of every human soul for its own sake, and had proclaimed a Kingdom of God which men were to enter, not on the ground of racial privilege, but through love and faith and righteousness. By its nature Christianity was a universal religion. It spread from Galilee into the Gentile lands by the same necessity that makes water rise to its level. Although Paul had never appeared, although there had never been a Roman empire in which races and creeds were being fused together, the new message would sooner or later have won the ear of the world.

It had begun to do so even in the primitive days when the church was still confined to Jerusalem. We learn from the book of Acts that among the first converts were "Hellenists"—Jews from the Greek-speaking countries. Apparently within a few months of its origin they had come to form a considerable section of the church. These foreign Jews must have been peculiarly attached to their religion, for it is impossible to think of any other motive which can have brought them to reside in Jerusalem. All their life, while they dwelt among the heathen, they must have cherished the hope of ending their days in the holy city, under the very shadow of the Temple. Like many devout Catholics who migrate for a like purpose to Rome, they had been disillusioned. In the outside world they had acquired a width of outlook which found nothing to satisfy it in the petty routine of Jewish ritual and legality, now seen too near at hand. They had looked to Jerusalem through an atmosphere which had idealised it, and the reality had proved sadly different. In this mood of disappointment they had become acquainted with the new teaching, and had found in it what was lacking in the orthodox Judaism. They had been drawn into the church and had accepted its beliefs in the light of conceptions which were often more Greek than Jewish. Before long, we are told, a division arose between the native Christians and these Hellenistic converts, who had found their leader in Stephen. After his death they were scattered to the various cities from which they had come, and this, according to the book of Acts was the beginning of the Gentile mission.*

For some time the Judaism of the Dispersion and the surrounding Paganism had been drawing together. Between the two types of religion there seemed to be nothing in common, and on both sides there was a strong feeling of antagonism. The Pagans regarded the Jews as a strange people, whose beliefs they either ridiculed or connected with some dangerous magic. The Jews prided themselves on their aloofness from Paganism, which filled them with horror as sheer idolatry or a worship of devils. Yet the gulf was not so wide as it was supposed to be by those who stood on either side of it. There were bridges over it, and this is recognized by Paul who is able, as a Christian, to take an impartial view. Sometimes he goes so far as to class Jews and Pagans together, not merely as hostile alike to Christianity but as similar in their religious attitude. For one thing, both Jews and Pagans relied on the efficacy of outward rites. The Jews were indeed convinced that their rites had been divinely ordained, and were not to be compared for a moment to the idolatries of the heathen. Yet the difference, as Paul perceived, was superficial. Jewish piety, no less than Pagan, was a matter of ceremonies, of meats and drinks,† holy days which were determined by the motions of moon and stars. Worship was all dependent on things belonging to the material world. On the other hand, both Jews and Pagans, in their different ways, were seeking after God. This is frankly acknowledged by Paul. The Jews believed in God as He had revealed His will explicitly in the Law, but the Gentiles, without knowing it, believed in the same God. They also possessed His Law, written in their deeper instincts and their inward sense of

* Acts 11:19 f.   † Rom. 2:15.

right. They were following this light, although they had allowed
it to grow so dim and distorted that it had misled them. None the
less beneath all the perversions of their religion they had an
authentic sense of God—the unknown God who had at last revealed Himself.

The two types of religion had many affinities, and were now
discovering that to a great extent they had a common basis. All
Eastern races had at one time been powerfully affected by Baby-
lonian, and later by Persian influences. These had played a great
part in the making of Judaism, and had contributed, in a hardly
less degree, to the religious thinking of Greece and the adjoining
lands. The result was that the religions of the ancient world had
largely the same ground-work. We think, for instance, of apocalyptic as a peculiarly Jewish mode of thought. We imagine the
Christian missionaries as faced by a grave difficulty when they
sought to convey to the Gentile mind their strange beliefs in angels
and demons, judgment, retribution, a new age on the point of
dawning, a Saviour sent from heaven. The truth is that these
ideas were all familiar, in one form or another, to the Gentile
religions. It has often been noted that the fables and fairy-tales
which we heard in childhood have their counterparts in India and
Arabia, and the reason is that they run back to the same primitive
source (perhaps Egypt in the age of the Pyramids) and have remained essentially the same under all the variations. In like manner the Pagans, as they listened to the Christian preaching, were
able to recognise many of their own traditions. This was doubtless
one of the reasons why they responded so quickly to the message.
It did not come to them as something entirely strange. Whatever
might be new in this Christian teaching, it was attached to ideas
which to a great extent were their own.

Between Judaism and Paganism there were thus real points of
contact, and under the conditions of the first century they had

approached more closely to each other. Within the Roman empire national barriers had broken down, and people of every race had been thrown together in the great commercial cities. It was now impossible to preserve the old animosities. Since they had perforce to live together, men learned a mutual toleration. They began to see a value in customs and modes of belief which had once seemed absurd or repellent, and did not hesitate to adopt them. Most of all in the field of religion a process of borrowing was constantly going on, so that the old cults ceased to be sharply divided. Paganism in its hundred separate forms, was fast coalescing into a single religion, made up of elements which they had all joined in contributing. This fusion was rendered possible by the pervading influence of Greek thought, which acted as a solvent of all contradictions. It was discovered that all religions, when skilfully interpreted in terms of the Greek philosophies, had very much the same meaning, so that they were equally valid and could be merged at will in one another. And while Greek thought thus modified the religions it was itself profoundly affected by them. The Eastern races now pouring into the West had their own heritage of culture, which reached further back in many instances than that of Greece itself. Their religions, more especially, had far more spiritual value than the Greek Paganism, and by means of them all higher thinking was, to a great extent, rejuvenated. Philosophy in its later stages had reached the point of exhaustion. Thoughtful men had begun to realize that it could do nothing to solve the ultimate problems; but it now joined hands with the Eastern religions, and found in them at least the symbols of truth to which it could not by itself attain. The word "knowledge" (Gnosis) as used by the first century thinkers, had come to denote not merely an activity of reason but a mystical apprehension, an insight which was at once intellectual and religious.

Judaism was never in danger of losing itself in the syncretism of the age. The other religions were varying forms of nature worship, and could easily blend together; but Judaism held fast to its central belief in the one invisible God. This monotheism could not be resolved into a mere element in a composite religion. Moreover, the Jewish tenets were definitely laid down in a sacred book, and were enforced by the ceaseless discipline of the Law. It was impossible to confuse them with those of any rival cult. But while Judaism continued to be a religion apart, it was now brought into close relation with the general religious movement. The Pagan cults, as they merged in one another, had softened or discarded many of the features which had made them offensive to Jewish sentiment. Their myths and ritual were understood in the light of philosophical ideas, and out of the old polytheism the conception was gradually emerging of one divine principle which revealed itself in manifold aspects. These might be called by the names of separate divinities, but for the enlightened worshipper they were only so many energies of the one God. With Paganism of this kind Judaism could reach some kind of understanding, and could borrow from it much that helped to illuminate its own teaching. To be sure, it would not admit the borrowing. It fell back on the theory that Pagan thinkers had somehow learned the truth from the Jewish scriptures—that Plato and the Stoics were the unconscious disciples of Moses. But in this roundabout fashion Jewish and Pagan beliefs were brought together. A Judaism grew up in the Dispersion which was impregnated with Hellenistic thought, and so prepared the way for a new interpretation of Christianity.

This Hellenising of Judaism was no doubt in process at various centres in the Roman world, but was chiefly identified with Alexandria, the intellectual capital. It found its leader in Philo, who is entitled in his own right to a high place among ancient thinkers, and has a supreme historical importance as the link between Greek theology and that of the Christian church. He was a faithful Jew, and never dreamed of changing Judaism into a Hellenistic religion. His object was just the opposite. Believing that Judaism had been ordained by God himself, he offered it as the one true religion for all men. Pagans had grown aware that the truth was not given them in any of their diverse creeds, and were trying to find it by selecting elements from one creed and another and fusing them together. Might they not be brought to see that the religion they sought for was already given them in Judaism? Philo therefore examines the book of Moses and the ritual of the Law, and shows that they embody in allegorical form all the results of Greek thinking. He thus offers a Judaism which is not antagonistic to philosophy but is only the full revelation of what it has taught imperfectly. This was an attitude not uncommon among liberal Jews of the first century, and is nowhere so well expressed as in Paul's speech at Athens. Paul was repelled by the idolatry he had witnessed in the Greek city, but could feel that underneath it there was a striving towards the true worship. Among the countless idols he had seen one with the inscription "To an unknown God," and he fastened on this as the heart-felt cry of the Gentiles. They were seeking to know God, and he now brought to them the knowledge which had been denied them. This was also the task of Philo, with the difference that he had no new revelation to offer. He gave back to the Greeks under the guise of Judaism what they had already learned, and what he himself had learned, from the current philosophy.

No clear-cut line can be drawn, therefore, between Jewish and Hellenistic religion. They stood to a large extent on common ground, and in the course of the first century they were coming more and more to reconcile their differences. It was understood on both sides that the same inward principles might be discerned under the varying doctrines and traditions. Many modern scholars have been led into false conceptions of the New Testament teaching by their failure to allow for this kinship between Judaism and Hellenism. In their study of Paul, more especially, they lay stress at every point on two conflicting strains in his thought. He was a Jew and also a Hellenist, and it is taken for granted that these two personalities in the one man were constantly at odds. The problem of how he sought to reconcile them is supposed to constitute the chief difficulty in the understanding of Paul. But the distinction, more often than not, is an arbitrary one. Paul inherited a Judaism which had become so Hellenised that he could not tell what was native and what was foreign. When he turned from a Jewish to a Hellenistic idea he was no more conscious of an incongruity than we are when we change from a Saxon word to one derived from Latin. Wherever the word may have come from it is now part of our ordinary language. So in the Judaism of the Dispersion there was much that went back to Pagan thinking and was yet recognized as Jewish. It is never quite safe to say positively of anything in Paul that he has taken it deliberately from a Gentile source, and this is equally true of other New Testament writings, like the Epistle to the Hebrews and the Fourth Gospel, which bear the impress of Hellenistic thought. Before we speak of foreign influences we must always remember that in the first century the boundaries between Judaism and Hellenism had been largely obliterated. The two modes of thought were feeling out towards one another. Intelligent men on both sides were growing aware that while they differed they had many fundamental things in common, and might express them either in the Jewish or the Hellenistic way.

Nevertheless it is true that between the Jewish type of religion and that of the Hellenistic world there was a cleavage which no attempt to reconcile them could fully conceal. Nothing is more remarkable than the mutual repulsion of the two cultures, the

Greek and the Hebrew, which were destined to count for most in the life of humanity. In the Old Testament we look almost in vain for any reference to the Greeks. In the whole of Greek literature, up to the time of Christ, there are only a few scanty allusions even to the existence of the Jews. Yet the two races lived almost in sight of each other in that Eastern corner of the Mediterranean. Both of them were endowed with high intelligence and were interested in similar problems, and might have learned much, on both sides, if they had come together. But while Greek thinkers were intensely curious about the wisdom of Egypt and India, and made difficult journeys in quest of it, they seem never to have been aware of the great religion which was close to their own door. We have here a riddle to which no satisfactory answer has yet been offered. The separation of the two peoples cannot have been due to mere geographical causes, for Greece was in constant intercourse from the earliest times with Tyre and Sidon, the natural gateways into Palestine, and from the time of Alexander onward Palestine was actually incorporated into the Greek world. There must have been some spiritual barrier of which Jews and Greeks were both obscurely conscious. They felt that they were made differently and would never understand each other. There was no hostility, but simply an instinctive feeling that they had better remain apart. Herodotus, who has so much to tell of foreign peoples, is silent concerning the Jews. It is not unlikely that in the course of his travels he visited Jerusalem, but he saw nothing there to excite his interest.[‡] Paul at a later date found himself at Athens, but seems to have been quite unmoved by the glories of its art and history. In his Epistles, written as they were in Greek cities, there is no suggestion that the culture with which he was in daily contact was in any way remarkable. Jews and Greeks lived in differ-

[‡] It is not improbable that Jerusalem is the "Kadytis" of Herod. II, 159 and III, 5.

ent worlds, and this was nowhere so apparent as in their religion.

The difference was brought clearly to light under the conditions which prevailed in the first century. In earlier times it had hardly been possible to discover any radical principles which were common to the Pagan religions. Every city or clan had its own gods, and its worship was only an aspect of its patriotism. If a Greek had been asked to define in theological terms what he believed in, he would have answered, "I am a Spartan or Athenian, and duly perform the rites prescribed by my city; what they may signify and why my well-being depends on them, it is not for me to enquire." But with the decay of civil liberty and the progress of speculation, this attitude was changed. Religion was now an interest in itself, and men were compelled to reflect on the inward meaning of their beliefs. Mere local associations fell away, and religion was something which concerned the individual soul, in its relation to a higher world. Certain convictions were thus disclosed which had always lain at the heart of Pagan worship. They could now be consciously apprehended and set forth in rational language.

The Paganism which the Christian mission encountered was by no means a uniform system. One of its chief characteristics was its infinite diversity. A hundred cults had been thrown together and blended with one another in all manner of combinations, and expounded with the aid of many philosophies. Yet the process of fusion had now been so long at work that it had resulted in a general type of religion. The situation was much the same as in the Middle Ages. As we study that period we soon discover that there was a great variety of belief. The common people in every region, almost in every village, had their peculiar ideas, reflected in crude legends and customs. Side by side with this popular religion there was that of the Scholastics, that of Dante and the mystics. Barbarism went side by side with sublime art. Gross materialism held its own against the loftiest spirituality. Nevertheless in this strange medley there was an attitude of mind which we at once recognise as mediaeval. It was distinct from any other before or since, and was due, in large measure, to that very mingling of elements which impress us at first sight as incongruous. This was likewise true of the first century. It was an age of the most varied contrasts which yet, in their sum, produced a uniformity. We can speak in broad terms of a Hellenistic religion, based on principles which can be traced through all the diversities. It is necessary to consider some of these principles which were distinctive of the first century Paganism, when regarded as a whole.

(1) In the first place, reason was accepted as the final reality. It had been the grand achievement of the Greek genius to discover that the world was rational, governed by a power which had its counterpart in the human mind. In the confidence that man carried in himself the master-key which would unlock all mysteries, the Greek thinkers of the classical period had turned away from religion. For Plato and Aristotle it was a hindrance in the quest for truth. It rested on vague conjectures, on myths and fancies which at best were childish and were often false and immoral. The time had now come for accepting reason as the one sure light. Stoicism, which in course of time had displaced the older philosophies, boldly put reason in the place of God. It held that the divine reality is nothing else than the Logos, the immanent Reason which pervades all things and becomes conscious of itself in man. But this deification of reason had been followed by a reaction, due partly to the inroad of the Eastern cults, and much more to the growing sense that reason by itself cannot apprehend the ultimate truth. If men are ever to perceive those things which lie beyond the senses it must be by some kind of revelation. Knowledge, in

the last resort, was a mystical knowledge, in which man's reason is assisted by a supernatural power.

The Greek mind had thus been forced into a position similar, in some respects to that of Judaism. It had come to the point when plainly it could advance no further. It was ready to confess with Paul that "the world by wisdom knew not God," and that if God was ever to be known He must Himself speak to men. None the less the idea persisted that the apprehension of God must somehow be rational. For the Hebrew prophets He was the holy and righteous one, and men could find Him only by the way of moral obedience. For Hellenistic thinkers He was the supreme intelligence. The path to Him lay through knowledge—if not a philosophical knowledge yet an enlightenment given from above. Men would have fellowship with God in so far as their reason could attain to the divine reason. This idea was deeply rooted in all Hellenistic religion, and the effects of it are everywhere traceable in the Christianity which grew up in the Gentile world. Paul protests against the value which his Corinthian converts set on knowledge, and declares in noble language that this must rank lower than faith, hope, love. Yet as a Hellenist he cannot himself escape from a reverence for knowledge. He was the Apostle of faith but he might also be regarded as the first of Christian rationalists. He is never content until he can find in reason some ground or evidence of what he has grasped by faith. It might seem from many of his utterances as if the aim of faith were to ensure a higher knowledge. This attitude of mind is still more marked in the Fourth Gospel, where knowing and believing are almost equivalent words. Eternal life is defined as nothing else than perfect knowledge—"to know thee, the only true God and Jesus Christ whom thou hast sent." ¶ At a later time Christianity was presented as a metaphysical system which was precisely formu-

¶ Jn. 17:3.

lated in the creeds. This was inevitable when the Hellenistic mind
had taken full possession of the gospel.

(2) Again, in the Gentile lands religion had always involved a
dualism. The distinction of divine and human was conceived as
one of essence. Man was of earthly substance, and as such was incapable of immortality, or of any true happiness or virtue. This,
in the Greek view, was the real tragedy of his existence, to which
all others were incidental. With all his effort he could never escape
from the fatal condition of his being—that he was man, and subject therefore to every kind of evil—pain, folly, adversity, sin,
death. The gods were different. In their veins, according to the
naive Homeric fancy, there flows not blood but ichor. Their
life-principle is of finer nature than man's, and so they live forever, and are exempt from suffering, and are wise and just and
strong. For man there can be no deliverance unless the substance
of his being can somehow be transformed.

This is the idea which underlies all Greek religion. Its ultimate
purpose was to effect not so much a change of will as a change of
essence. The culminating religious act was initiation into the Mysteries, when the worshipper was assimilated, by means of symbolic
rites, to the nature of the gods. He underwent a process of re-birth,
from which he emerged a different creature, divine instead of
earthly. With the advent of the Oriental cults a new vitality was
given to this conception, which was now generally acknowledged
to be the central one in all religion. The ethical motive was by no
means forgotten. It was assumed that no one could aspire to the
change of nature unless his will and passions were purified, and
the moral demands have never been stated more impressively than
by some of the Pagan teachers of the first and second centuries.
But there is always the thought in the background that everything
else is only preparation. Virtue is necessary before the soul can be
fitted for the higher privilege. The one great need of man is to be

lifted out of the mortal sphere. He will be free from all other evils when he has undergone the change of essence, and his condition will be hopeless until then.

This Hellenistic conception was destined to have a profound effect on all Christian thinking, and we shall have frequent occasion to return to it in later chapters. Jesus had contemplated a change of will. He never doubted that man exists already in the image of God, and his teaching all revolves around the idea of God as our Father. It is the tragedy of our life that we have wandered away from God, and so have frustrated His purpose with us. Nothing else is needed than to repent, and to recover our true welfare by turning again to God. The later teachers, with their Hellenistic background, were unable to state the Christian message in those simple terms. They could not escape from the feeling that besides the moral there must be the essential change. The object of Christ's coming, as they conceived it, was to effect this change. He had possessed in himself the divine nature, and had appeared on earth that he might impart it to men. When they had thereby been born again they would enter on a new life, and all moral excellence would follow of its own accord. Endowed with the higher nature they would do the will of God. Later New Testament thought is all determined by this Hellenistic conception, and here, more than anywhere else, it breaks away from the original gospel, and is conformed to the Pagan type. The contemporary cults aimed at a change of essence which could only be effected magically through ritual acts, and the church found itself compelled to take up the same position. More and more it drifted away from its conviction that faith was the one thing needful, and laid the emphasis on sacramental rites, or on a purely mystical experience. This was necessary since the object in view was not a moral change but a change of nature. At the same time a deeper conception of the work of Christ was now made possible, and this is apparent when we turn to such interpretations of the gospel as are offered us by Paul and John. These teachers are able to grasp the truth that man's nature stands in need of a radical renewal. Christianity does not consist in a mere reformation of the old life, but in the possession of a new and different one. "Ye must be born again"; the Christian is a "new creation," made over again at the very springs of his being. This was the truth implicit in Jesus' own teaching. He insisted on repentance, but for him the word had an infinitely deeper meaning than for John the Baptist. To repent was not merely to amend your life here and there, but to throw yourself utterly on God, so that henceforth His will becomes your will. Through the Hellenistic conception the great Christian teachers were enabled to give full effect to this demand of Jesus. They declared that his servant must be a new man, that his whole mind must become different. This Christian idea, however, was now involved with an alien one. The renewal effected by Christ was conceived as a mysterious change, not in man's will but in the constitution of his being.

(3) Once more, the inner motive of Hellenistic religion was not so much a faith in God as a sense of the ideal. At the heart of it lay the assurance that the visible world is only the shadow of another, which is reflected in it but lies beyond our senses. The Jewish mind accepted the present world as real. A time was indeed coming when it would pass away, and give place to a new and glorious order in which God would reign. But meanwhile this is the real world, and we must make the best of it, trusting in God and looking forward to the better age which is to come. The Greek mind was not much concerned either with the present or the future. It took for granted that all evils under which we suffer are inherent in the earthly conditions, which will always remain what they are now. There are not two ages but two worlds, over against each other. Man is to live amidst the changing things with

an abiding sense that they are only shadows, and that through them he may catch some glimpse of the higher realities. It is only in the great thinkers, such as Plato, that this idea comes to clear expression, but something of it may be traced even in the ordinary Paganism. It supplied the impulse to that enthusiasm for art which was so closely allied to religion in the ancient world. Earthly things were represented not as they were but as they might be, in a world of perfection. It was the same instinct which gave rise to the Greek philosophies. The Hebrew mind accepted the world as it was. God had created it and declared that it was good. But the Greek mind could never rest satisfied with things that were present and visible. It saw in them only appearances which testified to something that lay beyond them and gave them meaning. Plato, in his famous parable, compares man to a prisoner in a cave, where he sees nothing but shadows cast on a wall in front of him. He seeks to shake off his fetters and escape from the cave, and gaze on the realities which as yet he can only surmise.[§] This sense of the ideal which is also the real is the inner motive in Greek philosophy, and also in Greek religion.

Christianity in the Gentile world was imbued with the Greek idealism, and its message assumed a new character. Originally it had rested on the hope of the coming Kingdom. Jesus had proclaimed that a day was near at hand when the existing order would come to an end, and a new one would set in. Men were to sustain themselves amidst present evils with the prospect of this new age. They were to think of it as so near that they could overlook the brief interval, and live for it as if it were already come. But for the Gentile Christians this was not enough. They were not content to wait for a coming salvation since the higher world had always been and was present now. What they desired was to rise out of the bondage of this earthly existence and obtain the

[§] Plato, *Republic*, VII, 1, 2.

true life. The idea of redemption thus took on a new meaning. Outwardly the church maintained its belief in a crisis that was at hand and in a final Judgment, but these conceptions had ceased to have much more than a figurative value. The higher world was now regarded as a present reality. It was not necessary that the whole creation should be dissolved and a new order come into being, for by faith in Christ men could already win their deliverance. They had been prisoners in a world of shadows and now they were made free. From the time of Paul onward this was the governing idea in Gentile Christianity, and it brought with it a readjustment of all the primitive beliefs. The gospel was so interpreted as to offer the assurance of a present redemption.

There were two further elements in Hellenistic religion which might seem at first sight to be radically opposed but which were closely related, and sprang from the same root. In all times they are found to go together, and while they appear so different are constantly interchanging. On the one hand, Pagan religion in all its forms was sacramental. It made much of particular times and places, sacred objects, words and gestures which had a mysterious efficacy. This was all connected, in the last resort, with that idealism which was so deeply seated in the Hellenistic mind. It was intent on a higher world over against the visible one, and believed that in certain things the other world became actual. By means of these men could realise that it existed, and feel themselves in contact with it. In Judaism, and likewise in the earliest Christianity, there was nothing that could rightly be called sacramental. Forms and symbols were largely employed, as they must be in all religion, but it was clearly understood that they were only symbols. The temple and its institutions were holy because they were associated with the worship of the invisible God, and in some measure reflected his glory. No pious Jew imagined that God was actually present in wood and stone. He was exalted above all created things, and an object became holy when it pointed beyond itself to a Majesty in the heavens. So in early Christian worship the Lord's Supper was not a sacrament. It was observed by Christ's followers to keep them mindful that he had died for them, that he would come again, that even now they had fellowship with him. There was no thought that he was somehow made palpable in the outward rite. But for the Gentiles a holy symbol had a virtue in itself. It was believed that this material thing was a vehicle of the supernatural, so that by touching it you received something of the divine essence. The higher and lower worlds were utterly different, and yet sometimes they were mysteriously conjoined, and the spiritual nature was communicated through the earthly. Religion in the Pagan world was saturated with this sacramental idea, and it passed over into Christianity. Jesus himself had imposed no ritual. He had required that prayer should be offered in the simplest language, expressing with perfect sincerity the desires of the heart. He had taught that man's relation to God should be one of love and obedience. Yet we can see from the New Testament how the primitive Christian customs, when adopted by the Gentile churches, took on a sacramental character. This was due to no conscious departure from the earlier practice but to the inborn Gentile feeling that God must be approached through sacraments. As time went on the spiritual meaning of the religion was almost buried under the forms.

On the other hand, Hellenistic piety was mystical, and in this direction also it brought a new element into Christianity. As there was nothing sacramental in Hebrew religion, so there was nothing mystical. God was enthroned in heaven, and man's attitude to him could only be one of awe and adoration. It was forbidden even to utter his true name. A union of man's nature with the divine nature was, for a pious Jew, unthinkable. Jesus himself threw off the traditional conception of God as infinitely remote and apart. His whole aim was to impress on men that they might think of God as their Father, whom they could trust and love and with whom they could live in fellowship. But this fellowship, as he conceived it, was one of personalities. The Father in Heaven and His children on earth could be one in will although they were so far divided. There is no suggestion in Jesus' teaching of a mystical union, whereby the being of man could merge itself in that of God. This, however, was the whole purpose of Hellenistic religion. Since all man's trouble is due to his earthly nature there can be no help for him unless he can change that nature for the higher one. How can he become divine instead of human? How can he lose his individuality in God? This was the question which Pagan religion had always been asking, more or less consciously, and in the first century, under the combined influence of Greek philosophy and the Eastern cults, the answer was found in various types of mysticism. It was believed that man, although he belongs to this earth, can yet break the barrier which separates him from the divine. All being proceeds from the absolute being, and this must also be true of man. If he can only probe deeply enough into his own nature he will reach the point at which it flows out from the being of God. He will be able to identify himself with that divine life which is ultimately one with his own. Sometimes this end was attained by ecstasy, induced for the most part by artificial means. Sometimes it was achieved by intense contemplation. Gazing for a long time steadfastly on the stars a man lost consciousness of his little life and mingled it, like a drop in the ocean, with the life of the universe. Or he turned inward on his own soul, sinking down from deep to deep until at last he touched on absolute being and knew himself to be one with God.

Christianity, as it made its way among the Gentiles, was imbued more and more with the Hellenistic mysticism. The message of Jesus was interpreted in the light of ideas which were foreign to his own teaching. His thought was not metaphysical. He started from a faith in God which required no proof; he was concerned only with the will of God, and sought to bring men into fellowship with God by doing his will. Yet the mystical strain was implicit in his religion, and this is brought home to us as we read the Epistles of Paul and the Fourth Gospel. Here we have writers who come to the message of Jesus with the Hellenistic mind, and who seem at times to change it into something different. But they do not in any sense pervert it. They present it under forms which Jesus himself might not have recognised, but the truth they are seeking is none the less concealed in his gospel.

It is not difficult, therefore, to understand why the Pagan world responded to the new message, although on the surface it ran counter to all previous beliefs. Under forms derived from Judaism it appealed to needs and instincts which were not peculiar to any race, but were inherent in human nature itself. It was with this confidence that Paul pursued his mission. He tells us in the opening chapters of Romans how he offers his gospel to all men because there is no difference between Jew and Gentile when it comes to the greater issues of life. All are accountable to the one God, who has implanted in them some knowledge of himself, and who bestows his mercy through Christ on all alike. In the first century the Gentiles had become susceptible, in a peculiar degree, to this universal power of the gospel. Their separate religions were crumbling down, and little was left of them but the original substance which they had in common; and this, it was found, was in harmony with the Christian teaching. The new religion was not entirely strange, but answered to conceptions which lay at the heart of Gentile religion although they had never before been clearly realised. Christianity, it might almost be said, was welcomed by the Gentiles because they discerned in it their own faith, no longer obscured by errors and accretions but as it was, in its inner intention.

The idea that lay deepest in Hellenistic religion was that of deliverance. It is a strange delusion which in modern times has identified Paganism with a frank enjoyment of the life of the senses, oblivious of everything that was beyond. The characteristic Pagan mood, which we can trace everywhere in the Greek and Roman literature, was that of Hamlet when he exclaimed, "All the world is a prison." Men felt themselves in bondage to forces against which they were helpless, and from which they could see no hope of release. In the earlier days they had at least found forgetfulness in active devotion to the state, in whose freedom and well-being they could try to realise their own. This outlet was closed to them under the domination of Rome, and they were forced back on the conviction that bondage was inseparable from their human nature. The prison in which they felt themselves confined was nothing else than their condition as men. "O wretched man that I am; who shall deliver me from this body of death?" * In this outcry of Paul we can hear the voice of the whole Hellenistic world, oppressed with the knowledge that man's lot is hopeless because he is man, and that the higher life to which he aspires is forever closed to him. To this despairing world Christianity brought a promise of deliverance. Man had access to a power from above, in the strength of which he could shake off his fetters.

The new religion answered not only to a spiritual but to an urgent practical need. More perhaps than at any time before or since, the world of the first century was demanding moral guidance. This had formerly been supplied by the various cults, but these were now worn out, and were so much confused with each

* Rom. 7:24.

other that none of them had any clear authority. Philosophy, moreover, had long been criticising religion, and had done its work too well. It had proved that the ancient myths were incredible, that pious customs had no meaning or efficacy, that religion as commonly understood was nothing but a burden, imposed on the living by the superstition of a past age. Philosophy, which had discredited religion, was called on to supply its place. Life was plainly impossible without some principles which would give it basis and direction, and the thinkers of the time were fully awake to their responsibility. Philosophers abandoned mere questions of metaphysic and worked with a practical aim. They worked in deadly earnest, for it was evident to thoughtful men that without some moral foundation society would soon collapse. But the best efforts of the moralists had proved ineffective, for the precepts they offered had no sanction which could enforce them. In Christianity there had appeared a religion which was at the same time an ethic, loftier and more consistent than any other. This was what the age had been waiting for. There were countless earnest Gentiles who could make little of Christianity on its purely religious side, and who yet welcomed the help it afforded them in the actual conduct of life.

The Hellenistic world was thus open to the gospel, but could not receive it in the primitive form. This is at once apparent when we turn to those books of the New Testament which are associated with the Gentile mission. They reflect a mode of thinking which is not that of Jesus or of the earlier Apostles. The traditional terms are used with a new meaning, and ideas have come in, and have taken a central place, of which there seems to be no suggestion in Jesus' own teaching. From this it has been argued that in the hands of Paul and his successors Christianity became a different religion. They availed themselves, we are told, of certain beliefs

connected with the name of Jesus, and on this foundation built
up a religious system which had more in common with the Hellenistic cults than with the authentic Christian message. Ever since
then the religion of the church has not been Christianity but a
substitute for it, devised by those Gentile teachers. Now it may be
granted that the primitive beliefs were in large measure revised
in the course of the later mission, but this was not done with any
deliberate purpose. The revision was one which inevitably made
itself. As soon as a Gentile heard the message he apprehended it
in the manner that best conformed with his own thinking. Christ
was the Redeemer, and what could redemption mean but the
communication to man of the divine nature? He had come with
a revelation, and this must consist of a higher kind of knowledge.
He had brought men into fellowship with God, and this must be
conceived as a mystical union. So at every point the Gentiles
understood the gospel with some difference, and there arose that
type of Christianity which we call Hellenistic, and which might
seem to be a distortion of the message of Jesus. But it was essentially the same message, and the Hellenistic teachers were not
aware that they were making any serious change. Paul declares
vehemently that there could only be one gospel and that any one
who tries to supplant it with another is a man accursed.[†] What
seem to us now to be alien elements are due to nothing else than
the impact of Christian truth on a new kind of intelligence. The
Hellenistic mind was like a coloured window which gave its own
hue to the light.

To this extent there was a type of Christianity which can be
described as Gentile, and within the one general type we distinguish a number, all of which are represented in the New Testament. It must never be forgotten that in spite of the unity imposed
by Roman government the culture of the Western World was

† Gal. 1:9.

highly diversified. Each nationality preserved much of its former character. Each of the religions now blending together had still its peculiar beliefs. The various philosophies kept up their rivalry. To some extent the old civic spirit maintained itself, so that every important city stood for a tradition which made it distinct from others. Under such conditions the Christian message could not be proclaimed in a single uniform fashion, and there arose a number of interpretations which seemed often to be in conflict. None the less a broad similarity can be discerned in all of them. At the present day the nations of the West are sharply differentiated, each of them with its own type of art and literature, its own customs and politics and moral code. Yet they all start from the same general conceptions, so that we can group them together and speak of the Western mind. In like manner there was a Hellenistic mind, and a Hellenistic Christianity in which it was reflected. Various types of teaching are included under this name, and they need to be carefully distinguished, but in the final issue they are species of the same genius. The Gentile interpretations all have their root in those broad conceptions which were inherent in the Hellenistic culture.

It has to be admitted that these conceptions were not wholly adapted to the exposition of the Christian message. One has only to think of the two assumptions which lay, as we have seen, at the heart of Pagan religion. It was believed, for one thing, that God must be approached by way of reason. This religious knowledge was not, indeed, wholly intellectual, and was derived from a divine enlightenment concerning the nature of God and the secrets of the unseen and the hereafter. But it did not essentially differ from other knowledge. Religious thinking is nothing in itself but an exercise of the mind, and to identify it with salvation and fellowship with God must always be a fatal error. Jesus did not make this error. He spoke of things which are hidden from the wise and prudent and revealed to babes. He declared that those who see God are not the gifted and enlightened but the pure in heart. The New Testament teachers never question this position of Jesus, and insist that knowledge must take a secondary place; but in spite of themselves they are led to make·it a necessary element in faith. More and more the Hellenistic conception tended to encroach on the Christian. Already in the New Testament we have signs of the later development in which faith was confused with knowledge.

Again, the chief aim of Hellenistic religion was to discover some means whereby human nature might be transformed. It was assumed that man's earthly being was at fault and that he must undergo a new birth before he would be capable of a higher life. He must participate in the life of God as in some kind of ethereal essence. This idea found its way into Christianity, and gave a new character to the whole doctrine of redemption. Jesus had required a change of will, manifesting itself in active service of God, and this was never forgotten. But it was now assumed that the change of will would follow on a change of nature, and would otherwise be unattainable. By union with Christ a man must first receive into himself the divine substance, and when he was thus transmuted his will would right itself, his action would be conformed to that of Christ. As a consequence of this mode of thinking the moral interest tended to fall into the background. The main concern of Christian thought was to explain how the mysterious change was effected, and how men could feel assured that it had taken place in them. It has always been found, however, that when religion tries to get beyond the ethical it falls back on magic, in forms more or less disguised. At first it may connect itself with a profound philosophy, or with an expressive symbolism, but all this at last becomes magic and nothing more. This was the experience in Indian religion, which degenerated by

successive stages from the metaphysic of the Vedas and Upani-
shads into a gross materialism. In a less degree the same process
repeated itself in Christianity. It was unavoidable when once the
emphasis was laid on a semi-physical instead of a moral change.

Apart from the special conceptions inherent in Hellenistic
religion it must never be forgotten that the Gentile mind, even at
its best, was saturated with Pagan beliefs and Pagan estimates of
life. Judaism may have been narrow and legalistic, but it was
associated with a lofty ethic and with faith in the one God, who
was holy and righteous and throned above all material things.
The Law itself was an attempt to give embodiment in man's daily
living to the spiritual teaching of the prophets. Hellenistic religion, though it had now cast off much that was crude and childish in the old Paganism, had yet sprung out of it, and brought
into Christianity not a few elements which were purely Pagan.
This became evident later, when Pagan forms of worship were
taken over by the church, when Christian sentiment was in large
measure Paganised, when Christ himself assumed a mythological
character, hardly different from that of a heathen divinity. In the
New Testament period there never was much danger of such confusion. At every point the line was clearly drawn between Christianity and Paganism, and even when Gentile ideas were borrowed they were re-cast in the Christian mould. Maxims of Stoic
morality were brought into harmony with Jesus' own teaching;
the Platonic conception of a higher world was merged in the
Christian hope for the Kingdom of God. Nevertheless we can perceive at least the beginnings of the process whereby the Christian
beliefs were assimilated to the Pagan. This was apparent to the
New Testament writers themselves. At the outset all interest
centres on the conflict with Judaism, but even Paul, in his later
Epistles, has grown aware of a new and more serious menace.

"False teachers" have arisen in every community—men who are infecting Christian worship and doctrine and morality with the Pagan leaven.

The Hellenising of Christianity was thus fraught with many dangers, but in the main it served a great and necessary purpose. For one thing, the message could not have been made intelligible unless it had been thus adapted to the Gentile mind. Jesus had taught under Jewish forms of thought, and his ideas needed to be lifted out of their original frame-work; otherwise they would have remained exotic, and might actually have repelled many who were best fitted to understand and welcome them. Paul had recognised, almost from the first, that unless it were set free from the Jewish Law the gospel could make little appeal to the Gentiles. The later Hellenising process was only the fulfilment on a larger scale of the principle for which Paul had struggled. He had declared that Christianity rested on faith, and the church grew conscious that faith was independent, not only of the Law, but of any given patterns of religious thought. However it might be interpreted, the Christian message, in its essential import, would be the same. It might be offered to the Gentiles in the forms most vital to their thinking, and would still remain the gospel of Christ.

Such an adaptation was the more necessary if the better minds among the Gentiles were to be won over. Paul could truly say, in the earlier days of the mission, "not many wise men after the flesh are called";‡ but there was no time when the new message only attracted the ignorant. Paul's Epistles are themselves sufficient proof that the audiences for which they were written were intellectually of a high order, able to appreciate great language and thought that was often difficult. As the religion became better known it made an ever more powerful impression on superior

‡ I Cor. 1:26.

minds. No doubt in this there was a danger, and in some respects it might have been better if the church had never entangled itself with the wisdom of this world. Yet religion has always suffered when it has allied itself with ignorance. Not only has it fallen in general esteem, which means little, but intrinsically it has sunk to a lower level. Unless it can hold its own with the best culture of its time, it deteriorates sooner or later into a superstition. So if Christianity was to maintain itself in the Gentile world and preserve its true message, it could not refuse to take its part in the intellectual movement; and this it could only do when it adopted the current modes of thought. The name "Christian" was at first given by way of ridicule. It was intended to mark the believers as a fanatical group, which insisted that Jesus should be called the Messiah; and for the Gentiles this was only a barbarous title, which signified nothing. That rational men should so excite themselves over a meaningless name was mere absurdity. But when the name Messiah was exchanged for Lord, Son of God, Eternal Word, the teaching had to be taken seriously. It could be seen that the question at issue was nothing less than that of the nature of God and His purpose with men. The Christian answer to this question might be mistaken, but it could not be disregarded. It carried with it a challenge to all existing belief, and must be examined and refuted. In the time of Paul Christianity had appeared to be a mere fanaticism, but the Apologists of the second century can take for granted that it is a new philosophy, and defend it on this ground. There could be no better indication of a change of attitude on the part of thoughtful Gentiles.

By the interpretation in new terms the message was not only made more intelligible but was able to disclose more of its import. Jesus, although he had been born a Jew, had far transcended any racial limitations. It was, indeed, one of the tragedies of his life that he was obliged to express his thought under forms that too often were unequal to it. Take, for instance, his claim to be Messiah. No other name was offered him within the Jewish tradition which answered even remotely to his inward sense of his calling, but the Messianic idea was a national one, with many implications that were alien and repellent to him. He accepted it reluctantly; he tried to put new meanings into it; to the very end he hesitated to assume a title which was only too likely to mislead. So with much else that belonged to the substance of his teaching. He had to pour the new wine into old bottles, aware all the time that the wine would break the bottles. In many ways the Greek forms were more adequate to his purpose than those which he had himself employed. They were the outcome of centuries of profound thinking, which had brought many things to light which Judaism had never surmised.

This was especially true of that element of mysticism which may be regarded as the chief contribution of Hellenistic thought to Christianity. God was conceived as the absolute Being, with whom, in this world of change, the soul desires to make itself one. With the aid of this conception the church was enabled to reinterpret its message. It presented Jesus as possessing in himself the divine nature, so that in union with him man participates in the nature of God. The whole idea of the Christian redemption was brought into harmony with this Hellenistic mode of thinking, and it has often been held that the gospel was thereby distorted. An ethical religion was changed into a mystical one. This may be true in so far as Christian faith was now allied with a metaphysic, peculiar to the Hellenistic world. Its assumptions would have meant little to Jesus, and for the most part have grown foreign to ourselves. Yet it may truly be said that the later creeds give utterance to something which was present in the mind of Jesus, and which he could only express imperfectly in the language of Jewish apocalyptic. He was not, properly speaking, a mystic, but there is a sense in which mysticism is a necessary element in all religion. Before God can be known and served and worshipped there must be the certainty that he is real and living, and that we can meet him an an inward presence in our own souls. Jesus, above all others, had this certainty. We can make little of his religion when we think of it merely as an ethic, for through his ethical teaching he was ever seeking to impart his assurance of God and of the reality of the higher world. Paul and his successors were intensely conscious of this other side of Jesus' message, and through the conception given them in Hellenistic mysticism they brought out explicitly what was contained in the message itself. The Fourth Evangelist makes Jesus declare himself in language which could not have been literally used except by some one familiar with the ideas of Greek and Oriental thinkers, and Jesus, we are often told, could not have spoken in that manner, and the Evangelist has therefore coloured or perverted the historical message. But it may be fairly argued that in the Fourth Gospel, more surely than in the others, we hear the voice of Jesus. He may not have used those words, but they declare something that was ever in his mind. Behind all that he actually said there was the call to an inner communion with God, the revelation of an unseen world. By means of the Hellenistic ideals all this that was implicit in his thought is made articulate.

In the view of some modern writers Christianity was overpowered by the forces which it encountered in the Gentile world. It had set forth to conquer the alien culture but it was itself conquered, and what we now call Christianity is little else than the old Pagan religion, modified here and there. The creative power in the later faith of the church was Hellenistic and not Christian. Such a view, however, is utterly contrary to the facts. In the world of the first century there was no force which was strong enough to offer serious resistance to Christianity, much less to absorb or master it. The century was indeed a great one, perhaps the greatest of all the centuries, even apart from the outstanding fact that it gave birth to the new religion. It saw the culmination of the whole history of the ancient world. For more than a thousand years the minds of men had been active in every field of knowledge, and at last there had come the harvest. The diverse races had been drawn together into one political system, and had gathered into a common store all the treasure they had accumulated in the past ages. Everywhere scholars and thinkers were co-ordinating and applying the manifold wisdom they had inherited. But the creative period had come to an end, and for the time being everything was stationary. We learn from Tacitus that when Augustus took the empire in hand he laid down the principle that no further territory should be added.[¶] All energy should be devoted to the maintenance and consolidation of what had been already won. It might appear as if a similar decision had been reached in the realm of thought. Everything we possess from that age is derivative. Literature and art have lost their vigour; philosophy can produce nothing new. Look where we will there is no one who ventures on any fresh enterprise, or tries to contribute anything of his own. All are intent on conserving, or throwing into new combinations, what has previously been gained. It is absurd to think of Christianity as the creation of that age which created nothing. On the contrary, the one creative power was Christianity itself. It laid hold of the various interests of the time and vitalised them by allying them with its own message. In this process it no doubt seemed to change its character, and to lose itself in one and another of the Hellenistic movements, but all the time it was asserting the power that was in itself. A plant may be removed to a different soil and climate in which it developes, after a few seasons, into a new variety. It has not been

¶ Tacitus, *Annals*, I, 12.

mastered by its surroundings, but has mastered them. By a force inherent in itself it has adapted the new conditions to its purposes, and drawn out of them a fresh life. It was this that happened when Christianity became a Gentile religion. In the strange environment it seemed to change its nature, but it was itself the living power which subdued the alien forces to its own need.

CHAPTER IV

THE RELIGION OF PAUL

PAUL HIMSELF tells us that he was acclaimed in his lifetime as the leader of a particular school. "Every one of you saith, I am of Paul, I am of Apollos, I am of Cephas." * This attitude towards him has persisted ever since. In every age there have been those who looked to Paul as their master, and have done battle for what they considered his special type of Christianity.

Paul denies, however, that he was a party leader, and was not aware that the opinions for which he stood were in any way peculiar. He wished to be regarded simply as an Apostle of Christ. He declares that he differed from other Apostles only in this,—that his work was one of "planting." † Those who succeeded him might add to his message and confirm it. His aim was to lay the foundation on which they could build.‡ In this estimate of himself Paul was fully justified. He cannot be assigned to any given school of Christian thought. As soon as we class him with one group of teachers we discover that he had as much or far more in common with some other. He was not a moralist or a mystic or an apocalyptist or an ecclesiastic, but all of them together. The attempt has often been made to identify him with some one doctrine, and to make this the touch-stone of what is truly Pauline. Luther fastened on the doctrine of Justification by Faith, and the Protestant church has since looked to Paul as its chosen Apostle. But this doctrine is prominent only in two of his Epistles, and elsewhere his thought proceeds along quite different lines. It would not be

* I Cor. 1:12. † I Cor. 3:6. ‡ I Cor. 3:10.

difficult to show that not a few of his ideas have their logical issue in the Catholic position.

Many would acknowledge that Paul was not the leader of any sect or school, but would still make him responsible for the cleavage between the Jewish and Gentile churches. Not only did he bring the Gentile church into being, but he founded it on a new interpretation of the Christian message, in which he broke off from the Apostles before him and to a large extent from Jesus himself. What he represents is not so much a special type of Christian thought as a new religion, which for all later times has obscured the original gospel. A generation ago it was not uncommon to speak of Paul as the second founder of Christianity.

This view, however, is being gradually abandoned in the light of closer enquiry. For one thing we are learning to see that Paul was not the creator of Gentile Christianity. It began with the Hellenists at Jerusalem, and he was himself the product of the movement which he is supposed to have originated. Before he came on the scene it had made considerable progress, and for the first half of his career he was only an assistant, and not the most conspicuous one, in the Gentile mission. After starting his own great enterprise he still made it his rule not to preach the gospel where it had been preached already.¶ He recognised that the earlier Gentile missionaries were on the same footing as himself and were proclaiming essentially the same message. They had anticipated him in some of the most important fields, including the two great capitals of Rome and Alexandria which were destined to take the lead in the future development of the church.

Again, so far from breaking with the Jewish church, Paul was anxious to keep in fellowship with it. As the first and most necessary step in his mission he sought to win the approval of the elder Apostles. He worked in partnership with men like Barnabas and Silas, who belonged to the primitive community. He was a per-

¶ Rom. 15:20.

sonal friend of Peter, and on one occasion stayed with him for a fortnight as his guest.[§] To the end of his days he acknowledged the primacy of Jerusalem, and it was during a visit to the Jerusalem church, for the purpose of healing all past differences, that he was arrested, and his work as an active missionary came to an end.

In his teaching, as in his outward relations, he remained in sympathy with the church before him. He was careful to preserve all that he deemed essential in the primitive tradition, and indignantly denied that he sought to introduce another gospel. That his ordinary preaching was not much at variance with that of the other Apostles is sufficiently evident from the first letter to the Thessalonians. Here he addresses a church which he has newly founded, and reminds it of those elementary truths to which his message, during his brief sojourn, had been confined. There is hardly a verse in the Epistle to which Peter or James would not willingly have assented. In other Epistles he speaks to converts who have made some progress in the faith, and feels at liberty to discuss Christian ideas in their deeper implications. But he still takes the primitive teaching as his foundation. His thought, with all its involutions, may be compared to a great musical composition which is built up around a simple melody.

It cannot be too much emphasised that Paul's quarrel with the church before him was on a matter of practice, not of belief. Were Christians still bound to the observance of the Law? The answer to this question no doubt involved far-reaching consequences,—moral, theological, religious,—and Paul demonstrates, with wonderful insight, what they were. But it can be said of almost any difference, however trivial in itself, that great issues depend on it. The Covenanters made their protest against a certain form of church government, and it is often pointed out that nothing vital was at stake in that controversy. Men can be good Christians just as well under bishops as under presbyteries, and

§ Gal. 1:18.

all the zeal and sacrifice expended in that quarrel went for nothing. But the battle-ground must not be confounded with the battle. The Covenanters, whatever we may think of their particular aims, were fighting for human rights, for liberty, for pure religion; and it was the same with Paul. In his conflict with the Judaists the question of the Law itself mattered little. He seized on the one obvious difference between the new religion and the old, and made this the starting-point of his message.

To this day the legal controversy which bulks so largely in Paul's writings has obscured our whole judgment of his teaching. His religion has come to be entangled in our minds with an issue which belonged to his own day, and has now ceased to have anything but an historical interest. For this reason it is argued that Paul has little to teach us, and that his dominance in Christian thought has been a calamity, binding our religion to old-world conceptions which it has long outgrown. The truth is that his message remains essentially the same when the legal controversy is left entirely out of account. It is not only the same but can be apprehended more clearly. He seeks to impress on us that faith is the vital Christian principle, that Christ is the one Lord to whom we owe obedience, that through Christ we enter on a new life, that this life is controlled by the Spirit. These were the things which Paul believed. He states them in terms imposed on him by the controversies of his time, and when we so look on them we are apt to miss their import. When they are lifted out of their accidental setting they are the convictions which form the substance of Christianity. The church held fast to them before Paul came on the scene, and has always held to them, and must continue to do so if it is to remain a living church.

The term "Paulinism" is, indeed, a misleading one, suggesting as it does that there was a peculiar type of religion of which Paul was the author and representative. Countless books have been written on the subject of Paulinism, and the practice invariably is to collect all Paul's teaching as it has come to us in the Epistles and so consider it as a single whole. But in this body of teaching which we call Paulinism three things have to be distinguished. First of all, there are the beliefs which he took over from the primitive church. Several times he refers explicitly to "that which I received," and under this formula he might have included the greater part of what he writes. He had received from those before him all his knowledge of the earthly Jesus. He had received the fundamental beliefs which he works out to their deeper issues. Even in the details of his thinking he was guided, far more than he knew, by the earlier teachers. Before he started on his own mission he had been working for many years under their direction, and it cannot be supposed that he suddenly discarded all that he had learned from them. His Epistles contain the harvest of all that had been ripening in his mind during those years of preparation. We cannot tell, and he could not have told himself, how much he had received.

Again, we must make allowance for all that he took over from Hellenistic Christianity. It needs to be remembered that Paul was not only a Hellenist by birth but had spent practically his whole Christian life in Hellenistic communities. His first knowledge of Christianity was indeed acquired in Jerusalem. He apparently came to the city very shortly after the Crucifixion, when the recent tragedy and all that had led up to it would be subjects of constant discussion. He was an ardent Pharisee and would hear the story first from the side of Jesus' enemies. Later he would come in contact with Christian teachers, most notably with Stephen, who disputed, we are expressly told, in the synagogue of the Cilicians.* With a strong bias against it, and yet with a secret

* Acts 6: 9.

attraction, he thus made acquaintance with the new message. Two years after his conversion he returned to Jerusalem for the purpose, he tells us, of meeting Peter, and would learn from this immediate disciple everything he had to teach. It is absurd to maintain, as some have done, that Paul knew little or nothing of the original gospel. Although he had never seen Jesus in the flesh he was well informed on what he had done and taught, and on the beliefs of his followers. Nevertheless his main associations were with Christian communities in Gentile cities. His fellow-workers were all Hellenists like himself. His Christianity, therefore, was of the type which was growing up in the Gentile world, under the influence of Gentile ideas. Before he began his independent mission he had been a Christian for fourteen or seventeen years,[†] and all this time Hellenistic Christianity had been developing under the care of earnest and gifted men. Paul would listen to them with deference and his mind as a Christian would insensibly be moulded by them. So it is quite improbable that he simply created those peculiar ideas which are found in his writings. We are now unable to compare him with any others than the primitive Apostles, and wherever he differs from them we take for granted that he falls back on his own reflection; but it is necessary to allow for the intermediate influence. A man of science makes a discovery which seems to the popular mind to have sprung full grown out of his own brain, but chemists and physicists are aware that he has only perfected what hundreds of others have been thinking of, and that he could never have succeeded unless they had laboured before him. It can hardly be too much to say that a large part of what we call Paulinism was in no way peculiar to Paul, but belonged to Hellenistic teaching generally. He brought to his work a powerful original genius, and stamped his

---

† According as we interpret "after fourteen years," in Gal. 2:1. Most probably he means after the three years already accounted for.

individuality on everything he touched, but his material had been given him. His own task was to arrange and combine it and fill it with the breath of life. Ever and again he makes use of theological terms which have perplexed all later expositors, but he does not feel it necessary to explain them. They belonged, apparently, to the current language of the Gentile church, and he can take for granted that all his readers will understand him. This is particularly striking in the Epistle to the Romans, written to a church which he had never visited and which only knew of his teaching by hearsay. His object is to remove misgivings which had been caused by false reports, and to assure the Roman Christians that there is nothing in his message to which they can take exception. The doctrines on which he insists as common to all believers are those which we usually describe as Pauline; this, indeed, is the Epistle which has always been accepted as the classic presentation of Paulinism. So it is more than likely that we must look outside of Paul for the true origin of most of the Pauline ideas. He adapted and matured them, but they represent the work of Hellenistic thinkers in a time before his influence made itself felt. These doctrines were, indeed, inevitable when once the attempt was made to interpret the gospel to the Gentiles. A new attitude of mind was brought to bear on the Christian beliefs; they were understood in the light of those conceptions which were native to Gentile thought. A theology emerged, almost of its own accord, which we now associate with Paul, but which is more properly to be regarded as that of the Hellenistic church.

In the general body of Paulinism there is, however, a third element, which must be attributed to Paul himself. He was sensitive and receptive in an unusual degree, and was born into that Hellenistic world of the first century in which all manner of cults and philosophies were confused together. Modern scholars have busied themselves with tracing out the affinities of his thinking, and the task is an endless one. It can be shown that in the most literal sense he was "debtor to the Greeks and the barbarians, to the wise and the unwise." [‡] There is scarcely one of the spiritual movements of that age which has not, in one form or another, left its imprint on the thought of Paul. None the less he was one of the most original minds in history, and while he acknowledges frankly how much he had received he was yet passionately aware that his gospel was his own. "I did not receive it from men, neither was I taught it, but it came to me by revelation of Jesus Christ." [¶] It is this individual element in his teaching which is rightly to be called Pauline, and he tells us himself how it is to be distinguished. There was something in his thought which was plainly due to revelation. It could not have been given him from tradition or from any process of reflection. It was such a knowledge as he could only have obtained by an immediate insight. His mind had responded to the mind of Christ, which had borne in upon him irresistibly the true meaning of the new religion.

It has been the habit of most students of Paul to devote themselves almost wholly to his doctrines, assuming that his theology and his religion were one and the same. Sometimes, it must be granted, he lends himself to this misunderstanding, and confuses the truth he believes with the theories by which he tries to explain it. He is nowhere more terribly in earnest than in the Epistle to Galatians, where he contrasts the gospel, as a living message from God, with the formalities of Jewish legalism. Yet he is himself guilty of the very error he condemns, and insists on his own doctrinal scheme as if it were itself the gospel. The Epistle is a strange mixture of profound religious insight and fantastic, often puerile argument, and no clear line is drawn between them. We might al-

‡ Rom. 1:14.   ¶ Gal. 1:12.

most conclude that Paul's faith in Christ was inseparable from a number of historical and doctrinal opinions which he had taken over from tradition, and which we can now see to have been ill-founded and artificial. None the less his faith was one thing and his theories about it were quite another; and it is always possible to discern the real intention behind the apparent one, the substance beneath the form which was imposed on it by the mind of the age. The doctrinal system which we know as Paulinism is for the most part a sheath or vesture which conceals within it what is vital and individual in Paul's religion.

This becomes evident when we look for a moment at the nature of this doctrinal system. Countless efforts have been made to discover in it some kind of logical cohesion, but it is now generally admitted that this cannot be done. Paul's ideas continually intersect, and frequently contradict each other. He lays hold of any idea that suits his immediate purpose, careless of how it may harmonise with what he has said elsewhere. He reasons, now as a Jewish Rabbi, now as a Hellenistic thinker. He finds his proofs in the Old Testament, in Roman law, in the facts of nature, in ordinary custom or sentiment. The impression he is apt to leave on us is that of a clever advocate who makes use of any argument which happens at the moment to support his case. This, indeed, is how he often impressed his contemporaries. They regarded him as one who was all things to all men, who had no settled opinions but kept veering from one side to another with the one object of attaining his own ends. This judgment on him was not unjust in so far as he sat loose to all special theologies, using them only as instruments which he was always willing to exchange for others when occasion required. But the reason for this vacillation was just the opposite to that which his enemies assumed. He had intense convictions, so real to him that he cared nothing for formal consistency. His one aim was to assert those

convictions in whatever way he might best enforce them. They
were not part of a logical scheme to which as a thinker he felt
bound to adhere, but were rooted in his very being as a Christian
man.

It needs to be observed in this connection that there is little in
Paul's thought which can rightly be called philosophical. This
is the more surprising as philosophy, in that age, was the medium
of all intellectual intercourse. No worker in any field of knowledge
could expect a hearing unless he could place his convictions on
some kind of philosophical basis. It had become fully apparent,
long before the end of the first century, that the Christian teacher
could find much in Greek philosophical thought which would
help him in the interpretation of the gospel, and the chief aim of
Paul's successors was to make use of this instrument, lying ready
to their hands. Paul has sometimes been represented as doing
likewise. He changed the gospel, we are told, into an intellectual
system, and was thus responsible for the confusion which has
ever since existed in the Christian mind. A religious message was
identified with a body of doctrines, intelligible only to the abstract
thinker. The truth is, however, that Paul takes little to do with
anything that can be called philosophy. He lived in a philosophical age, and had been educated at Tarsus, which was famous for
its Stoical schools. He must have been well acquainted with the
general nature of philosophical thought, and avails himself frequently of terms derived from philosophy. When he was at Athens, according to the book of Acts, he made a speech to a select
audience in which he based his argument on Stoic doctrine.
This, however, was an experiment, and not a successful one. He
never repeated it, but made the resolve that henceforth he would
preach nothing but "Christ and him crucified."* Throughout his
letters he speaks of "man's wisdom" only by way of disparage-

* I Cor. 2:2.

ment, declaring that by means of it men cannot know the things of God, which must be spiritually discerned.

So far, then, from trying to philosophise the gospel, this is the one thing which Paul is determined not to do. He feels that it must speak for itself, that it must carry with it its own convincing power, and otherwise is ineffectual. The Epistles are full of argument, but their logic is of a kind which irritates and baffles every expositor. This may partly be because his method is more often that of the Rabbis than that of Aristotle, but it is due much more to the character of his thought. He has not arrived at his conclusions by a logical process. He relies on principles which to the Christian mind are self-evident, although they are not capable of the usual proofs. His gospel, as he frankly confesses, is "to the Greeks foolishness," † and vindicates itself not by man's wisdom but by demonstration of the Spirit and of power.‡

So in his appeal to the Gentiles Paul avails himself more of the religion than the philosophy of his time. Much has been made in the modern enquiry of Paul's relation to the mystery cults which were so widely diffused in the first century. As with all discoveries when they are still novel the importance of this one has been much exaggerated. Some writers would hold that Christianity, in the hands of Paul, becomes nothing more or less than an oriental cult, in which Jesus takes the place of Attis or Serapis, but this is an obvious caricature of his true position. He takes the Christian message as it was given him by the primitive church, and interprets it, in the main, by means of Jewish ideas. His Judaism, however, is of the Hellenistic type, and he is drawn particularly to those speculations which had entered Hellenistic thought through the mystery cults. It may be doubted whether he had any direct acquaintance with those cults, but the Hellenism of the time was an amalgam in which elements from many quar-

† I Cor. 1:23.   ‡ I Cor. 2:4.

ters were compounded. The Greeks had contributed most, but the barbarians with their strange mythologies had brought in a number of conceptions of high religious value. Paul was open to all suggestions which might throw light on the central mystery of the gospel, and in the philosophies he found little help. They reflected this world's wisdom, and knew nothing of those divine purposes which lie beyond it. But those other conceptions, whatever may have been their source, belonged to the sphere of religion. They had manifestly sprung out of the desire to know God, and Paul responded to them. He was seeking to convey the gospel to the Gentile mind, to which it was largely unintelligible, and here was a common ground on which Christianity and Hellenism could meet. Out of the diversified elements which made up the thought of his time, Paul was instinctively attracted to the mystical beliefs which had filtered in from the East. With the aid of these he could in some measure explain the meaning of the work of Christ.

All this, however, belongs to the shell or circumference of Paul's religion. He was the spokesman of the Gentile church, and in his interpretation he employed modes of thinking which were congenial to that church as a whole and were not peculiar to himself. To understand Paulinism we must look for that which was personal in his religion. All the rest was given him by the church before him or by the environment in which he worked. There was something which he knew to be his own and which had come to him, he tells us, by revelation. He speaks at various times of "my gospel," "the gospel which I preach," and when he so expresses himself he does not refer to those special doctrines which we are accustomed to call Pauline. He speaks of the gospel as his in so far as it has become a living power in his own life. Others may stop short with the formal beliefs; he has grasped them in their inner purport and allowed them to work in him so that they have changed him into a new man. What he seeks to communicate is this vital apprehension of the gospel. He attacks the Judaists because they lay the whole stress on mechanical observances. He attacks the false teachers because they turn religion into a matter of theory and speculation. He disowns the party at Corinth which called itself by his name because it followed him only in his particular mode of stating the Christian beliefs. This, he tries to impress on them, was not his gospel. They had failed to understand him unless his doctrines had conveyed to them some sense of what the message had meant to himself, and what it would mean to all who truly responded to it. They might prefer one statement of it to another, but all genuine teachers, Paul and Apollos and Cephas alike, were intent on the one truth which constituted the gospel. The Kingdom of God, as Paul knew it, was not meat or drink, and neither, he might have added, was it any doctrinal system. It was an inward condition of righteousness and peace and joy in the holy Spirit. Paul had attained through Christ to this condition, and his one aim was to make it known to others and enable them to share it with him. The term "Paulinism" ought to be used not of forms and ideas which Paul had borrowed but of that knowledge of Christ which was personal to himself. Here we must look for his real contribution to Christian thought.

His knowledge had come to him by revelation, and could not have come otherwise. All true insight must be direct and individual. Your sense of right is worth little unless it resides in your own conscience. You have no apprehension of beauty if you need always to follow some one else's judgment. Most of all, the knowledge of God must come to you as an immediate gift, or you will never attain to it. A religion which is only a tradition from the past, or a fashion of your time and neighbourhood is of little value. You must in some way have met God for yourself. You must know him because he has spoken directly to your own soul.

Paul's revelation had come to him in the moment of his conversion, and it is here that we must seek the key to his gospel. Everything else in his teaching is only his endeavour to explain to himself what had been given him in that immediate experience. He had then apprehended what Christ had been, and what was involved in his message. Paul's theology is often presented, under the searchlight of modern enquiry, as a composite of many illassorted elements, Jewish and Hellenistic. The impression is left on us that his mind was stuffed with odds and ends of religious belief, and that he merely scrambled them together into a nondescript system. It is no wonder that the Pauline teaching, as thus understood, has been largely discredited, and that many earnest souls are now anxious to get back from Paul to Christ. But those various elements which are supposed to be everything are only the raw material out of which Paul made something of his own. We need to look through the vehicle to the vital content. A truth had been given him which was not "from man or through man but by revelation of Jesus Christ."

What was it that happened to Paul in that moment of his conversion? Our accounts in the book of Acts deal only with the circumstances, which are worked up dramatically by Luke's imagination. Even if we accept his story as literally true, it tells us little of what we chiefly desire to know. What was the inward experience of Paul in that sudden illumination from which he emerged as a dedicated Apostle? In at least four passages he makes express reference to the event,[¶] and in many others the memory of it appears to colour his thought. Each time he makes mention of a vision, the outward reality of which he never seems to have doubted. "Have I not seen the Lord Jesus?" "He appeared to me also, as to one born out of due time." But the

¶ I Cor. 9:1; I Cor. 15:8; II Cor. 4:6; Gal. 1:15, 16.

emphasis is laid, not so much on the vision, as on the inward revelation which had been given along with it. "God who makes light
to shine out of darkness shone in my heart." "It pleased God to
reveal his Son in me." Paul's experience was evidently the same
as happens in every conversion, although in most cases it is not
accompanied with any supernatural circumstances. Many have
tried to describe the mysterious change of which they were conscious at some given moment of their lives, but perhaps the most
helpful of all the records is that of Pascal,—one of the few men
in history who may be deemed comparable in mental endowment
with Paul himself. His nature, moreover, was curiously similar to
that of Paul, combining a hard intellectual power with a strong
moral sense, a passionate temperament, a mystical cast of mind.
After his death a fragment of paper was found on his body, carefully preserved in a small linen bag. It contained a few incoherent
jottings, thrown down apparently within the very hour when he
had passed through the convulsion which had changed his life. It
gives us, therefore, what may be called an actual photograph of a
soul in process of conversion.§ "Fire: the God of Abraham, Isaac
and Jacob. Not the God of the philosophers and the wise. Certainty, certainty. God of Jesus Christ. My God and thy God: thy
God shall be my God. Forgetfulness of the world and of all but
God. Joy, joy, joy, tears of joy. I have fallen away, I have fled
from him. May I not fall away from him for ever." In these burning phrases, uttered when the ecstasy was hardly over, we have
the best commentary on the brief allusions to his own experience
which Paul wrote down after a lapse of years. A light had broken
on him. He had won certainty after a long, futile struggle. He had
been filled with an unutterable joy, and a new sense of the fellowship of God.

Paul's conversion has often been explained as nothing more

§ A full account is given in Viscount St. Cyr's *Pascal.*

than his acceptance of a belief which he had hitherto rejected. He came to see, as in a flash of lightning, that Jesus was indeed the Messiah, that the Law had been superseded, that the Christian account of God's purpose was the true one. All this was no doubt involved, but the changes of opinion were only secondary. It was not Paul's intelligence that was converted but his whole nature and outlook. He became, as he is never tired of telling us, a new man, living henceforth in a new world. The conversion has to be understood quite apart from any of the doctrines which we associate with Paul. These came by way of reflection, when he had set himself to revise all his thinking in the light now vouchsafed to him. The conversion itself was the flowing in of a divine power. He had been seeking God, and now God, by his own act, had found him. Again and again when Paul speaks of knowing God he corrects himself and puts it the other way. "To know God, or rather to be known by him." "Then shall I know as also I am known." "To know the love of Christ, which is more than knowledge." He had become aware that it was no longer he that lived, but a higher power had taken possession of him; and this was the ultimate meaning of his conversion.

It is from this point of view that we must understand the religion of Paul. We think of him as a theologian, building up a doctrinal system which must be explained from his previous training, and by the study of writers who belonged to his world and may possibly have influenced him. All this is useful, and throws light on much that is puzzling in various aspects of his thought. But it leaves us quite in the dark when we try to apprehend what is vital in his teaching,—what is specifically Pauline. His doctrines themselves are unintelligible when they are considered merely as doctrines, for by means of them he is always trying to tell us something of the revelation which had come to him, not by a rational process but in an ecstatic experience. This, indeed, is the chief value of the doctrines, and all enquiry which neglects it is beside the mark. In the study of such a poem as the lament of David over Jonathan, it is necessary to know something of the historical conditions, of the social and religious ideas of that distant age, of the nature and structure of Hebrew poetry; but the lament is inspired by the passion of friendship. That is the one key to it, and unless you take it into account you can make nothing of the poem. At the heart of Paul's theology there lies the revelation which had come to him through Christ. All the rest is subsidiary,—an attempt to convey in terms of doctrine what cannot be so expressed. Now and then in passionate outbursts Paul forgets his doctrines altogether, and it is there that we see most clearly into his inner mind.

The truth is that the teaching of Paul is radically simple. We are wont to think of him as difficult and obscure, never content until he can state even ordinary facts in some roundabout way. As early as the second century the author of II Peter acknowledges that in the writings of Paul "there are many things which are hard to understand, which they who are unlearned wrest to their own destruction"; * and this criticism has been echoed many times since. Yet in the last resort the thought of Paul is simple. It might almost be summed up in a single sentence,—that through Christ we have access to a divine power which will do for us what we cannot do ourselves. Paul was once asked in the middle of an earthquake to declare the substance of his message, and at once he answered, "Believe in the Lord Jesus Christ and thou shalt be saved." † This was indeed his one demand, of which everything else was only an expansion.

It has often been remarked as strange that Paul's account of Christianity, apparently so abstruse and complicated, has a force

*II Pet. 3:16.   † Acts 16:31.

of appeal which is not to be found in any other. In his own day he was by far the most successful of all missionaries, and he has supplied the energy for all the religious revivals in times since. Endeavours have constantly been made to find a substitute for Paul. The gospel has been re-stated in forms that appear more reasonable, and more congenial to new ways of thinking; but somehow these other presentations do not have the same power. Ever and again the complaint is made in our own day that while our modern Christianity is more attractive and more intelligible than the old evangelism, it does not quicken and awaken in the same way. Why is it that the plain man is unmoved by a simpler gospel, but responds to the message of Paul, which perplexes even the trained theologian? The answer is that Paul's interpretation is simpler in its essence than those which are offered in its place. It is indeed associated with a number of doctrines which at this distance of time have grown obscure and often doubtful; but these for the most part can be disregarded. There is a truth at the centre of it which every one can recognise, and which is vital in all religion. Man in his helplessness can throw himself on God and find forgiveness and new life. Paul had realised this truth with such intensity that he was able to enforce it, as no other teacher has done, on the minds of others.

So it may fairly be claimed that Paulinism, rightly understood, is no mere type of Christianity but is the religion itself, in its ultimate meaning. Paul never doubts that this is so. He calls himself the ambassador of Christ. He believes that Christ is speaking with his voice. He can say "be followers of me, as I am of Christ." Yet it has always been recognised that the message of Paul is peculiarly his own. In his lifetime he was regarded as a schismatic, and even his own converts were half doubtful of him. After his death he stood out as the greatest of the Apostles and the pattern for all Christian men, but while his writings were diligently read they had little influence on the general thought of the church. He was allowed a place by himself, and the later theologians carried on their work apart from him. His teaching has never been fully accepted. There have been those in every age who said "we are of Paul," but at best they have laid hold on some of his ideas and magnified them, and have quietly discarded all the rest. There must be reasons why the Pauline teaching has never commended itself to the church at large, and they are not hard to discover.

For one thing, the very truth and greatness of Paul's message have stood in its way. He asserted the Christian demand in its full extent, without compromise. He brought to light what was finally involved in the new gospel. Few men, if any, have been able to go the whole length with Paul, for the very reason that they cannot fully accept Christianity itself. Those elements of Paul which the church has incorporated in its creeds are for the most part those which lie on the circumference, and which belong not to Paul's own religion but to his age. The difficulty has always been with the essential Paulinism, which lies behind the doctrinal structure and which Paul had received not from men but by revelation of Jesus Christ. This was his true religion, and when we consider its cardinal principles we can well understand why the church has held aloof from Paul.

(1) In the first place, he grounded his teaching in the conception of grace, with its correlative that man's attitude to God must be one of faith. Before he became a Christian he had assumed, like others, that God was a task-master who paid strictly for service done. This idea was worked out most fully in Judaism, but was taken for granted in all religions. It was, indeed, the natural assumption. Man finds, in his common experience, that he only receives what he has worked for. This is the rule that obtains everywhere, and since the world's order appears

to be founded on it must we not conclude that it also holds good in our relation to God? It was revealed to Paul, by his knowledge of Christ, that God does not deal with men according to that rule. He is the infinite Giver, who by His own grace, apart from our deserving, bestows on us all the things that are most worth having. As He sends rain and sunshine on the evil and the good, so He offers His salvation; and the part of man is simply to open his heart to the bounty of God, aware that he has nothing of his own and must be willing to receive. This attitude of receptivity, of utter self-surrender to God, is what Paul calls faith, as contrasted with all previous trust in our own righteousness. In his anti-legal polemic, which is apt to impress us now as wearisome and academical, he is trying to drive home a simple religious truth. God does not bargain with us but gives freely, and the Cross is the eternal symbol of the divine grace. Faith is the act in which we respond to it, and by faith alone can we be saved. This is a message which men can never bring themselves wholeheartedly to believe. They cannot rid themselves of the old assumption that from God, as from their fellowmen they can receive nothing but what they have earned. In every creed of the church there is some effort to adjust Paul's conception to that other which he threw aside.

(2) Closely related to his doctrine of grace and faith is that of the Spirit. He had learned, as part of his revelation, that on those who trust Him God bestows a divine power. The whole Christian life, to Paul, is life in the Spirit. By nature we are children of this world, and are subject to all its limitations, but as Christians we are endowed with an energy from a higher world, and in the strength of it can do what seems impossible. The mind is illuminated with a new kind of knowledge; the will is renewed and all moral achievement is brought within our reach. Paul was a Hellenist, and fell heir to the Hellenistic idea that man's weak-

ness is due to his earthly nature, which must undergo a radical change. His teaching is affected by this idea, and he appears to think of a heavenly essence, mingling with the earthly substance and transmuting it. To this extent his conception of the Spirit is entangled with a magical theory, more Pagan than Christian. But apart from the doctrinal frame-work he was not indebted for his belief to any suggestions, either from Jewish or Pagan thought. From the moment of his conversion he had realised that something which was other than himself had taken possession of him. His life was controlled by a higher power to which he yielded himself without reserve. At this point also the church has found it necessary to part company with Paul. His doctrine of the Spirit has been formally preserved, but has been qualified, and to a great extent neutralised. It has proved impossible even for the most ardent souls to commit themselves wholly to the Spirit, and room has been made, under various disguises, for the old authority of the Law.

(3) Again, Paul was conscious that in some mysterious way he was now united with Christ, and here, perhaps, we touch on the conception which is most intimately Pauline. It pervades his whole religion, and marks its intensely personal character. All Christians can join in the confession "Jesus is Lord," but with Paul this loyalty to Christ merges in a sense of actual identity. He thinks of Christ as the inner principle of his own being. Here again it is possible to discern the Hellenistic influence at work in Paul's expression of his belief. The aim of the prevailing cults was to bring the worshipper into union with his divinity. When the rites of his initiation were completed he was divested of his garment and clothed with another, in token of the divine nature with which he was now endued. Paul would seem at times to fall back on similar ideas. He speaks of the convert as rising from baptism into newness of life, and as casting off the old man and

putting on the Lord Jesus Christ. But he is only seeking to describe, in the religious language of his time, a profoundly Christian experience. Nothing is more remarkable in the writings of Paul than the note of passion which breaks in of its own accord whenever he speaks of his devotion to Christ. He may be in the middle of an abstract argument, but all at once he soars into rapture. It is absurd to explain this passion from an effort to conform Christian ideas to those of the Pagan cults. The very mark of it is its perfect spontaneity. It is not due to any outside influence but springs out of that element in Paul's religion which is most purely Christian. He is over-mastered by his love of Christ. He speaks of himself as the "slave" of this Lord, who owns him soul and body. And as always happens in a great affection he has a sense of oneness with the object of his love. Christ is not some one other than the man Paul but in some mysterious way is his more essential self. The phrase which occurs most frequently in the writings of Paul is the mystical "in Christ." It escapes from him in all manner of connections, often when he is speaking of quite ordinary things, and bears witness to a mood which was habitual with him, giving direction to everything he did and thought. The term Paulinism has come to be used vaguely, and covers a great deal which was the common property of Gentile Christianity, but we can be sure that whenever he tells us of that union of his own being with that of Christ, we hear the authentic voice of Paul.

(4) Again, Christianity is for Paul the religion of liberty. "Christ has made you free"; this idea is ever and again repeated in different words, and may almost be taken as the central motive of Paul's message. He thinks of the Christian as released from all earthly bonds; to his own Master he stands or falls; he judges all things but is himself judged by no man.[‡] On one mem-

‡ Rom. 14:4; I Cor. 2:15.

orable occasion Paul made his appeal to Caesar. Amidst all his earlier troubles he had carried with him the proud consciousness that he was a Roman citizen, and in an extremity could defy any lower tribunal and demand a sentence from Caesar himself. This privilege he had forborne to use, but in the end, tired out by the law's delays he fell back on it, with disastrous consequences. It is one of the ironies of life that a man's worst calamities result, almost always, from his advantages, and this was the experience of Paul. His appeal to Caesar proved a delusion, but as a Christian he had a higher privilege which he was using constantly. From all human judgments he could appeal to that of Christ, and in this assurance he passed through the world with a splendid sense of immunity, He sat loose to all tradition and opinion, and went fearlessly on his own way. In the course of his Epistles he has occasion to answer many questions, and never fails to lift them to a higher plane, and to make his decision by the one standard of the mind of Christ. It is not too much to say that Paul was the first man in history who was really free. There can, indeed, be no true liberty which is not founded on Paul's conception of man as a spiritual being, who lives in this material world but is subject to another, and who cannot, therefore, accept any earthly authority as final.

The idea of Christianity as the religion of freedom was, in the full extent, peculiar to Paul,—so much so that the church has never risen to the height of it. This was the chief cause of the hostility which followed him in his lifetime. He had declared that all shackles were now removed, and even his best converts were afraid to go with him beyond a certain point. They could not but feel that some restraints ought to be preserved,—the opinions of great Apostles, good customs and traditions, the general sentiment of mankind. In the later church Paul's doctrine of liberty was frankly abandoned. He had claimed for every

Christian a complete autonomy, and it was recognised that under such conditions there could be no settled creed or ethic, no leadership, no organised community. With human nature as it is, an unlimited freedom would mean anarchy, and the effort of the church was to impose discipline and to strengthen its control over its members. Paul was himself aware that his principle of liberty could not be put fully into effect. He finds himself obliged constantly to qualify his demand, and to allow for circumstances, consideration for others, common prudence, established law and practice. Yet he is never in doubt as to his principle, and insists that it belongs to the very essence of the Christian faith. Even when he is obliged to make concessions he maintains that the Christian is responsible only to his Lord, and therefore is absolutely free.

These, then, may be singled out as the distinctive elements in what may rightly be called Paulinism. It has been Paul's misfortune to be read as a theologian, who supplies the proof-texts for a number of approved doctrines; but to understand his real teaching we need, as a rule, to leave the doctrines out of sight. He did not think of himself as a theologian. He was the messenger of a new religion which had brought life to him, and would also do so to the world. His mind was set on the life-giving principles which were for him the substance of Christianity. He does his best to explain them, and brings to this task the knowledge he had acquired as a Rabbi, the memories which had clung to him from his youth in Tarsus, the ideas which had found currency in the Hellenistic church. But by means of all this he seeks to convey the truth which had come to him by revelation. This he can only do in very imperfect measure, for it is impossible to express in terms of reason the verities which are beyond reason. As Paul himself declares they cannot be known except by the Spirit which searches the deep things of God.[¶] He possessed this spiritual

¶ I Cor. 2:10.

knowledge, and apprehended the gospel in its inward meaning, but his difficulty was to impart to others what was clear beyond question to his own mind. All that he could do was to present in the form of reasoned doctrine what he had received by vision. The church accepted his doctrine but missed the things of which it was only the vehicle. It fastened on the externals of Paul's teaching, on the arguments and analogies by which he tried to drive home his essential thought. His theology was substituted for his religion.

There are other reasons, however, why the church at large has never fully responded to Paul. It has to be admitted that his message, with all its intrinsic truth and greatness, suffers from grave defects, which make it appear no more than an eccentric type. They are usually attributed to his involved and often arbitrary methods of thought, but this is a mistaken view. His message, when all is said, is clearly distinguishable from his doctrines, and is simple and self-evidently true. No presentation of the gospel, it may be repeated, takes such an instant hold of the ordinary man as that of Paul. Without much difficulty he can penetrate through the doctrines and grasp the truth behind them. Moreover the doctrines are by no means so obscure as is generally assumed. Theologies far more intricate have succeeded from time to time in securing the assent of the church. One has only to think of the subtle metaphysical creeds which were formulated at the great Councils and imposed themselves on Christendom for more than a thousand years. For that part the Pauline doctrines themselves were elaborated by the Reformers into complex systems, far more abstruse than anything in Romans or Galatians, and yet those confessions became the basis of flourishing churches, and were expounded week by week to companies of plain men and women who found little trouble in comprehending them. The difficulty of Paul has consisted not in his doctrines but in just those principles which constitute his religion. Take, for instance, his doctrine of liberty. To most men since, as in his lifetime, it has seemed to entail a moral danger, and while formally assenting to it they have quietly set it aside. Or take his conception of union with Christ. Such a union, it has been reasonably felt, is only possible to rare saints and mystics, and the ordinary Christian is conscious of an insincerity when he pretends to it. Even faith, as Paul employs the word, involves a frame of mind of which most men feel themselves to be incapable. He declared that salvation is by faith, and from this it would follow that no one could be saved unless he throws himself, with utter self-surrender, on the grace of God as revealed in Christ. A demand of this kind would certainly exclude the great majority of people who call themselves Christians, and faith has been interpreted by the church as a mere acceptance of certain approved beliefs. The intellectual act is taken as an equivalent of that great act of will which was plainly in the mind of Paul.

For this failure of his message Paul was himself very largely responsible. While he proclaimed the authentic gospel he did so in a one-sided way, so that it may fairly be held that he represents a type of Christianity and not the whole religion. This was inevitable, for he was a unique man, and had come to Christianity through a unique experience. He had received the gospel by a revelation, and the whole power of the revelation lay in its immediate, personal quality. Before other men can enter fully into Paul's religion they would require to have just the same kind of revelation as had come to himself. But in a Christianity on which all can agree there must be a common basis, and there can be no real Christianity unless it appeals to all. Jesus meant his gospel for the world, and, however lofty any presentation of it may be, it fails of its purpose if only a select few can respond. Paul's Christianity has never been accepted by the whole church, and in the nature of things it can never be. The reason may indeed be that it is too purely Christian, but the church rightly feels that its salvation must be within the reach of all. From this point of view the greatness of Paul's teaching was its grand defect; the gold without alloy could not become current coin. It is not a little significant that the Pastoral Epistles, written by some follower of Paul who dilutes his master's doctrine, have exercised a more practical influence on the life of the church than the genuine letters of Paul. By their very inferiority they gave it something which it lacked to make it a working religion. Paul is one of the most individual of all thinkers, and for this reason he is one of the most vital. As we compare him with any of the theologians who have come after him we feel at once that in spite of its outworn forms his message still pulses with life, while the others belong to a dead past. This is because he speaks from a revelation which came directly to himself; he puts us in contact with his own soul. But this individuality which is the strength of Paul's teaching is at the same time its weakness. He was himself aware that he could not fully bring home to his readers what he most desired to say unless he could add his presence to his words. "My little children," he writes in Galatians,§ "would that I could be with you now and change my voice,"—that is, vary my tones, as cannot be done in a letter. His words cannot have their true effect apart from the living voice, with all its modulations. It may fairly be said of all Paul's writing that he speaks by letter because he cannot be visibly present, and tries to put into his language the very tones of his voice. His style has an intimate quality which has rarely been equalled, but the thing he attempts is impossible. At best we can only half understand him since we do not hear that personal note which gave convincing power to his message.

It is here that the difference between Paul and Jesus is most

§ Gal. 4: 20.

clearly evident. Paul speaks for himself, and is greatest when he is most individual; Jesus speaks out of the general heart of man. Paul was indeed a cosmopolitan, if there ever was one. He was the most widely travelled man of his age; he could think in two languages and was imbued with the culture of Jews and Greeks and barbarians; he had the quick and mobile temperament which enabled him to become all things to all men. Jesus had seen nothing of the world outside of his native province; his intercourse was confined to people of a given class; he was probably unacquainted even with the names of the great thinkers who had done most to direct the lives of men. Yet of these two it was Jesus who had the universal mind. As we listen to him we quite forget the place and time in which he lived and the traditions which had helped to form him. He can be understood without any historical knowledge, for he speaks to us as if he belonged to our own age and country. With Paul we can never forget that he was a Hellenistic Jew of the first century. Every verse he wrote is coloured with the peculiarities of his mind and character. So in our approach to him we are always conscious of a barrier. The man himself, with his singular personality, comes between us and his message.

None the less the message is in substance that of Jesus. It has been the radical error of most interpreters of Paul, especially in our own day, to assume that he was an innovator, who cannot be understood unless we leave all previous Christianity out of account. This is precisely the error against which Paul himself protests in his criticism of the parties at Corinth. He asserts in the strongest terms that there can only be one gospel, and that his whole endeavour is to proclaim it, in the light of his own revelation. He calls himself a steward of the Christian message, whose one duty it is to be faithful to his trust. What he describes as "my gospel" is nothing else than the familiar gospel, which in the fullest measure he had made his own. His apparent innovations were only two, and his aim in both of them was not to change but to preserve. On the one hand he severed Christianity from the Law, and this was regarded at the time as a wilful departure from the original teaching. He knew, however, that by disentangling it from the Law he had not altered the gospel but had laid bare its essential nature. Matter, as seen by the physicist, is different from what it appears to the ordinary man. But the physicist has not changed the properties of matter. He is the true conservative, who removes our false assumptions and discloses the facts as they have always been. Paul made the great disclosure that salvation is by faith and not by works. He did not thereby pervert the gospel but clarified it, and this was how he himself understood his work. He claims that he has the mind of Christ, that he is thinking in the same manner as Jesus had done. The more we examine his teaching in all its implications the more we realise that he was profoundly right.

His other innovation, at first sight a more serious one, was in throwing the whole emphasis on the death of Christ. He changed the centre of gravity in the Christian religion, making everything else depend on a mysterious redemptive act, for the sake of which Christ had come into the world. To many this has appeared to be the fatal weakness in his teaching. He seems to leave out of account all that Jesus had himself intended. About the ministry in Galilee he has nothing to say; the Parables and the Sermon on the Mount seem to be forgotten. Paul had determined, as he expressly tells us, to know nothing of Christ after the flesh and to think only of the Lord who died and rose again.* It is maintained that he thus changed the nature of Christianity, assimilating it to those mystery cults which had their vogue in the Hellenistic world of his time. This, however, is a mere travesty of Paul's

* II Cor. 5:16.

message. He knew the life of Jesus, and was awake, as few others have been, to its significance. He knew the teaching of Jesus, and although he seldom quotes it literally his own ethic is entirely moulded by it. But he sees the life, not in its manifold detail, but gathered up as into one burning focus in the Cross. In that crowning act Jesus revealed himself, in all the height and depth of his nature, as he could not do in his daily living. Through the Cross, too, we have the full revelation of that divine love which Jesus proclaimed and manifested, and on which we can utterly rely. It was not the weakness but the strength of Paul's religion that he concentrated on the one fact of the Lord's death. He thereby presented the Christian message in all its simplicity. He made it possible to look away from all side-issues and apprehend the one truth which supremely matters, and which includes in itself all others. There was here no innovation. Paul was intent, as he always was, on the inner meaning of the gospel, which gives it power to renew the lives of all men as it had renewed his own.

Paulinism, therefore, is not to be regarded as merely one of the interpretations which were placed, in early days, on the new message. It is not, properly speaking, an interpretation, but a statement of the message itself. The church was separating into many schools of opinion, each under its own leader, and Paul seeks to get behind them all. He asks, "Is Christ divided?" Is there not a gospel which transcends and embraces all the different accounts of it? Paul was concerned with this ultimate gospel. He was confident that it had been revealed to him in that moment when he had seen the Lord on the way to Damascus. It is true that he makes much of certain doctrines, but they do not constitute his religion. For the most part he borrows them from the thinking of his time, and does not hesitate to pass from one set of doctrines to another, for all this reasoning about the truth is nothing to him but a means to an end. What he seeks to communicate is not a theology but a living faith. In so far as it might be conveyed by doctrines they were useful, but he had no interest in them for their own sake. He declares in one place that he had been appointed not to baptise but to preach the gospel.[†] It was not that he disparaged baptism, which he considered the necessary seal whereby faith was made effectual, but that the ordinance which confirmed it was a formal one and might just as well be performed by others. In the same manner he might have said that he was not appointed to frame a doctrinal system. This also was a necessary task and he was willing to take his part in it, but his aim was to create the faith which found expression in the doctrines. This, he believed, was his peculiar work. He had received the gospel by revelation, and through him it could be imparted with something of the immediacy with which it had come to himself.

Paulinism, therefore, was not a particular type of Christian teaching. If Paul had so desired he might have been the greatest of party leaders. He might have founded a church which called itself by the name of Paul and held its own triumphantly against all rivals. As it was, he had to yield to other teachers even in his own communities, and in later times there has never been a Pauline church, although all the creeds have been built out of fragments of his thought, like villages out of the ruins of an ancient palace. He failed as a party leader because he was so great a Christian. Where others insisted on their interpretation of the gospel he was concerned with the gospel itself. He sought to make men realise what it was in its essential nature, the divine truths on which it rested, the new life in which it fulfilled itself. As we trace the history of Christian thought in the century which followed Paul's death we are surprised to find how completely his teaching has fallen into the background. New theologies have

† I Cor. 1:17.

come to hold the field and the church proceeds on its way as if Paul had never existed. Yet with all this apparent neglect there is a growing reverence for Paul. He stands out, ever more conspicuously, as the great Apostle, the pattern of what all Christians should strive to be.[‡] This is what Paul himself had desired. He laid little store on his theology, and would have felt no resentment if he had known that it would be forgotten or misunderstood. What he wished to impress on men was that inner meaning of Christianity which was to be apprehended not by man's wisdom but by faith. It became evident, as time went on, that this had been his real achievement. He had taught the world to know the gospel. Above all other men he had caught the purpose of Jesus, and was the spokesman not for any one variety of Christian thought but for Christianity itself.

[‡] He so appears in the 1st Ep. of Clement, the Epp. of Ignatius, the Pastoral Epp.

CHAPTER V

THE RIVALS OF PAUL

PAUL WAS the greatest of the early teachers, and from this it has sometimes been inferred that he was the only one. All later Christianity is made dependent on the work of Paul. It may have found for itself a number of channels, but each of the later streams must be traced back to the great lake which was the teaching of Paul. The study of Christian history has been largely misled by this assumption that Paul was the one Apostle. All other Christian thinking has been related to his mission, and from this point of view has been misunderstood or condemned. From the time of the Reformers onward it was considered self-evident that in the second or third generation the church had become corrupted. It fell away from the doctrines of Paul and thus drifted into error.

The truth is that Paul was only one of many teachers, whose authority was at least equal to his own. As yet there was no settled creed, and all were free to interpret the gospel in their own way, under the guidance of the Spirit, and so far from providing the standard for Christian thought Paul was regarded with grave suspicion. It was known that the chief Apostles were doubtful of him, and other missionaries, entering into his communities, had little difficulty in persuading his converts that he had deceived them. In all his Epistles we find him on the defensive. The Christian movement was developing, and of this he was well aware, under influences which were frankly opposed to him.

There are two reasons for the common estimate of Paul as the one authoritative teacher. On the one hand we are now able to recognise his surpassing greatness, which was not apparent to his contemporaries. When we speak of the Elizabethan drama we think only of Shakespeare. The others appear as his satellites, and yet we know that they worked independently, and that some of them stood higher than he did in the judgment of their day. So Paul had fellow-workers who are now remembered only because they moved within his orbit, but this is our estimate, not that of the first century. Again, Paul is the only teacher who left a written record behind him. His is the one voice which we can still hear, and so we get the impression that no else was speaking. Early Christian teaching was all by word of mouth, and Paul himself normally employed the oral method. He turned to writing, partly because he was the founder of scattered churches with which he wished to maintain a personal relation, and partly because he was conscious of a literary gift. His enemies could not but acknowledge that "his letters are weighty and powerful," * and he was fully aware of this himself. As an orator he seems to have been unimpressive,† and perhaps if it had been otherwise he would never have troubled to write; but he knew that in the written word he could do himself justice. Too much has been made sometimes of the purely occasional nature of his Epistles. They are taken as ordinary letters, written off-hand for an immediate purpose, and we wonder why anything so produced should be so excellent. But they are not casual letters. He deliberately put his best into them, and meant them to be circulated and preserved. He made the writing of them one of the most important features of his missionary work, knowing that he had here found his most effective mode of utterance. Since he thus wrote it down carefully we still possess

---

* II Cor. 10: 10.
† In this sense we must understand the words "his bodily presence is weak."

his message, while that of his fellow-workers has been lost. But the spoken teaching had the same value in its own day as the written one, and often counted for much more. An accomplished speaker can reach a far wider audience and make a much deeper impression than a writer, and this was particularly true in the ancient world, where readers were few. The historical church, as it emerged from the first century, had been shaped for the most part by men who had taught only by the living voice.

It cannot be too much regretted that we know so little of those oral teachers. We should be ignorant even of their existence if it were not for chance references in the book of Acts and in Paul's own writings. He deals with them, as a rule, in a controversial spirit, and we have no choice but to accept his judgments, which are admittedly those of a hostile critic. Most of our difficulty in understanding the early Christian movement is due to this lack of first-hand evidence. If only one of Paul's adversaries had written an answer to his Galatian Epistle, we should not, perhaps, have been much richer theologically, but we should at least have known far more of the question at issue and of the workings of the early Christian mind. As it is, we have to move in the dark, and meet continually with problems which baffle us. We are in the position of the scientific enquirer when he has to deal with forces of which he knows nothing and the presence of which he can only infer from their effects.

A number of movements have thus to be reckoned with which ran parallel with the mission of Paul. Little is known of them, and even that little has come through biassed witnesses, but it does not follow that they were negligible. They played an essential part in the making of Christianity, and account for much that now seems extraordinary. Why was it that the later church departed so widely from the teaching of the New Testament? As we pass into the second century and watch the growth of ritual and ecclesiasticism and the Greek metaphysical creeds it might seem as if there were indeed some ground for the old theory of a gradual corruption of the faith. But much would be explained if we had better information of what had been going on beneath the surface. All that we know about the early period is from the record which happens still to survive. There were teachers who are not even names to us, and who were yet among the chief builders of the future church.

One thing must be borne in mind as we try to form some picture of the varied Christian activity of the age of Paul. The church was making its way among the Gentiles, but was still subject to the Jewish influence. Every community was made up largely, and in many cases predominantly, of Jews, and their opinions on all matters of doctrine carried peculiar weight. To all appearance the church had become Gentile, and was learning to express its message in terms of Gentile thought, but there was no complete transformation. Jewish and Gentile ideas maintained themselves side by side, and modified each other. It is this mingling of two different strains which accounts, in large measure, for the diversity of teaching in the first century. Christianity was adjusting itself to the new world of thought, but the adjustment could be made in countless different ways. As yet there was no clear standard of doctrine, and every teacher sought to reconcile the two traditions after his own fashion. Thus there emerged many interpretations of the gospel, some of which have left their record in the remaining books, while the character of others can only be surmised.

It is possible, however, to draw a broad dividing line between the diverse types of teaching. Paul had a profound instinct for what was truly Christian, and was also a man of liberal spirit. He made it his rule not to encroach on fields where the gospel had been preached already, although he was well aware that it had not been presented in just the manner which to his mind was the right one. He could feel satisfied that men with whom he disagreed were yet faithful to the essential principles of the gospel, and that he had no right to interfere with their work. Again and again in the course of his letters he has occasion to criticise other teachers, but for the most part he admits that with all their short-comings they proclaim the gospel. "Some indeed preach Christ even of envy and strife, and some of good will. Notwithstanding, every way whether in pretence or in truth Christ is preached, and therein I do rejoice, yea and will rejoice."‡

On the other hand, especially in the later Epistles, he is obliged to speak of doctrines which he condemns as false. They are put forward as Christian, and were finding converts within the church, but in his judgment they were alien to Christianity and he warns his readers again them. It was not that he measured them by some approved creed and found them wanting, for as yet there was no set creed. Christians were permitted and encouraged to think out the message for themselves and to express it in the forms which most appealed to them. Paul allowed himself the widest liberty in his own speculations, and could not justly deny the same liberty to others. But he rightly feels that what he seeks to interpret is the gospel. Wherever his guesses may lead him he is always intent on elucidating some truth involved in the inner principles of Christianity. Those teachers whom he condemns, however they might play with Christian phrases and ideas, had never apprehended the gospel, and had no real interest in it. His criticisms on them are not grounded in mere theological prejudice but in his sense that they are not truly Christian. From this point of view the conflicting movements in the church of the first century can best be considered. They might all appear to be equally

‡ Phil. 1 : 17, 18.

legitimate, since Christian doctrine had not yet been defined, and every one who had been baptised in the name of Christ might claim to be led by the Spirit. Yet there were some teachers who kept their hold on what was distinctively Christian, while with others the Christian interest was secondary. Their ideas, carried to a logical issue, would allow no place for the new message. This division, it may be said, is a vague one, but to Paul and to the other New Testament writers, it was sufficiently clear.

Paul never speaks directly of Stephen, with whom his own Christian career was so closely associated, and who, in a very real sense, was his predecessor. The activity of Stephen may have been confined to only a few weeks, but it had momentous results for the whole later history of the church. It was not Paul but Stephen who was the real pioneer of the Gentile mission. He worked among the Hellenists at Jerusalem, and after his death his followers returned to their native Gentile cities, carrying with them the Christian message as Stephen had taught it. The main lines of his teaching may be inferred from the long chapter in Acts which purports to be the speech he delivered at his trial.[1] This it can hardly be, for it has no relevance to the charges brought against him, and is more a theological tract than the defence of a man on trial for his life. More likely we are to see in it an outline of Stephen's teaching which was drawn up by his disciples, and it may possibly be the very earliest piece of Christian literature which has survived. Luke must have known that it had a peculiar value when he interrupted his narrative at a point of crucial interest to make room for it. The main theme of the chapter is that in the Christian church the history of Israel has reached its consummation. In all times past the true Israel has been a remnant, disowned by the nation at large, and now

[1] Acts 7.

Jesus has been rejected and his people have been cast out, although through them God's purpose with Israel has come to fulfilment. It is evident that Stephen still moved within the limits of Judaism. He thought of Jesus as the Jewish Messiah, the prophet greater than Moses whose coming had been foreshadowed by all God's messengers before him. But through the national conception Stephen was feeling his way towards a larger one. In his manifesto we can see the first effort of Christianity to break through the shell of Judaism. God does not dwell in temples made with hands or confine his promises to one particular race. The church is the standard-bearer of a universal religion.

Paul never alludes in so many words to the teaching of Stephen, but in one of his Epistles, in some respects the most important one, he probably has it in mind. There is good reason to believe that Christianity first came to Rome through the followers of Stephen, and a large and vigorous church grew up, which would adhere in the main to Stephen's type of Christianity. When Paul wrote his Epistle to the Romans he had never visited the Roman church, but was doubtless well acquainted with its general character. In the course of his mission he had constantly been meeting Christians from the great capital; two of them, Aquila and Priscilla, had for some years been his closest associates. For that part, he would never have presumed to write his letter unless he had first informed himself as fully as he could on the conditions of the church he addressed. He is able to assume that it holds a religious position which is broadly similar to his own, but in one respect he appears to take issue with it. In his Epistle to the Galatians he had vehemently assailed the Jews, who still looked to the Law for salvation. In Romans, although the line of argument is much the same, the note of bitterness is absent. He holds that the Law has failed, not because it is wrong, but because man with his sinful nature cannot live up to it. He goes out of his way to defend the Jewish people. He points out that God had chosen them and endowed them with high privileges, and declares that if they have been rejected their fall is only temporary, and that a day is coming when Jews and Gentiles will share together in the divine promises. All this is strangely different from the uncompromising attitude of Galatians, which was written not very long before, and the change must be due to a difference in his two audiences. The Galatians had over-rated the Jewish claim; the Romans had disparaged it. As may be gathered from the later sections of the Epistle they were accustomed to speak of their Jewish brethren contemptuously as "the weak," while those who disregarded the restrictions of the Law were "the strong." Paul takes care to assert his pride in his Jewish race and antecedents, and to protest against the misjudgment of his people.

The Roman attitude may have been due, in some measure, to local sentiment. Jews in Rome had fallen into disfavour, and about the time when Paul wrote his letter a large number of them had been expelled from the city. The common prejudice may have affected the church, and made it anxious to dissociate itself as much as possible from its Jewish origins. But the real cause of the estrangement has probably to be sought in the inherent nature of Roman Christianity. It was struggling to maintain itself at the centre of the Gentile world, but it had started from Jewish pre-suppositions and had never been able to escape from them. Paul had laid hold from the first on the inner principles of the gospel, and in his effort to affirm them the Jewish forms fell away of their own accord. He availed himself of Gentile ideas, not because they were Gentile but because they expressed more adequately the thought that was in his mind. The Roman Christians had none of his insight into the essential newness of the gospel. As they had received it from Stephen's followers it was bound up with Jewish ideas which they had sought to disguise by purely external changes. The result was a sort of inverted Judaism. This is strikingly illustrated in such writings as the Epistle of Barnabas and the *Didache*, which possibly originated in the Roman church at a somewhat later time. The authors of these tracts are intent on proving that Christianity is entirely different from Judaism, and their method is to show that Jewish ordinances are reversed in the practice of the church. "We fast on Wednesday and Friday, not like the hypocrites on Monday and Thursday." * Fasting is still regarded as one of the primary religious duties, but its whole character is supposed to change with the shifting of the day. It was with such an attitude that Paul had to deal in his Epistle to the Romans. The "weak," unable to shake off their Jewish sensibilities, abstained from animal food; the "strong" made an ostentation of using it, to show that they were free from the Law. Paul seeks to impress on both parties that they were subject to the same error. Christianity has nothing to do with meat and drink. The religion of outward rule has now given place to the religion of the Spirit.

In the light of the Roman Epistle we can thus discern a type of thought which was destined to prevail ever more widely. Rome was the capital city, and in course of time the Roman church imposed its own religion on the whole Western World. This religion was Christian, and Paul never questions its validity. He acknowledges at the beginning of his letter that when he comes to Rome he expects not only to impart but to receive "some spiritual gift," and this is not to be taken as a mere empty compliment.† He is aware that the Roman church, along its own lines, has developed a Christianity from which he has something to learn. But it was an imperfect Christianity, based on conceptions which belonged in large measure to the past. Judaism had been formally abandoned, but the substance of it still lay as a dead weight on the

* *Didache,* VIII: 1.   † Rom. 1: 11, 12.

new revelation. Behind the letters of Paul we can trace a growing consciousness that the Law was a far stronger force than he had at first supposed. The Law as a system might be discarded, but the Law stood for a principle, for a religious attitude which would persist under many disguises. The gospel and the Law would always be found in conflict with each other.

From some meagre indications in the book of Acts we learn of another type of belief, the nature of which it is hard to determine. Paul, we are told, on his arrival at Ephesus, fell in with certain disciples who were acquainted only with the baptism of John, and had not even heard that there was a holy Spirit.[‡] This means, no doubt, that the idea of the Spirit had no place in their religion. All Jews were familiar with the Old Testament conception of a supernatural power which descended from time to time on God's chosen servants, and which would be bestowed on all his people in the new age. What the Ephesian disciples had not learned was that the promised Spirit had now been given. One of them, apparently, was Apollos, who carried on a mission on their behalf, "speaking and teaching diligently the things concerning Jesus, though he knew only the baptism of John." He met with Aquila and Priscilla, who expounded to him more perfectly the way of God," that is, the full Christian gospel as they had learned it from Paul.[¶]

What was the nature of this religion followed by the disciples at Ephesus? This is one of the most perplexing questions in the early history, and if it could be answered with any confidence the whole background of the Christian mission would be illuminated. The mysterious disciples were presumably Jews, and by Luke's account had already become Christians. Like other Christians they practised the rite of baptism, but attached to it only the sig-

[‡] Acts 19: 1 ff.   [¶] Acts 18: 26.

nificance which it had for John. By undergoing the rite they professed repentance, and obtained the assurance that their sins were forgiven and that when the Kingdom came they would enter it. For the church generally, ever since the day of Pentecost, baptism had signified the gift of the Spirit, but of this the Ephesian disciples were not aware.

If they were Christians, therefore, we must think of them as belonging to some group which had come into existence apart from the church, and this is at least conceivable. Jesus in his lifetime had won a considerable following, and there may have been those who believed in him, although they had no connection with the body which had formed itself at Jerusalem. It is very strange that after the Gospel period we never hear again of Galilee, and are given to understand that all the believers migrated to the capital, and were henceforth identified with the church. This is hardly possible. Of those common people who heard Jesus gladly by far the greater number must have remained in their native province. Some of them must have continued to treasure his message, and may have transmitted it in some literal fashion without any knowledge of later doctrine. One may conceive of groups of believers in the first century, and they may have spread as far as Ephesus, in which no gospel was taught except that which Jesus had proclaimed in Galilee. This, however, is in the highest degree unlikely. Two different communities, both recognising Jesus as their Master, can hardly have existed side by side for many years without learning something of one another. Moreover a community which held exclusively to Jesus' own teaching would not have made a central feature of the baptism of John. Jesus himself did not baptise, and made no demand for this or any other outward ceremony. Baptism is precisely one of the things which would be wanting in a religion founded wholly on his Galilean message.

It is more than probable, therefore, that in the account of Acts there is some misunderstanding on the part of Luke. Those men at Ephesus may be regarded as disciples not of Jesus but of John the Baptist. We know that John's movement was much more important and enduring than we might gather from the Gospels. His disciples continued to revere him after his death, and we hear of a Jewish sect more than a century afterwards which called itself by his name. There are indications that the Fourth Evangelist, working in that very region of Ephesus, was acquainted with the sect, and had it in view when he wrote his Gospel. The disciples whom Luke describes as Christians would therefore be disciples of John, but while accepting John as their prophet they may well have allowed some place to Jesus. He, like John, had proclaimed the nearness of the Kingdom of God, and had called on men to repent. It would be natural, and indeed almost inevitable, that the disciples of John should also speak of Jesus, and borrow some elements of his teaching. The church, from the outset, had made much of John. It had linked him closely with Jesus in its records, and had taken over from him its rite of baptism. The sect which he had founded would be no less ready to look for suggestions to the church.

However we regard it, the episode in Acts is significant and instructive. It serves to remind us that factors were at work in the early Christian movement which must always be reckoned with, although we know little of their nature. In many indirect ways some knowledge of Jesus had penetrated into the outside world. His name was not altogether a strange one; an interest in him had been awakened and a vague rumour of his message was in the air. This, we may believe, was one of the chief reasons why the Christian mission, when it had once begun, made such rapid progress. It did not find men entirely unprepared. There were many, like Apollos, who already knew something about this message, and who only required to have it expounded to them more perfectly.

With Apollos, however, we encounter another type of teaching which entered into rivalry with that of Paul. Luke tells us that Apollos, whatever may have been his previous beliefs, received instruction from Aquila and Priscilla and was baptised into the Christian faith, He tells us further that he was a man of exceptional gifts and training, and came from Alexandria, the home of a Judaism in which the traditional beliefs were blended with Greek philosophy. He was an "eloquent," or perhaps the Greek word should be translated a "learned" man. The background of other teachers was Jewish, but Apollos brought to his task a mind furnished with the wider culture of the time. He was "mighty in the scriptures," and by this is implied not merely that he knew them well, but that he was able to pierce into their inner import. In other words, he was an adept in the allegorical method as practised in the school of Philo. When Apollos became a Christian he employed in the service of his new faith the ideas and accomplishments which he had acquired in Alexandria.

Almost from the first he took his place as a conspicuous teacher, and when he was sent on from Ephesus to Corinth he was quickly accepted as a leader of the church. To many of the Corinthians his account of the gospel was more attractive than that of Paul, so that a party formed around 'him which distinguished itself from those which followed Paul and Peter. He possessed gifts in which the others were wanting, and was qualified to appeal, as they could not, to a Greek community. It cannot be too much regretted that so little is told us of the work of Apollos, for of all the early teachers of whom we only have passing glimpses he is perhaps the most remarkable. With him a new element entered into Christian thought, and one which was destined in increasing measure to shape all later theology.

Our whole knowledge of him is derived from the brief notices in Acts and those chapters of I Corinthians where Paul deals with the divisions which had sprung up in Corinth after his departure.§ For those divisions it would appear that the coming of Apollos had been largely responsible, although Paul is careful to lay no blame on him personally. Wherever he speaks of Apollos his tone is one of friendship and even of admiration; and if he criticises, it is certainly not out of jealousy of a rival teacher who had been more successful than himself. All that concerns him is the teaching of Apollos, and he throws no doubt on its genuinely Christian character. He acknowledges Apollos as his fellow-labourer, who has furthered the cause of Christ, and has done a work which is the necessary complement of his own. He takes care to explain that if he has seemed to speak of Apollos disparagingly it has been only to enforce a principle. "These things I apply to Apollos and myself by way of illustration." * What he deplores is the spirit of division which has begun to manifest in the church. Men have come to think of the gospel as broken up into a number of messages, and are putting their separate leaders in the place of Christ.

Paul admits, however, that the teaching of Apollos was different from his own, and from the passage in Acts we can infer the nature of the difference. Apollos had approached the gospel with a mind which had been trained in Alexandria. He had sought to reconcile it, after the manner of Philo, with the rationalism of the Greek thinkers. It is possible, for that part, that he had been an actual pupil of Philo. An intellectual man, with strong religious interests, he could hardly have avoided some contact with the revered teacher who was the pride of his race and who was lectur-

§ I Cor. 1:10–3:23.   * I Cor. 4:6.

ing at that time in his own city. However this may be, Apollos was one of the links, and perhaps the principal one, between the new religion and Alexandrian doctrine; and for this reason his conversion was hardly less momentous than that of Paul himself. It was chiefly through Paul that Christianity became a Gentile religion, but Paul took little to do with Gentile thought on its philosophical side. Through Apollos and his successors the gospel came to be interpreted philosophically, and was thus brought into the main current of the world's intellectual life. Before long the whole Gentile church was attracted, as the Corinthians had been, by the new mode of teaching. Theology, as we know it from this time onward, took its main direction from Apollos rather than from Paul.

As may be gathered from the Corinthian letter Paul clearly saw a danger from the movement which was now beginning. After the opening chapters he makes no further allusion to the Apollos party, but the thought of it is constantly in his mind. The whole Epistle is a warning against the undue emphasis laid on "knowledge." Christianity is not to be changed into a speculative system, for it consists in a life, inspired by the example of Christ and his living power. The Epistle culminates in the beautiful thirteenth chapter in praise of love, the greatest of all spiritual gifts. Augustine in a later time was to frame his theology in protest against the intellectualism which was usurping the place of religion, and this is also the motive of the first Epistle to the Corinthians.

In the world of Greek culture it was necessary that the gospel should explain and defend itself by means of philosophy. Paul had himself realised this when he was called upon to state his beliefs before a typical Greek audience at Athens. So long as he argued on the line of Stoic doctrine he found an attentive hearing, but when he began to speak of Christ and the Resurrection some mocked, and the others slipped away. Yet the Christian religion, as Paul knew it, consisted in those truths which to the Greeks were foolishness. A philosophical statement could not but leave out the vital element in the message. From the Christian point of view the wildest enthusiast who spoke with tongues was on a higher level than the most accomplished rationalist. He had at least grasped the fact that there was a world beyond man's reason, only to be known by revelation. It will always be true that the effort to intellectualise religion is by its nature futile. What you believe on logical demonstration you do not really believe; for that which is proved by argument can just as easily be disproved, and of this you are secretly aware. Not only so, but the premises on which reason builds are always insecure. At this distance of time we can plainly see that the accepted Greek theories of the creation, of the moral law, of the nature of divine being, were mere hypotheses, and this, we may be sure, is equally true of the science and speculation of our own time. Perhaps no form of religion is now more utterly discredited than that which in the last century claimed the name of "Positivism," since it rested wholly on admitted facts. We have found, with the advance of knowledge, that those facts were all doubtful; and each generation makes the same discovery that it cannot rely on any previous conclusions. Religious faith, if it is to be worth anything, must stand clear of the shifting ground of men's opinions, even though they bear the appearance of assured knowledge. Faith must carry within itself its own certainty.

It is the strength of Paul's own teaching that he grounds himself on truth which has come to him by revelation. We can easily challenge his arguments, and he does not himself put much confidence in them. Again and again when he has expressed himself in rational terms he is careful to add, "I speak after the manner of men." What he rests upon is the intuition of faith. He knows that his belief may seem contrary to reason, but he asks us to accept it because he has received it from Christ through the Spirit. Whatever our philosophy may make of it, "the foolishness of God is wiser than men."*

It was just the other way with those teachers of whom Apollos was the first representative. They were learned men, skilled in the best dialectic of their day, and their message, to the Greek mind, had a more convincing power than that of Paul. But the power was all in the argument itself. Behind it there was no demonstration of the Spirit, but only some hypothesis which might or might not be true. Like the theologians who succeeded them they aimed at constructing a system which could not be overthrown since it rested on solid foundations of reason, but it was just those foundations which were unsound. Unawares to themselves these subtle thinkers were like the foolish man in the parable who built his house on the sand.

At the same time Paul gladly recognises in Apollos his fellow-workman. All through his Epistle he makes it clear that knowledge, although it must be considered secondary, has a real value, and what this value is he aptly describes in his metaphor, "I planted, Apollos watered." † Philosophy can do nothing to create faith, but when faith is present, philosophy can nurture and unfold it. Everything that can make men think about their religion is helpful, for man is a reasoning creature, and can have no real hold on his religion unless he can bring it into some conformity with his reason. Nothing is so unstable as a mere emotion, and if faith has no other support than a passing impulse, even one which has manifestly come from the Spirit, it cannot maintain itself. The function of reason in the Christian life is to preserve and foster what has been given by faith. It serves also as the necessary instrument for the discovery of new meanings in the Christian message. We are often told that the various theologies have

* I Cor. 1:25.   † I Cor. 3:6.

been only for a time, and must therefore be regarded as intrinsically worthless. But there has never been a theology, honestly
thought out, which has not brought to light some truth of permanent significance. Under the conditions of one particular time
this truth has become fully apparent, and has taken its place as
an integral element in Christian thought. It is not too much to
say that the theologies to which we owe most are those which bear
the clearest impress of their own day. They are now out of date,
but there was something which God was revealing by his Spirit
in that time, as in no other, and it was secured for the Christian
mind as a lasting possession.

It was so in that early period when Christianity allied itself
with the Alexandrian teaching. The Greek thinkers had viewed
man's life in its relation to the world as a whole, and this also
had been the aim of Philo. He was a faithful Jew, but he had
sought to combine the religious beliefs of Judaism with a cosmical philosophy. The God of Israel was also the Creator, and
the life of man was bound up with the whole scheme of things.
According to Philo's allegory the high-priest's breast-plate was a
symbol of the world, and armed with this consciousness of man's
oneness with God's universe he made his approach to God on behalf of the people.[‡] Through the Alexandrian influence a similar
interest now entered into Christianity. The Christian puts his faith
in Christ, but if Christ is truly the Saviour he must have a value
not merely for the life of man but for the whole order of which
man is a part. He must be accepted as in some way the principle
of creation, the controlling power of the universe. It is easy to
point out that Christian thought was diverted into false channels
by this endeavour to attach a cosmical significance to Christ.
Faith in him is quite independent of any view we may hold concerning the nature of the world. When the gospel is confused with

‡ Philo, *De Monarchia*, VI.

physical and metaphysical theories it ceases to be the gospel, and this became ever more apparent in the course of those fruitless controversies which occupied the church from the third century onward. But the work of the Greek theologians was, sooner or later, inevitable. If an absolute value is ascribed to Christ he must be co-ordinated with the universe. Religion cannot be enclosed in a charmed circle and taken by itself. Man's life is involved with the whole of existence, and if we confess Jesus as Lord we must believe that he is somehow at the centre of everything. "All things were made by him, and without him nothing was made that was made." [1] This was the interest which came to the fore-front in the Greek theology, and which led to the adoption of the Alexandrian doctrine of the Logos. Christ was boldly identified with the divine principle in which God went forth from Himself and formed the world. He has therefore not only a religious but a cosmical value. Whatever we may think of the solution we cannot but recognise the problem, which has indeed become more urgent now than it was in the early centuries. As the universe unfolds itself in the light of modern physics and astronomy we cannot but ask "what of our religion?" If the Christian message is true it cannot be isolated. It must in the last resort be harmonious with this infinite world of God from which our little human life is inseparable. We must have confidence that by faith in Christ we apprehend what is central in the meaning of the universe.

Paul does not question the right of Christian teachers to interpret the gospel philosophically. He warns the Corinthians against making too much of knowledge, but grants that it is fully consistent with life in the Spirit, and is, indeed, a necessary element in this higher life. Apollos, like himself, is working in the cause

[1] Jn. 1:3.

of the gospel, watering where he has planted. But there were forms of teaching, apparently Christian, which he is obliged to condemn. In the later Epistles, more especially, he has occasion to speak of doctrines now making their way into the church which to his mind were false, and endangered the very foundations of the faith. As time went on these doubtful forms of Christianity won an ever larger following, and in the writings subsequent to the death of Paul we hear of them constantly.

Nothing is definitely known of the origin of these heresies, but it is not difficult to see how they would arise, almost of their own accord, under the conditions of that time. All races were now mingled together in the one empire, and their religions tended to disintegrate, and then to fuse together in an endless variety of combinations. Men had ceased to hold seriously to their own beliefs, and at the same time had grown familiar with the beliefs of others. Christianity appeared when the eclectic movement was in full process, and thoughtful men could not but perceive that in this new message there was something valuable and unique. It had a contribution to make, more valuable perhaps than any other, to a new composite religion.

This effort to blend Christianity with other cults took two directions. The majority of the Pagan thinkers remained outside of the church, and were content to borrow from it occasional ideas which struck them as novel and suggestive. Most of the Gnostic systems of which we have notices in the early Fathers are of this character. Christian elements are present in them, but only as a kind of spice, added to a compound which is obviously Pagan. Here and there, however, there were teachers who professed themselves Christians, and in whose speculations the Christian beliefs were dominant. They went so far in their Christianity that it was impossible, in the free atmosphere of the early church, to refuse them baptism; but their Christian interest was little more than intellectual. It hardly affected their conduct, and did not radically change their religious outlook. The Christianity which they taught did not exclude many borrowings from other sources, for the most part frankly Pagan.

The difficulty with these men was that they worked within the church. It had no official authority to forbid them entrance, and the confession "Jesus is Lord" was so indefinite that almost any one could read his own meaning into it. The church, moreover, left its members to the direction of the Spirit, and strange opinions, like strange modes of utterance, could be ascribed to the spiritual impulse. The very extravagance of an idea might only be the mark of its supernatural origin. Not only so, but the men who held such opinions were usually men of intellectual gifts. Ordinary Christians looked up to them, and took for granted that these men, with their superior knowledge, must have a deeper understanding of the gospel. They naturally took their place as teachers and leaders.

Tests were gradually devised by which those doubtful converts could be distinguished from others. They preferred, for that part, to form sects of their own, called by the names of their more eminent founders. The controversial writers of the second and third centuries are able to direct their attacks against those specific sects, confessedly opposed to the church. In the New Testament writings the dangerous nature of the heresies is recognised, but they are still treated as Christian. This, indeed, was what made them dangerous. Under cover of their Christian profession the dubious teachers were welcomed as brethren, and travelled at their will among the communities, diffusing their strange doctrines. All the New Testament writers, from Paul onward, find it necessary to counteract the mischief wrought by the "false teachers." Sometimes they are dealt with explicitly and at length, as in Colossians, I John, Jude, II Peter, the Pastoral

Epistles. Elsewhere, as in the opening chapters of Revelation, in Hebrews 13, Philippians 3, Acts 20 they only receive incidental comment. The case of the Fourth Gospel is peculiar. It can hardly be questioned that the Gospel has the same background as the First Epistle of John, and that the heretical doctrines are constantly in the writer's mind; but he does not expressly mention them, feeling no doubt that in a narrative of the life of Jesus he could not directly introduce a controversy which belonged to his own time.

It cannot be made out that the same form of heresy is condemned in all these writings. This, indeed, is altogether improbable, for the very mark of the false teaching was its tendency to dissolve from one form into another. It had arisen out of the blending of Christian ideas with Pagan, and while the Pagan cults had all the same family likeness, they varied with race and locality, and wherever Christianity was planted there was apt to spring up beside it some new belief of hybrid character. Many attempts have been made to find some definite connection between the New Testament heresies, but this is wasted labour. Nothing can be said except that they were all due to the mixture of Christianity with Paganism. Towards the end of the first century the conditions must have been much the same as in the middle of the second, and we then encounter a medley of Gnostic systems, resulting from countless permutations of similar myth and theory. They are all different and yet so much alike that it is at once possible to identify any one of them as Gnostic. This is equally true of the later New Testament period. The heresies are never the same but they may be classed together, and the resemblances must be explained from no direct connection but from that interaction of Christian and Pagan ideas which was in process everywhere.

The character of the false teaching is most clearly indicated in two New Testament writings, which also illustrate the different forms which it was wont to assume. One of these writings is almost certainly from the hand of Paul himself. He had heard of a movement which was making dangerous progress in the church at Colossae, which he had never visited but for which he held himself responsible, since it owed its origin to one of his assistants. This Colossian heresy is peculiar in so far as it was affected by Judaism as well as Paganism, and insisted on dietary rules and the observance of holy seasons. According to one view it was fundamentally Jewish, and was derived from the monastic community of the Essenes.§ This is hardly conceivable, for the Essenes were the most exclusive of the Jewish sects, and confined themselves to their isolated settlements east of the Jordan. It cannot well be imagined that they carried on an active propaganda in the middle of Asia Minor. There is, in fact, nothing that need surprise us in the apparent affinities between Essenism and the heresy at Colossae. Ascetic theories are common to many religions, and wherever they are held they give rise to the same kind of practices. Nor is there anything remarkable in the admission of Jewish observances into a Pagan heresy. The peculiar customs of Judaism had made a strong impression on the ancient mind, and had been taken over, to some extent, by various cults. Little was known of the Jewish religion in its moral and spiritual aspects. To the common eye it was chiefly made up of unintelligible rites and formulae, but these were supposed to have some mysterious efficacy. Jewish charlatans were able to traffic with this superstitious feeling towards their religion, and were among the chief practitioners in those magical arts which were so much in vogue. Jewish sorcerers like Simon and Elymas make their appearance in the book of Acts, and were doubtless to be found everywhere.

§ Importance was given to this story by Lightfoot's acceptance of it in his classic commentary on Colossians.

However it may have been touched superficially by Jewish influences the Colossian heresy was essentially Pagan. Paul indicates some of its principal tenets, but he does so, unfortunately, in the terms employed by the sect itself. Like all similar groups, both in ancient and modern times, it seems to have depended largely on a high-sounding jargon. Many scholars have tried to decipher those specimens of it which are quoted by Paul, but the task is a hopeless one, since the occult language had probably little meaning, and for that very reason had a hypnotic power over minds of a certain type. It was closely connected with the performance of secret rites and the display of sacred symbols, and if there was any central idea in the jumble of strange words and ceremonies it may be found in that "worship of angels" * on which Paul lay a special stress, and which determines his line of thought in the Epistle. The heretics professed themselves Christians, but while they believed in Christ they felt that something more was necessary. Living on this earth man is surrounded with dark forces which need to be appeased. Christ has redeemed him from sin, but if he is a moral being he is also a creature of the material world and must reckon with the sinister agencies which govern it. The Colossian teachers aimed at securing a complete deliverance. Through Christ man can obtain peace with God but he must also propitiate the angels who rule in the lower sphere.

This mode of belief has often re-appeared in Christian history, and one might almost regard it as the prevailing one in our own time. The material forces are no longer conceived in the ancient manner as angels, but we still endow them with something like a personal existence and think of them with adoration. Religion for multitudes of people is a mixture of Christian faith with the worship of physical and economic laws. It is for this reason that Paul's argument in Colossians has much more than a theological

* Col. 2 : 18.

or historical interest. In his answer to the false teachers he takes his stand on two principles which he holds, as a Christian, to be indubitable. On the one hand Christ, by his death on the Cross, has vanquished all hostile powers. This world has been overcome, and there is now no purpose in the Pagan submission to the "elements,"— the spirits which rule in the material order. Such worship is nothing but a humiliation,[†] since the Christian, by his faith in Christ, belongs to God, who is the absolute Lord. On the other hand it is argued that the Christian life has become different from the natural one. The Colossian teachers, despite their lofty phrases and pretensions, were still on the material level. They attached value to outward shows, to things of baser substance which perish with the using. They took for granted that man is no more than an earthly being, enslaved by the terrors of this world and craving for its benefits. The purpose of Christianity is to change men's nature and lift him into a higher world, in which he becomes free.

The Colossian heresy was typical, in its main intention, of others which are known to us only from bare allusions. They all sought, in their various ways, to combine the faith in Christ with the Pagan veneration of material forces. Thus in the book of Revelation we hear of sects in the Asian cities which had grafted sensual rites on Christian worship.[‡] The Epistles of Jude and II Peter are directed against forms of teaching in which the message of redemption was entangled with Gnostic mythologies. In all such types of belief the object was that which Paul exposes in his Epistle to Colossians,—to make up for the insufficiency of the gospel and assert the claims of the visible and material. As a result Christianity was half emptied of its meaning and was assimilated to those Pagan religions which it was seeking to overthrow. If such teachings had been allowed to prevail they would

[†] Col. 2:23. [‡] Rev. 2:14, 20.

have made the new message an ingredient, and perhaps a minor one, in a composite religion which was intrinsically Pagan.

There was another type of heresy which might seem, at first sight, of just the opposite character to that of Colossae. It aimed, not at materialising the gospel, but at making it more purely spiritual. Christian facts were resolved into symbols and abstractions, and were viewed through a haze of metaphysic which appeared to idealise and magnify them.

The First Epistle of John was written in answer to this heresy, and there is reason to believe that the Fourth Gospel had a similar purpose. Reference to the same type of teaching may be detected in most of the later New Testament writings, and in the Epistles of Ignatius, shortly after the close of the first century, it stands out as the typical heresy, the most dangerous of all perversions of the Christian faith. It is commonly known as Docetism, since it rested on the strange belief that Christ had only appeared to be a human being. The disciples had mistaken him for a man like themselves, but what they had seen was nothing but a phantasm in which the divine nature had veiled itself for a short time. This theory of the Person of Christ was extended to his teaching. He had expressed himself in ordinary human language, but all that he said was to be understood in a higher, spiritual sense. His message had nothing to do with the merely physical side of man's existence. Paul quotes a maxim which apparently was current among some members of the church at Corinth; "Meats for the belly and the belly for meats,"—that is, the physical life must be left to its own impulses.[1] Men are concerned as Christians with purely spiritual things, and the body, with all its desires and needs, may be treated with indifference.

As we see it now the docetic position was absurd and childish,

[1] I Cor. 6:13.

and we cannot but wonder that it was ever taken seriously by intelligent men. But with all its crudity it stood for a sincere belief in the divine worth of Christ. At this distance of time, when the origins of Christianity have melted into a remote past, we do not appreciate the difficulties of those who were close to the events. There were some yet living who had actually seen Jesus, and the memories of his life were still so recent that they were encumbered with many trivial details. How was it possible to conceive of this contemporary as a divine being? Any one can feel the sacredness of an ancient cathedral; it needs some effort to have the same sentiment towards a building that has risen up before your eyes. By means of the docetic theory the Christians of the first century were able to look at Jesus with something of the perspective in which we can see him now after two thousand years. He had indeed lived as one of themselves, but with this difference,—that he had only appeared to share in the everyday life. His true existence had been entirely separate from the gross material world. We must remember, too, that for the Hellenistic mind the distinction of divine and human was one of essence. . The higher nature, by its very definition, was apart from matter, and it was unthinkable that Jesus was the Son of God and at the same time subject to earthly limitations. The Hellenistic Christian found himself in a hopeless dilemma, and welcomed the escape from it which was offered him by the docetic heresy. Living on this earth Jesus had still preserved his divine essence. He had not submitted himself to change and mortality and contact with earthly things. What men had mistaken for a physical body was only a semblance, through which the divine nature had for a moment made itself visible.

This type of thought, so far from appearing childish, was chiefly attractive to those who prided themselves on their finer intelligence. We can gather from the First Epistle of John that some of those more enlightened members had separated from the main body of the church, and that their secession had caused grave misgivings.§ Might it not be that they had advanced to a higher knowledge of which the plain believer was incapable? The purpose of the Epistle is to allay such doubts. Certain tests are offered by which every Christian may examine himself, and discover whether the true life is in him, and it is shown that the separatists, when so tested, are found wanting. They have failed in right belief, in right conduct, and above all in love to their fellowmen. The very fact that they held proudly aloof from others was evidence that they knew nothing of the gospel, which has, as its foundation, the principle of love.

The heresy which is treated at length in the First Epistle of John appears to be glanced at in the Epistle to Hebrews. Here, too, we learn of Christians who have ceased their attendance at the common meeting, convinced, apparently, that they do not need the fellowship which might be helpful to the uninstructed.* Perhaps it is with such people in mind that the writer dwells on the earthly life of Jesus, who became at all points one with his brethren and so fitted himself to be our High-Priest. We need also to read the Fourth Gospel against the background of the docetic heresy. The evangelist builds on the great thesis, "The Word was made flesh," which is often taken as a strong affirmation that while Christ appeared in the form of man he was all the time the eternal Word. Almost certainly the emphasis is the other way. Although he shared in the divine nature Christ became flesh, and his whole significance is made to depend on this reality of his earthly existence. Apart from this there is no security that the divine life which dwelt in him can be imparted to men.

Between the docetic heresy and that other which combined the worship of Christ with that of the material forces there might

§ I Jn. 2:19.   * Heb. 10:25

seem to be a radical division. In the one, the spiritual character
of the gospel was pushed to an extreme; in the other it was more
than half obliterated. Yet on closer examination it can be seen
that the two heresies were closely akin, and that both of them had
their origin in the Pagan habit of mind. The Docetists, like the
angel-worshippers, were pre-occupied with the world of matter;
only they viewed it from the negative side. Their one interest was
to make out that the life of Christ was not material, and in this
anxiety to spiritualise it they over-reached themselves. Spirit, as
they were led to conceive it, was only matter of a finer and more
ethereal kind. It is a well-known fact in religious history that
when a morbid attitude is taken to the physical side of life the
result may be either a strict asceticism or a gross self-indulgence.
The bodily impulses may be either suppressed or glorified, and
which of these courses may be followed is largely a matter of
chance. The same man may change almost in a moment from the
one attitude to the other, and the libertine of to-day is the hermit
of to-morrow. So in the docetic and the paganised types of Christianity we may discern the same underlying motive. They both
construed the gospel in terms of matter, negatively in the one case
and positively in the other. Jesus had brought an inward and
moral revelation, but this was set aside, and his work was related
to the physical world.

This affinity of the two heresies came fully to light in the later
Gnosticism, of which they marked the incipient phase. The Gnos-
tics, like the sectaries of John's Epistle, claimed to be "spiritual
men," in contrast to the mass of Christians who were unable to
rise above the earthly plane. Yet their profound speculations were
hopelessly confused with myths and magical ceremonies. This
was inevitable, for the Gnostic thinkers, like the heretics at Colossae, never shook off their bondage to the "elements of this
world." Their spiritual ideas were simply those of Pagan nature-
worship, sublimated by a philosophical process, and could not

give rise to anything of religious value. There are many in our own time who look for a higher religion which will emerge eventually from the new scientific theories. They point out that the crass assumptions of the older physics are now being transcended. Matter has been resolved into something invisible and impalpable, and by way of the laboratory we seem to be returning to a spiritual conception of the world. This may be partly true, but matter, however it may be rarefied into motion and energy, does not cease to be material. As Christians we apprehend a world of different nature, in which love, faith, goodness are the sole realities. The modern endeavour to achieve a scientific religion is the same, in essence, as that of the semi-Pagan teachers of the first century, and the New Testament criticism still holds good. That which is born of the flesh is flesh and that which is born of the Spirit is spirit.[†] The natural man receiveth not the things of the Spirit of God, neither can he know them, for they are spiritually discerned.[‡]

It might be contended, however, that all the Hellenistic teachers had fallen into the same error as the heretics. Paul himself made free use of suggestions offered him by the Pagan thought of his time, and he did not pervert the new religion when he brought into it those foreign elements. In Paganism there was much that was worth preserving and that served to illuminate the Christian message. Why was it that certain types of teaching, similar, it might seem, to that of Paul, were recognised by Paul himself and by the church generally as false? To answer this question we need to look more closely at some of the criticisms made in the New Testament.

It is shown, in the first place, that the heretical doctrines were often in contradiction to cardinal beliefs. A wide latitude was allowed to the Christian teacher. He was fettered by no set creed,

[†] Jn. 3:6.   [‡] I Cor. 2:14.

and was welcome to all theories, wherever he might find them, which helped him to present his message more effectually. But what he presented must be the message. Jesus was the Lord; he had died and risen from the dead; he was to judge the world and bring in the Kingdom of God; his people must put their faith in him and follow his way of life. These were the certainties apart from which there could be no Christianity, and they must not be forgotten or obscured. So amidst the variety of the early teaching it was always possible to draw a line between the true and the false. Paul had differed from James and Peter but they gave him the right hand of fellowship because they perceived that he taught the gospel to the Gentiles as they did to the Jews. Under different forms they proclaimed the same message. But teachers were now arising who thought of Jesus as one Lord out of many. They denied the reality of his life and death. They separated the Kingdom of God from Jesus' way of living. It was evident that they were not interpreting the Christian ideas but were putting others in their place. However they might clothe their thought in Christian language their teaching was contrary to the gospel.

Again, much of the New Testament criticism is directed against the moral conduct of the heretics. They are described as crafty, self-seeking, proud, sensual, guilty of every kind of open and secret vice. Charges of this sort must always be viewed with suspicion. In every age it has been the habit of controversialists to blacken the personal character of their opponents. This is the easiest and also the most effective way of discrediting opinions from which you differ, and it cannot be assumed that the strictures in the New Testament are always just. Most probably the heretics in that age, as in later times, were for the most part men of decent life, honest in their thinking, anxious in their own fashion to help on the Christian cause. It is a historical fact that in the second century the most earnest Christians were often found in the Gnostic camp, and were attracted to it by the pure and lofty character of some of the heretical leaders. Nevertheless the ethical line of argument was justified. Whatever those teachers may have been in their private lives, the doctrines which they held could have no other effect than to weaken the moral law. They taught explicitly that the higher knowledge had nothing to do with practical behaviour. The "spiritual man" was held to be superior to others in virtue of an inborn quality of his nature, irrespective of the manner in which he lived. Such doctrines, as the Epistle of John points out, not only destroyed morality but fostered an arrogant, unlovely temper which was utterly inconsistent with the Christian law. Men are often better than their opinions, and this may well have been true of the heretics who are denounced so unsparingly in the Pastoral Epistles and the Epistles of Jude and II Peter. But opinions in the long run are sure to have their outcome in action. The truth of a doctrine may fairly be tested by the conduct which will result from it when it is accepted as a rule of life.

Again, a special stress is laid on the divisive character of the heresies, and this is urged as conclusive proof that they cannot be truly Christian. Wherever these teachers appeared they formed coteries which broke off from the main body of their brethren, and took no interest in the common life. Here also it may be argued that the spokesmen of the church were on delicate ground. From the outset it had been the Christian position that all believers must follow the guidance of the Spirit. It had been fully recognised that when men were earnest in their convictions they could not but differ, and the new teachers had a right to claim that in holding their peculiar doctrines they had only gone where the Spirit led them. Yet between the ordinary divisions in a Christian community and those occasioned by the heresies there was a clear distinction. It was possible for Christians to differ, and to differ very widely, while they still agreed on the fundamental things. Paul does not require of the parties at Corinth that they should abandon their several views. He only enjoins on them that with all their diversities they should remember that they were one in Christ. The effect of the false teaching was to destroy this essential unity. One group of Christians ceased to take part in the common worship and despised their brethren and believed that as spiritual men they were different in nature from the others. As the writer of I John is never tired of insisting, love is the very substance of Christianity. "He that saith he is in the light and hateth his brother, is in darkness, even until now." ⁋ Divisions that were caused not merely by doctrine but by scorn and self-assertion had clearly no place in Christianity. The heresies were due, in fact, to the intrusion of Pagan sentiment into the life of the church. For the Pagan there was a radical distinction between free men and slaves, between the intellectually gifted and the ignorant, and the separation of spiritual from ordinary men meant nothing but the reappearance in the field of religion of this arrogant temper. It was rightly felt that when once the idea of brotherhood was disowned there could be no Christianity.

The church was alive, almost from the outset, to the dangers involved in its Gentile mission. Converts from heathenism could not all at once discard their old practices and beliefs, and their religion, however sincere, was mingled with elements which were contrary to the gospel and might lead, sooner or later, to its destruction. Christian teachers did their best to combat the danger, but could accomplish little. All they could do was to reason with those who were in error and rebuke them, and even so they could make no effectual protest, since as yet the church had no fixed standards and no real powers of discipline. Moreover it did not wish to deal too strictly with its misguided converts. Nothing is

⁋ I Jn. 2:9.

more charming in Paul's Epistles than his tenderness to the "weak brother,"—the Pagan who had not yet been fully Christianised. This tolerance was due, not merely to a spirit of charity, but to a just instinct which governed the wiser minds of the church in their opposition to the false teaching.

They felt, for one thing, that Christianity could not make its way in the Gentile world without some admixture of error. The Gentiles were ready to welcome the new religion. There was much in their own higher thought which had prepared the way for it. There were some aspects of its teaching to which they could respond with their whole hearts. Yet the Christian outlook was so different from the Pagan that they could not all at once accept or understand it. Some interval was necessary before those who had dwelt long in darkness could grow accustomed to the light, and meanwhile they could only see as through a mist. A new truth is always liable to many misconstructions, and continues, perhaps for ages, to be blended with error. None the less it is the truth and is gradually making itself clearer and pervading the minds of men. Without the initial period in which it is seen imperfectly it could never find entrance at all. So the rise of the false teachings marked a necessary phase in the progress of the Christian mission, and this was recognised by broad-minded thinkers like Paul. They were aware of the danger, and tried to root out the weeds which might choke the grain. But their chief object was to make sure that the grain was planted. This they could never do if they troubled too much about the weeds.

Again, heresy was the price which Christianity had to pay, and must always pay, for liberty. In the first age, above all others, this was felt to be the great Christian interest. Christ had made us free; his people must submit to no authority but that of the living Spirit. There were false voices which were too easily mistaken for the voice of the Spirit, but they were not to be suppressed. All who confessed Jesus as Lord must be left free, and no one had the right to judge them when they claimed to utter the mind of the Spirit. The heretics availed themselves of this privilege and remained in the church, diffusing ideas which were often quite alien to the gospel. The risk was great, but if it had not been taken there would have been no Christianity worth preserving. At all costs the church held to its principle of liberty, and it cannot be doubted that this liberty, in spite of all drawbacks, justified itself. It has been the chief tragedy of the church in its later history that again and again the progress of thought has been arrested. Men who appeared with some new message have never had the chance of speaking it, because no one as yet could decide whether it was true or false, and it seemed wiser on the whole to silence them. This might easily have happened in the earlier time if the church had not held to its position that the Spirit must be left free. We know, for instance, that the Fourth Gospel was at first regarded by many Christians with grave misgivings, and if their view had prevailed our religion might have lost one of its most glorious possessions. But the church was still willing to trust the Spirit. Freedom was allowed to all teachers, even when they came forward with ideas that seemed novel and startling. Undoubtedly the door was thus opened to many dangerous influences, and the Christianity of a later age would have remained purer if they had been excluded. But the true found entrance along with the false. Without the heretics there would have been no room for Paul and the Fourth Evangelist.

The heretics themselves, for that part, were helping the church towards a better knowledge of its message. Along paths which we now see to have been erroneous they were feeling their way to the truth. It is the same in religious enquiry as in any other. For a long time, perhaps for centuries together, it proceeds along mistaken lines. Astronomers take for granted that the sun goes round the earth; political thinkers agree that no society can hold together unless its members are separated into classes and all power is concentrated in the hands of one man. It cannot be said that all this was false thinking, and that those who held to it were wilfully blind to the truth. We acknowledge, rather, that if we now see the facts differently it was they who led us forward. There could have been no true science without that groping through error. In matters of religion the church has always been too ready to brand as false teachers those who have deviated from a given path. They have been accused of evil motives, and are remembered in history as the men who corrupted the gospel. But their errors were those of pioneers who had no map by which to travel, and took roads which often led them into swamps and forests when they were seeking for the fertile plain. None the less those explorers in their aimless journeyings sometimes made discoveries which have meant much to the world, and even when their toil was fruitless they taught all later travellers what should be avoided. It may be that in the history of Christian thought there is nothing that can be swept aside as false teaching. What is condemned as error is found in the end to have done some service to the truth.

CHAPTER VI

APOCALYPTIC CHRISTIANITY

THE GOSPEL, in its original form, was apocalyptic. This is impressed on us by the very word "gospel," which means nothing else than the good tidings that the Kingdom of God is near. It had long been foretold that the present order of things would at last come to an end and a new age would set in, suddenly and miraculously, in which God would reign. Jesus had brought the message that this Kingdom of God was at hand. He had proclaimed himself the Messiah through whom it would appear.

The apocalyptic hopes had grown out of old mythologies and historical traditions, and it has been held that a religion which was based on them could have little intrinsic value. Even the precepts of the Sermon on the Mount must be considered questionable in so far as they depend on a mode of thinking which we can now see to have been mistaken. Attempts have therefore been made to deny or minimise the apocalyptic strain in Jesus' teaching. It is argued that all sayings of this character were attributed to him at a later time, or must be understood in some vague symbolical sense. But such efforts to explain away the language of the Gospels are arbitrary and are also unnecessary. The worth of Jesus' message was not affected, one way or another, by the forms in which it was delivered. Every teacher is obliged to put his new convictions in the framework provided for him by the time in which he lives. As he expresses himself in the current forms of speech so he must employ the common ideas, and the substance of his thought can be detached, without much difficulty, from the wrappings in which it is conveyed. When Jesus spoke of the Kingdom of God he made use of apocalyptic terms, but he sought by means of them to affirm his belief in a higher spiritual order. The vehicle of his conception makes no difference to the conception itself. In the minds of many scholars there is a nervous fear of any "modernising" of New Testament beliefs. It is maintained that every idea must be kept in its original setting, and must be understood exactly as it may have been by the author himself. This principle is undoubtedly a sound one, but the question arises, "How did the author understand the idea?" Was he intent on it for its own sake, or was he thinking more of the truth which it served to express? Water from a spring has to be carried in some kind of vessel, usually the first that comes to hand, but the thirsty man accepts the vessel with hardly a thought of its crude material and workmanship. The one thing he cares for is the water. So it may be said that the ideas of any great teacher need to be modernised before they can have the same meaning for us as they had for himself. He was trying to convey some living truth, and when we concentrate on the vessel, the bygone forms in which he gave it, we miss his intention. As we study his words we need to ask ourselves continually, "How would he say this now?" The ancient forms have grown useless, but into new ones, intelligible to ourselves, he would put the same essential meaning.

The whole subject of apocalyptic is often thrown into wrong perspective by the assumption that in this mode of thought there was something abnormal and occult. It is supposed that since Jesus spoke in this manner he had some twist in his mind. He must have had access to a secret tradition, or he belonged, perhaps, to some visionary group which stood apart from ordinary Judaism. But in that age there was nothing peculiar in the apocalyptic ideas. They were taken for granted, at least in outline, by all pious Jews, who thought of the world as haunted by angels and demons, looked for a judgment and the breaking in of a new age, waited for a Messiah who would deliver Israel and bring the purpose of God to its fulfilment. Apocalyptic was not a strange heresy, entertained by a few eccentric teachers, but was the acknowledged background of the common religion. In our own day we hold the scientific view of the world, and our thought of God and his ways with men is adjusted to it. In the time of Christ, men thought apocalyptically. A thousand years hence our scientific view will no doubt appear just as fantastic and out of date as the old apocalyptic one, but for religious purposes they are both valid. We cannot think of the great human problems unless we relate them to some universal plan. Our conception of the plan will always be inadequate, but all that we require of it is the larger setting in which we can frame our thought of God and of the final issues of our lives.

In many ways the apocalyptic scheme was better fitted than any other to the ideas of Jesus. Its value consisted in the very fact that it was not scientific but flexible and imaginative. At a later time the Christian beliefs were embodied in precise creeds, and this, to all appearance, was a great advance. The truth which had formerly been conveyed in shadowy pictures was now set forth in reasoned terms, so that men knew definitely what they were expected to believe. But in course of time the philosophies which underlay the creeds lost all their meaning. Religion was tied up with statements which had to be accepted as literally true, but to which the minds of thoughtful men could no longer yield assent. Those creeds, which made everything so clear and logical, have become the chief stumbling blocks to religion, and ever and again the cry arises that they should be discarded, and replaced by some new one which will define our faith in terms of modern knowledge. But if such a creed could be devised it would only be acceptable for a short time. In matters of thought there can be no finality, and one age cannot impose its theories on the next. In any case it is impossible to express rationally what is real and vital in religious truth. The warning of Paul will always hold good that "we know in part," and the part which is apprehended by knowledge is at best a superficial one. Apocalyptic, however, does not try to define. It does not pretend that its forecasts and symbols are to be taken literally as statements of fact. It makes appeal not to logic but to feeling and imagination, and has the same advantage over doctrine that poetry has over prose. Jesus employed this symbolical language, with the result that his own account of his message is still the only one that is fully adequate. In our prayers and hymns, and whenever we try to give utterance to heart-felt beliefs, we fall back on his imagery, not merely because it was his, but because it best expresses what is in our minds. It gives force and reality to what might otherwise be bloodless abstractions.

So from the outset apocalyptic was the natural medium of Christian thought. The disciples had arrived at their convictions by no process of reasoning but by an immediate, ecstatic experience. They knew that Jesus had come from God, that he had brought a deliverance, that his Kingdom was on its way. Why they so believed they could not explain, and they knew that in any explanation they would leave out that burning certainty which was the very essence of their faith. All they could do was to think in pictures, describing in the language of vision those hopes of which they felt assured. They saw the heavens opened; they looked for the return of Christ in clouds of glory; they spoke of this world dissolving and giving place to another in which God would reign. All this, it might be said, was irrational, but it is the function of apocalyptic to make palpable, almost to the senses, what might seem to belong to the world of ideas. That is why apocalyptic is a genuine and necessary instrument of religious thought. It provides the forms apart from which the truths of religion lose half their meaning, like the words of a song without the tune.

Jesus, then, threw his message into the apocalyptic mould, and there is no reason to doubt that he shared in a general way (for no other was possible) in the beliefs which were current in his land and time. It has been supposed that he only held them conventionally, much as an intelligent Catholic will bow before a sacred image, with the full knowledge that it has no value in itself and serves merely as a vehicle of purely spiritual ideas. But it seems apparent that Jesus looked forward, like the people around him, to an actual day when a new order would be established, and God would visibly judge the world and bestow eternal life on his servants. He believed in the reality of angels and demons, in a heaven which was the dwelling-place of God, in the whole apocalyptic scheme of man's destiny. Nevertheless, while he thus shared in the traditional ideas his mind was set on the deeper truth involved in them. This is the manifest difference between the apocalyptic of Jesus and that of the contemporary Jewish writers with whom he might seem to have so much in common. They are concerned with the outward concomitants of the new age,—convulsions of nature, hosts of angels, an earth made tenfold more beautiful and fertile, endless joys reserved for God's people. Jesus takes all this for granted. He scarcely touches on the external aspects of the Kingdom and they plainly have no interest for him. He thinks only of the new life, the new knowledge of God to which men will attain when the world's order will be changed. In one sense it might be said that apocalyptic has no real place in the teaching of Jesus. At most it is only an accompaniment of his thought and does not affect its substance. When we speak of the principle of justice we no doubt have in our minds some dim picture of assemblies and police and judges, but these are only accessories. The grand idea of a society ruled by justice would remain the same although the visible agencies were left out of account. So when Jesus speaks of the Kingdom of God he troubles himself little with those outward conditions which he yet assumed to be necessary. There is reason to believe, on purely critical grounds, that many of the apocalyptic sayings attributed to him in the Gospels were introduced at a later day. This is almost demonstrable with regard to the 13th chapter of Mark and its parallels in Matthew and Luke. Jesus himself was much less apocalyptic in his thinking than the reporters through whom we hear him. None the less he thought apocalyptically, and in that age he could not do otherwise. His outlook on the future and the unseen, and the crisis now approaching, was much the same as that which is set before us in the Jewish writings. With him, however, the apocalyptic scheme is always secondary, and in his more ethical teaching it hardly appears at all. It is little more than the frame or background for a purely religious message.

After the death of Jesus the apocalyptic ideas came for a time to overshadow all else in the minds of the disciples, and this, when we try to realise their situation, was not surprising. All their thought of Jesus was now associated with the tremendous events with which his life had closed. He had been crucified and had risen again and had been "declared Son of God with power."[*] Those who believed in him were waiting from hour to hour for his return and for the end of the present world. They were in no mood for quiet reflection on the meaning of Jesus' message. Their one interest was in the mysterious future which he had foretold, and which was now on the very point of inauguration. So among the sayings of Jesus they fastened on those in which he had spoken

* Rom. 1:4.

of what was coming, and expanded them with the help of others from the writings of prophets and apocalyptists. They had guesses and premonitions of their own which crept into the record of what Jesus himself had said. The Gospels, it must always be remembered, took shape in that early period when the Christian mind was wholly possessed with forebodings of the end.

One book in the New Testament is known emphatically as the "Apocalypse," and it appears, at first sight, to stand wholly by itself. Countless readers have wondered why the New Testament should include this strange book, so utterly different in character from the others. But so far from standing alone it represents what at one time was the normal Christian outlook. Like John at Patmos the believers were in the Spirit whenever they met together on the Lord's day; and under this influence they fell into trances, and saw visions of things in heaven and judgments which would shortly come upon the earth. For the most part those visions were momentary, and were perhaps forgotten by the seers themselves as soon as the transport was over. Yet they arose out of a mood which in some measure was habitual. Sometimes, when the vision was peculiarly vivid, it was put on record, and was incorporated in Christian belief. Apocalyptic, it may fairly be said, was the earliest form of New Testament literature. Before it occupied itself with reflection on its message the church was intent on preserving those intimations which had come to its prophets through the Spirit. The Book of Revelation is probably made up, to a great extent, of those early prophecies, expanded by the later author and adapted to his special purpose. No other book is entirely of the same character, but fragments of apocalyptic are scattered here and there through all the New Testament writings. Not only in the primitive time but for long afterwards the church ranked its prophets along with its apostles and teachers. Paul himself tells us that if there were anything of which he might boast it was his visions, in which he was caught up to the third heaven and saw things which it was not lawful for man to utter.[†] In one passage (2 Thess. 2) he forecasts a whole series of events which will lead up to the final crisis, and it is so different from anything else in his writings that its authenticity has often been doubted. But with his other gifts he had that of a prophet, and there is no reason why he should not have left us at least one example of how he exercised it. Christian thinking began with apocalyptic, and this never ceased, even with minds of the highest order, to be one of its characteristic aspects.

Nevertheless the main current was steadily turning in a new direction. Already in the first generation apocalyptic ideas were losing their hold, for it was growing more and more evident that they did not correspond with facts. The church had anticipated that Christ would return immediately, and he had not returned, and with every day that passed it became less likely that he would ever do so. For a time the disappointment was so keen that many Christians gave way to doubt and despair. Echoes of this mood are clearly discernible in the closing verses of Revelation, and in some chapters of the Epistle to the Hebrews. The writer of II Peter expressly tells us that many were saying, "Where is the hope of his coming? For since the fathers fell asleep all things remain the same as they were at the beginning." [‡] It seemed to these waverers that the whole Christian hope had been a delusion. The church had staked everything on the assurance that the final act was now in progress, but nothing had happened, and it was now apparent that the old order was to go on indefinitely. There were others, however, in whom the very disappointment had produced a stronger and clearer faith. It caused them to reflect more deeply on the meaning of the Lord's promise. He could not himself have been mistaken when he foretold that he would come again to

[†] II Cor. 12:4.   [‡] II Pet. 3:4.

bring in the Kingdom. The mistake must have been in the minds of his followers, and they must now set themselves to discover what he had really meant. It is not too much to say that the true understanding of the Christian message grew out of the failure of the original hope.

The church thus moved away from those apocalyptic beliefs which at first had meant everything. They were never formally abandoned, and have not been to this day, but they were blended with ideas of a philosophical or a purely religious nature, and were sometimes wholly dissolved in them. Thus Paul, while he never gives up the earlier apocalyptic, is confident of an inward and present redemption, of which the future one will be only the consummation. He thinks of Jesus as not merely the Messiah, but the divine Lord. He describes a resurrection at the last day, which will be accompanied with all the circumstances foretold in apocalyptic, but will manifest the new life which is already hidden with Christ in God. So the writer to the Hebrews works with the conception, derived through Philo from Plato, of an eternal, ideal world, over against the changes and shadows of the present. He still conceives of the future under apocalyptic forms, but merges them in those others, given him in Greek speculation. In these various ways the primitive scheme was retained, as an integral part of the Christian faith, but was modified and spiritualised. The process was carried to its final issue in the Fourth Gospel, where the writer sets himself deliberately to re-interpret all apocalyptic ideas in terms of their spiritual meaning. The Messiah becomes for him the eternal Word; the Kingdom of God is divine life; the Judgment consists in the sentence which every man passes on himself by his attitude to the light; the return of Christ is nothing else than his coming back to his people as an inward and abiding presence. In this manner the whole Christian message is re-written in the light of purely spiritual ideas which, to this evangelist's mind, were adumbrated in those of apocalyptic. His method is no doubt determined, in some measure, by the need of explaining the gospel to the Hellenistic world. Apocalyptic was a Jewish mode of thought, foreign, in many respects, to the Gentiles, and needed to be replaced by one that was more congenial. But the new presentation was due much more to a growing sense among Christians themselves that the apocalyptic forms were inadequate. Jesus had employed them because the Jewish tradition had no others to offer him, but they were incapable of expressing the full purport of his message. This became increasingly apparent to the later teachers, and soon after the beginning of the second century there was a strong reaction against all apocalyptic. For a long time the book of Revelation was denied a place in the New Testament canon. It was confessedly of an earlier date than some of the accepted books, and there could be no denying its extraordinary value. But the apocalyptic outlook was now alien to Christian thought, and in view of such fanatical movements as Montanism was considered by many to be dangerous. The effort was made to sever Christianity entirely from that type of belief out of which it had grown.

After the first age, therefore, there was a gradual drifting away from apocalyptic. Not only had the primitive hopes proved delusive but it was admitted ever more explicitly that they had never been truly in harmony with the Christian faith. What Christ had brought to men was an inward deliverance, and the old conception of a visible drama in which he would play the central part was at best symbolical, and the aim of Christian thinkers was to pierce through the symbols to the reality. In popular religion, however, apocalyptic ideas continued to hold their ground. The ordinary man does not care to think abstractly. Instinctively he tries to grasp by his senses the truth offered to his reason. He conceives of the future life in terms of place and time and physical experience. He can best understand the fellowship of Christ when he associates it with a literal meeting, as when one friend greets another after long separation. And this is not to be set down to mere superstitious fancy. In a very real sense the instinct of the common man is right, for religion means nothing unless it brings us the feeling of actuality. The objects with which it deals exist just as truly as those which we can see and handle. We miss them altogether when they are resolved into bare ideas, projected from the mind itself. The value of apocalyptic is precisely this,—that it makes the Christian teaching concrete. Its pictures may often be crude and fantastic, but they help us to visualise the things we believe, and thereby to make them real, so that we lay hold, as the writer to the Hebrews puts it, not of the shadows but of the very image of the things.¶ Apocalyptic, when it is so regarded, must always have a place in genuine religion.

We can understand, therefore, why it was never abandoned, although it ceased to be dominant, as in the primitive age. It held its own even in those interpretations of the gospel which aimed expressly at replacing it with more spiritual conceptions. In some sections of the church, and perhaps with the great majority of unreflecting Christians, it remained very much the same as it had been at first. There are many signs that it was the Jewish converts to Christianity who adhered to it most fervently. It was of Jewish origin, and much of it had little meaning apart from Jewish history and tradition. The men who translated the ancient apocalypses, which in the first century had their chief currency in the church, must have been Jews. It must have been Jews, too, who were mainly responsible for Christian books composed on the ancient model. But there was much in the apocalyptic beliefs which also had a fascination for Gentiles. The Book of Revela-

¶ Heb. 10: 1.

tion is the most Jewish of the New Testament writings, saturated with the ideas and imagery of the Old Testament and betraying even in its defective Greek the hand of an author whose own language was Hebrew. Yet it is addressed to Greek churches in Asia Minor, and the author can take for granted that this is the kind of message to which they will respond. In like manner the apocalyptic discourse which Mark attributes to Jesus forms part of a Gospel which almost certainly had its origin at Rome. The taste for mystery is common to all men, and the Gentiles welcomed those Jewish speculations on the mysteries of the other world. Not only so, but while Jewish apocalyptic might be strange to them, they were steeped in mythology. Their native religions consisted of little else, and they fastened eagerly on the mythological elements in the Christian teaching. They were able, without much difficulty, to fuse their own myths with those which were now offered them, and an apocalyptic grew up in the West which owed almost as much to Pagan as to Jewish sources. When Dante makes his journey through Hell and Purgatory his guide is not some Hebrew or Christian seer but Virgil. Between the Pagan apocalyptic and the Christian he can see no essential difference, and thinks of them both as represented in the Roman poet. It may, indeed, be argued that the sixth book of the *Aeneid* has done more than anything in the Bible to shape some of the conceptions of the other world which prevail to this day in popular Christianity. Into the teaching of the missionaries the Gentiles were able to read their own beliefs that a Golden Age was approaching, that the powers of evil would be overcome, that after death there would be a Judgment in which the good and the wicked would have their places assigned them. These beliefs in their Pagan form were blended with the old apocalyptic.

It was not difficult, therefore, for the Gentile mind to assimilate such ideas as pervade the Book of Revelation. To be sure they were Jewish in origin, and could not be understood without some knowledge of their background in Jewish tradition. But their Jewish character, instead of repelling the Gentile mind, would only make them more attractive. There is always a charm in the exotic. New cults are constantly arising in our own time and win numerous adherents, on the strength of little else than their connection with some remote part of the world. They may be unintelligible, but this, for a certain type of mind, is only the proof that they conceal in them some profound meaning. In the first century, Judaism made this kind of appeal in a pre-eminent degree. The Jews were regarded as a mysterious people, who had been entrusted, in a distant past, with a secret wisdom. Ever and again in Greek theosophical writings, like those collected in the Hermetic literature, we meet with Hebrew catch-words, and scraps of legend suggested by the Creation story in Genesis. The writers of our New Testament continually introduce Hebraic turns of expression, and this has been attributed to their imperfect knowledge of Greek, or to their use of documents composed in Hebrew or Aramaic. For the most part, however, the use of Semitic colouring appears to be intentional. Luke is an educated writer, whose native language is Greek, but he frequently goes out of his way to Hebraise his thought and style. He is aware that his Greek public will be more impressed by his story if it carries with it the suggestion of a foreign land and a strange people. So for the Gentiles the Christian forecasts of the future were the more significant when their Jewish imagery was preserved. They were concerned with mysteries, with the unseen world and the hereafter, and if they were cryptic in their language this only strengthened the conviction that an oracular voice was speaking. It must not be forgotten, too, that for more than a century the Old Testament was the one Bible of the church. Gentile Christians had grown familiar, just as we are now, with its peculiar idioms, and did not feel that they were harsh or unnatural. Jewish apocalyptic was studied along with scripture, as containing a fuller exposition of prophetic hopes and visions. The author of the Pastoral Epistles lays down the principle that every writing inspired by God is profitable for teaching, reproof, correction and training in righteousness; § and the apocalyptic books were numbered among those inspired by God, although they were not technically scripture. For some time after the church became Gentile they were assiduously read, and Christian thought was moulded by them.

Apocalyptic is thus a well-marked element in all New Testament teaching, but it appears in three forms which need to be carefully distinguished. The New Testament writers might almost be classified according to their attitude towards this aspect of their thinking. They all believe in the Christian message, but their Christianity is plainly of different types, and the type to which each of them belongs is clearly indicated by the manner in which he relates his faith to those conceptions which had supplied a framework to the original gospel.

For the most part, apocalyptic ideas were held in conjunction with a moral and spiritual message. Little effort was made to reconcile the two modes of thought, for they were not felt to be in contradiction. It has been remarked that the theology of Paul appears to run in two parallel lines which never meet. He thinks of a redemption which is given here and now, and yet he declares "we are saved in hope," "we groan within ourselves, waiting for the redemption." * He conceives of Christ as present now with his people, so that the very mark of the Christian is that he lives "in Christ"; but this mystical conception is combined with the

§ II Tim. 3:16. The Greek is best rendered as above.
* Rom. 8:24; 8:23.

primitive one that Christ has ascended into heaven, and will only be re-united with his disciples when he returns in glory. In like manner Paul knows of a resurrection which is experienced now, in the act of faith. We are risen with Christ, and must seek those things which are above; by dying with Christ we rise with him; we are called to newness of life, as men now risen from the dead. This note is struck in every chapter of the Epistles, and yet along with it there is the other, that while we live in this mortal flesh we look forward to a resurrection. Paul dwells on this great final event in the longest and most elaborate chapter in all his writings,[†] and describes it with a wealth of dramatic detail in glowing apocalyptic language. So in all his thinking we have the two strains, running side by side, and for later expositors this has offered a baffling problem. How can Paul have held the two incongruous views together? How were they related in his own mind? But the answer appears to be that he was not aware of an inconsistency. He passes frequently, almost in the same sentence, from one view to the other, and seems to assume that both were necessary. It is much the same with the writer to the Hebrews. He understands Christianity in the light of a Platonic idealism as the faith by which we apprehend the higher world and so live, amidst the things of time, for the unseen and eternal. But he still holds firmly to the belief that Christ is presently to return, that men will be summoned to a final Judgment, that the living servants of God will be gathered, in a new Jerusalem, to those who have gone before. This attitude of Paul and the writer to Hebrews was the normal one in the later New Testament period, and has continued to be so through the whole history of the church. Apocalyptic was retained as an essential element in Christian teaching. It might not be logically consistent with other interpretations, but it combined itself with them by a natural process, so that there

† I Cor. 15.

was no sense of a contradiction. One thinks of an ancient castle which has gradually been added to and transformed, and has so become a new one, almost without men's knowledge. A trained architect may be able, with little difficulty, to distinguish the primitive keep from the buildings of one century and another, but for all practical purposes the structure is now one, in all its parts. This analogy may be applied to the elements which make up our Christianity. They belong to different times and necessities and do not properly cohere, but they have all become adjusted to one another and none of them could be removed without injury to the whole.

It has sometimes been held that the apocalyptic beliefs were preserved for no other reason than that they were primitive. Christian thought had passed beyond them, but they were so closely associated with the original message that some place had to be made for them even when they had ceased to have much meaning. They were like those parts of the human anatomy which were necessary in some remote phase of evolution and still survive, although they are nothing to us now but an encumbrance. There are not a few modern thinkers who would have us free our religion of everything that is merely apocalyptic, and so give larger room for those truths which belong to its substance. This, however, is a mistaken endeavour. If there was ever a man who had an instinct for the inner meaning of the gospel it was Paul. He seized on what was new and distinctive in it, and broke away, with a splendid audacity, from all that kept it bound to outworn tradition. But while he discarded the Law he clung, almost passionately, to the apocalyptic hopes. They seemed to be out of keeping with the rest of his thought, but he felt that they represented something vital and must be preserved. This was equally true of Jesus himself. His teaching, like that of Paul, is full of apparent contradictions. He thinks of the Kingdom of God as future and at the same time present. He ascribes everything to God's own action, but is always insisting on man's responsibility. He offers a spiritual gospel which is yet interwoven with the seeming crudities of apocalyptic. Scholars are always trying, by ingenious methods. to remove those contradictions, but the truth is that they exist, not so much in the thought of Jesus or of those who transmitted it, as in the very nature of things. Is God a transcendent power outside of us or a presence in our own souls? Is the true life here or hereafter? Why it should be so we cannot tell, but in all such ultimate questions both answers are right, and a religion which allows for only one of them will never satisfy. It may be more harmonious and intelligible, but it leaves us with the sense of a vital thing which is wanting. Paul was conscious of this, and whenever he lays stress on his more inward interpretation he is careful also to make room for the old apocalyptic ideas. The redemption is already achieved, but we are still waiting for it, and looking for a glory which will be revealed. His thought may be here inconsistent, but he knows, as a fact of Christian experience, that both things are true. It is safe to affirm that the church will never be able to leave the apocalyptic ideas out of its religion. In some form they will hold their own, not out of deference to ancient modes of thinking but because they answer to a real necessity. Religion must conform itself to the mysterious facts.

In normal Christianity, therefore, the apocalyptic and the more spiritual accounts of the gospel were simply laid side by side, with no attempt to fit them together. They belonged, apparently, to opposite types of religion, but there was truth in both of them, and they were both allowed their place in Christian teaching. There were minds, however, which felt the need of reconciling them. Since it was the same message that was proclaimed, now in the apocalyptic and now in the purely religious form, the two forms must be inwardly related, and the one must be only a variant of the other. This is the assumption which underlies the Fourth Gospel and the First Epistle of John. The apocalyptic ideas are not abandoned. They lie always at the back of the writer's mind, and give direction to all his thinking. But he seeks to merge them in his own conception of the message by interpreting them in what he considers their true significance. Jesus had spoken of the Kingdom of God, but by this he must have meant eternal life. He had claimed to be the Messiah, but had thereby declared himself the Son of God, the Logos in whom resided the divine nature. He had said much of a coming Judgment, but in this manner he had impressed on men the solemn fact that by their attitude to his message they would reveal their true nature, as children of light or of darkness. All the Apocalyptic beliefs are thus subjected to a process of reflection and are found to embody great spiritual truths. Apocalyptic becomes a symbolism, and the task of faith is to pierce through the imagery to the truth behind it. This is done by the evangelist with marvellous skill and insight, and it cannot be denied that his method justifies itself. The meanings he discovers are truly present in the apocalyptic forms, which cannot be rightly understood unless we take them into account. At the same time there is something lost in his interpretation. He tends to resolve actualities into ideas, and the very purpose of apocalyptic is to lift religion out of the realm of abstraction. It takes those truths which mean so much to this evangelist and makes them real, like things that we can feel and see.

John's Gospel has sometimes been regarded as a protest against the apocalyptic tradition, but it might rather be described as an inverted apocalyptic. The effort is not so much to escape from the primitive conceptions as to give them a value quite different from their literal one. It might appear at first sight as if the apocalyptic and the mystical modes of thinking were exclusive of one

another. The one apprehends the truth through visual images;
the other seeks for it in the depths of the soul itself. Yet between
the two modes of thought there has always been a relation, difficult to explain. Almost all the great mystics have also been visionaries. Their one aim has been to detach themselves from the material world, but they have instinctively thought in pictures, and
their ideas have bodied themselves out in material form. It is a
curious fact that Christian mysticism has in all times fastened with
a peculiar sympathy on the Book of Revelation. Bernard, Teresa,
Swedenborg, William Blake have all devoted themselves to the
study of this book, which might seem of all New Testament writings to be the furthest removed from the mood of inward contemplation. Yet in the imagery of this book, often so crude and
sensuous, the mystics have found expression for their deepest
broodings on the spiritual life. It was by no mere accident that
Christian tradition assigned the Book of Revelation to the same
author as the Fourth Gospel. On critical and historical grounds
this identity of authorship cannot be maintained, but between the
two books there is a real affinity. Mysticism is the other side of
apocalyptic.

For the most part, then, there was a process of adjustment of
the earlier Christian beliefs to the later interpretation, but we
can also distinguish a type of religion which continued to be
frankly apocalyptic. The church at large had outgrown this mode
of thought, and was often inclined to view it with suspicion, but
there were sects, and in every community there were individuals,
that conceived of Christianity in terms of an apocalyptic drama
which had been unfolding itself since the creation and was now
nearing its climax. This apocalyptic Christianity has played an
important part in later history, and was no less prevalent in the
New Testament age.

Its attraction must be largely explained from the force of traditional belief. Millennarians in our own time hold firmly to a doctrine of scripture which was never questioned for many centuries. They argue that since scripture in every detail was inspired by God, its predictions must be literally true, and the course of history may be definitely mapped out by them. In the early period it was never forgotten that Jesus himself had spoken apocalyptically, that his immediate disciples had looked for his visible return, that the church itself had sprung into being out of this hope. The whole Christian tradition was on the side of the apocalyptic teaching. There might be some who tried to explain it spiritually, but they had been misled by false lights. The true believer was he who accepted the message just as it had been delivered. This was the attitude of perhaps the greater number of the apocalyptic Christians, and their doctrines were of little value. An apocalyptic faith has meaning only when it is accompanied with a real emotion. When Stephen in his dying rapture saw the heavens opened, when Paul was caught up into Paradise and heard unspeakable words, they had a right to believe what they heard and saw. Their visions, whatever may have been their nature, corresponded to something actual. But there can be nothing so dead as an apocalyptic taken over from tradition. The thing that gave it power is dried out of it, and nothing is left but an old-world mythology or a table of calculations, with no more religious quality than the figures in a ledger. Most of the popular apocalyptic has always been of this traditional kind, and thoughtful men are repelled by it. They can make allowance for everything in it that may seem fantastic and grotesque. Beliefs that in themselves are absurd may yet be the expression of a deep and genuine faith. But the thing that jars on us in most of the apocalyptic systems is their religious emptiness.

With many, however, those strange beliefs were no mere matter of tradition. It has always been found that apocalyptic makes its strongest appeal in times of crisis. To such times it owed its existence. Israel was struggling for bare survival against mighty empires, and could only expect deliverance from some miraculous act of God. The early Christian apocalyptic was likewise the outcome of a time of crisis. The Lord had departed, and his cause apparently lay in ruins, but the disciples took courage from their visions of another world and of a divine event which would bring them victory. After this earliest period the apocalyptic hopes suffered an eclipse, but they revived under stress of the persecutions which broke out at the end of the first century. The church was threatened with destruction by the invincible Roman power, and was conscious of its utter helplessness. Then the seer of Revelation came forward with his assurance that God was mindful of His people and would presently judge the world and bring in His Kingdom. It would not be difficult to draw a chart of Christian history and show that every period of war or pestilence has been accompanied with a great resurgence of the apocalyptic hopes. In no other way have men found it possible to discover a meaning in calamities that seemed in themselves quite purposeless. They have been enabled to look beyond the calamity, and even while it lasted to reconcile it with their faith in God and in His ways with men. Again and again during the past century the apocalyptic ideas have been thrown aside as outworn and childish, but they never die out, and it only needs the hour of crisis to bring them back. This is their justification,—that they keep open a door of hope when everything else has failed. This also is the proof that they are something more than an idle product of fancy. In their times of direst need men have little taste for vain speculations, and are seeking above all else for a sure foothold. They somehow find it in those apocalyptic hopes.

The chief danger which overhung the early church was from the side of the state, and this gave a peculiar character to New Testament apocalyptic. Jesus had declared that the earthly order would give place to the Kingdom of God, and his followers saw the power of this world concentrated in Rome, which was bent on destroying the church. The thought of Jesus was therefore construed politically. That material order which was shortly to be overthrown was the Roman empire. It represented the powers of evil, and had opposed itself to the cause of God, and was doomed to perish when Christ appeared in his glory. The New Testament apocalyptic is all pervaded by these ideas. There are signs that even in the lifetime of Paul a fanatical party was forming, which exulted in the belief that the downfall of Rome was near. The apocalyptic hopes were understood in this sense, and the church was thus exposed to serious danger. It was regarded as a secret society which under cover of religion was engaged in a dangerous revolutionary movement. The political reading of apocalyptic had a still more unfortunate result. It led to a narrowing and vulgarising of the Christian message, from which the church has never fully recovered. Jesus himself had held carefully aloof from the politics of his time, and had sought to make it evident that his one quarrel was with the evil in men's hearts. In later days his work was explained politically. It was assumed that he had come to destroy one system of government and set up another. His victory would be achieved when earthly power was transferred from those who were now abusing it to the Christian church. So in the Book of Revelation he appears as a conqueror who will lead his people in the final battle with his enemies, and ever since there has been a confusion in our religious aims. The triumph of some party, or of the church itself as an earthly institution, has been mistaken for the coming of the Kingdom.

The apocalyptic hopes were kept alive by the force of tradition and by the circumstances of a difficult age, but there was a further reason for the attraction which they never ceased to exercise, even when Christian thought was set in another direction. There have

always been minds which are by nature visionary. It is wrong to
think of apocalyptic as nothing but a survival from a distant age,
when men looked on the mysterious world with the eyes of children. Its specific forms may be explained in that way, but in
itself it is simply one of the various modes of knowledge. There
are those who think logically or scientifically, and base their religion on rational beliefs. There are others who think imagina-
tively, and feel the need of some kind of apocalyptic. If it had not
inherited the Jewish speculations the church would have devised
similar ones for itself, and has, in fact, been doing so, down to the
present day. We have to reckon not so much with the apocalyptic
tradition as with the apocalyptic mind, and its type of faith is
not to be regarded as perverse or defective but only as different.
The truth may be apprehended in this way just as legitimately as
in the other. Too often we associate an apocalyptic faith with
ignorant people, who are unable to grasp spiritual ideas in their
purity, and need to materialise them in order to grasp their meaning. No doubt it is the fact that a millennarian excitement always spreads most easily among the multitude, and we say, in
most cases justly, that this is due to the want of proper instruction.
Those who know nothing of the historical background of the
Bible understand in some literal sense ideas and descriptions which
must be taken symbolically. But the belief in apocalyptic is not
by any means confined to the ignorant. Paul was the greatest
mind of the early church, but he was confident that he would see
Christ returning on the clouds; he wrote that sublime vision of
the last day with which he closes his chapter on the Resurrection,
and also the strange prophecy of the Antichrist in Second Thessalonians. Tertullian was one of the most learned of the Fathers,
but in his later days he threw in his lot with the wild millennarian
sect of the Montanists. The most towering intellect of modern
times was probably Sir Isaac Newton, who finally turned away
from his mathematics and devoted himself to the prophecies of

Daniel and Revelation. There are men still of whose culture and intelligence there can be no doubt, and whose religion is strongly apocalyptic. It is not that they are uncritical or eccentric. There is something in their nature which responds to the Christian message in that form, and which cannot be fully satisfied with any other.

It is possible to distinguish two types of mind, at first sight very different, to which apocalyptic is a natural means for the apprehension of truth. On the one hand there are those who think through their emotions. Ideas in the abstract mean little to them, and need in some way to be brought within reach of the senses. Apocalyptic provides an instrument by which the truth can be so conveyed. The great mystics, as has been noted already, have also been apocalyptists. Their religion was all the more profound and intimate because it was associated with visions, often in the highest degree extravagant. The minds of those men were so constituted that the Christian beliefs came home to them most forcibly when they were thrown into imaginative forms. There is, however, another side to apocalyptic which has been too generally overlooked. We think of it as attractive to highly emotional and often unbalanced natures, so much so that any serious interest in apocalyptic theory is taken as the mark of some mental disturbance. But apocalyptic, in the last resort, is a mode of knowledge, and makes its appeal to speculative minds. The Jewish apocalypses were not the work of fanatics or dreamers. They were written, it is quite evident, by men who had pondered deeply on the social and political problems of their time, and still more on the religious problems. They were seeking an answer to those great questions to which all thinking eventually leads. For what purpose does the world exist? How did it come into being? What lies beyond the closed circle of our earthly life? Apocalyptic was the Jewish equivalent to that enquiry which in Greece took the form of philosophy, and in some respects it succeeded where philosophy failed. It is highly significant that Plato, at the close of some of his profoundest discussions, takes refuge in a myth which may fairly be described as an apocalypse. He feels that he has proceeded as far as thought can carry him, and has come upon a barrier which he can only surmount by this other kind of knowledge. In much the same manner Paul merges his theology, ever and again, in apocalyptic visions. He seems, indeed, to have thought of those revelations as the loftiest and most valuable part of his teaching. He tells us that by means of them he had learned secrets which he could only divulge to "those who were perfect,"—to those who were now mature in the Christian life and were capable of a higher knowledge.[‡] It may be inferred from his guarded allusions that this "wisdom of God in a mystery" was apocalyptic in its nature; the Spirit had revealed to him in vision those things of God which must be spiritually discerned. So in all times apocalyptic has been employed by great thinkers as a means to deeper insight. Some of them have made their own apocalyptic; others have taken up the traditional conceptions, and have found in them symbols of hidden truths which cannot be expressed in language. Apocalyptic has indeed come to us out of an ancient world, when men knew nothing of our science, and often put fantasy in the place of fact. But when it comes to the supreme questions all ages are very much on the same level. On the highest mountain tops you are little nearer the fixed stars than when you stood on the plain. So the apocalyptic symbols, devised two thousand years ago, are still valid for the loftiest purposes of speculation, and will never lose their interest.

Apocalyptic Christianity finds its classical expression in the Book of Revelation, which to the modern student is no longer a

[‡] I Cor. 2:6.

unique and mysterious, but a representative book. Although in its
present form it is undoubtedly the work of a single author, it is
made up of material which had been long accumulating, and
reflects a mode of thinking which prevailed among many groups
in the early church. They finally had their spokesman in a man
of genius, who gave power and beauty, and a new significance, to
what the others had said imperfectly. He wrote, it must never be
forgotten, for the special purpose of encouraging his fellow-
sufferers in a time of persecution. Grave injustice has often been
done him by the assumption that he put the whole of his Christianity into this book, and had nothing to say of many things
which we rightly deem essential to the gospel. But while he confines himself to his one aim we may be sure that all his thinking
was of the same general character as what he offers us in this book
of visions. Whatever else the gospel may have meant to him, he
looked at it in the light of apocalyptic ideas, and may be taken
as the chief exponent of a well-marked type of early Christian
teaching.

It has sometimes been made a matter of wonder that the book
was ever included in the New Testament. Its Christianity seems
at times to be little more than a veneer over sentiments which are
purely Jewish or Pagan, and which not merely ignore but contradict the teaching of Jesus. But we perceive, as we look deeper,
that it is a profoundly Christian book. In picture and symbol the
author gives splendid expression to the primary Christian ideas.
He believes that over against this visible world there is a higher
one, which overshadows the earthly life and in which it will reach
fulfilment. He believes that Christ has wrought a redemption,
that he has done so through his death, that his people will share
in his victory by following the same road of sacrifice. He takes
faith as the Christian watch-word. More emphatically even than
Paul he declares that salvation is by faith, though faith as he

understands it is the triumphant confidence that God is reigning, and will defend his own cause and establish his will on earth. It would not be difficult to show that all the great Christian beliefs have their place in this Book of Revelation, although they are presented, not in the form of doctrines, but as scenes of a drama which passes before our eyes. This does not mean that all reflection on Christian truth is absent. The author has thought deeply on the problems of man's being and destiny, and their solution in the work of Christ. His book, in one of its aspects, is a philosophy of history from the Christian point of view. But in his effort to reach out to a higher knowledge he uses apocalyptic as his instrument.

The seer of Revelation was a man of extraordinary gifts, and it cannot be supposed that all those who held his beliefs had the same feeling for their significance. In that time, as in all others, the ordinary millennarian was content to take the scripture promises literally, with little regard to what might be involved in them. Yet we cannot do justice even to the popular apocalyptic unless we allow for that deeper strain in it of which we are made conscious in Revelation. The people who looked for a visible return of Christ and a final Judgment had a real knowledge of their religion, although they could have rendered no clear account of what they knew. Perhaps in some ways they understood it better than many of the professed theologians. In all ages the apocalyptic Christian has been an easy mark for ridicule. His mind is occupied with extravagant fancies. He speaks of the mystery of the world in language which is utterly inadequate, like that of a child confronted with a glorious landscape. Yet the child may be seeing more of the glory than the cultivated man who has all the approved language at his command; and through his apocalyptic fancies the simple Christian may apprehend what is deepest and most vital in his religion.

In the Book of Revelation we grow aware of the wealth of meaning in apocalyptic thought, but at the same time we perceive its limitations. The New Testament would be much poorer without this book, but if all the writings had been of a similar character we should have had a sadly one-sided and distorted conception of the Christian message. In many respects our Christianity would have differed little from the faith of Islam. Both religions would present the same ideas of God, of the future life, of the moral ideal, of man's relation to his fellowmen. Without the other books we should not, for that part, have understood the Apocalypse itself. Its symbols do not become intelligible until we bring them into the light of that spiritual interpretation which was effected by Paul and the other teachers. There could have been no future for Christianity if it had never been disengaged from the apocalyptic setting, and this became apparent before the first generation was past. There were still those who maintained the primitive attitude, and looked for the visible manifestation of Christ and his Kingdom. Yet the church moved steadily away from this type of Christianity. It did so, not merely because the early hopes had proved illusory, or because the apocalyptic imagery was distasteful to a more enlightened age. Those old beliefs, we are often told in our time, have broken down, like other superstitions, before the march of modern science; but this is an erroneous view. It is not science but the Christian religion itself which has undermined apocalyptic. In the effort to disclose its inner principles it has gradually thrown off the original forms, and this was also what happened in the earlier time. There is, indeed, no suggestion in the New Testament that the apocalyptic ideas are incredible; all the writers accept them without misgiving. But they allow them more and more to fall into the background, for no other reason than that they cannot express in this manner what they feel to be the true meaning of the gospel.

It has always been found that a purely apocalyptic movement has its outcome, sooner or later, in some kind of Paganism. The mood of devotion is fostered for a time by the connection of religious ideas with a sensuous imagery, but the ideas are by and by forgotten, and the symbol is identified with the things it signifies. The picture of a departed friend is cherished by those who loved him, and brings back a thousand memories, and enables them to feel that he is still with them. A time comes when it passes into the hands of strangers, to whom it is nothing but a work of art or a piece of antiquity. This is always the fate of symbols, and between an apocalyptic faith and pure idolatry there is only a thin partition. When Christian hopes and certainties are wrapt up in a mythology they come at last to disappear in the mythology, which differs from the Pagan myths in little else than in the substitution of Christian names for Pagan. We are sensible of this even in certain parts of the Book of Revelation, and much more in the millennarian literature of our own day.

It was necessary for the church to state its message in other terms than the apocalyptic, but in doing so it still retained a place for those images and expectations which it had inherited from the first age. This also was necessary, and if the old forms had been simply discarded, something of inestimable value would have been lost. Paul did more than any one else to present Christianity as an ethical and spiritual religion, but to the end he clung almost passionately to the apocalyptic hopes. He is a profound religious thinker and at the same time a visionary, accepting in their literal sense what might seem to be nothing but old-world imaginations. To many it has appeared incredible that the two modes of thought should have existed together in the same mind, but between them there was a real affinity, and Paul was the greatest of Christian teachers because he held them both. He could not have attained to his marvellous knowledge of the new life in Christ unless he had also experienced his visions and revelations. Without them he would only have been a theologian, and in some chapters of his Epistles he assumes that character, and has nothing to offer us but lifeless dogma. He rises as if on wings when he thinks of the Lord's coming, and the glory that will be revealed.

Religion, according to the famous definition of Matthew Arnold, is "morality touched with emotion." As an account of religion this is miserably inadequate. Faith in God is not an emotion. Neither does it "touch" morality, but is the spring out of which it flows. You do not define painting as colour touched with form, or man as an animal touched with mind. Nothing is properly described when the very essence of it is left out or made secondary. But there is this much of truth in the definition,—that in religion everything else is inert unless emotion is added. Morality, intelligence, faith, worship must all be present, but there must also be the ardour which quickens them; and this is supplied by that apocalyptic symbolism which brings almost before our bodily eyes what would in themselves be mere ideas. The things most real to us as earthly beings are those which we can handle and see, but we believe that there is another order of reality, and in religion we seek to apprehend it. This is not possible until we clothe our hopes and aspirations in visual forms, making them real to the senses as they are to the believing soul.

The function of apocalyptic is to give this objectivity to what we discern inwardly. Christ is the highest that we know, and the world will at last own his sovereignty; the moral law has an absolute claim on our obedience; in fellowship with God we find life and blessedness. All this is true, but the confession in words is not enough. Our beliefs, almost of their own accord, embody themselves in the conceptions of a return of Christ in glory, a final Judgment, a consummation in heaven. It may be argued that these are imaginations. They have grown out of myth and tradition, or are projected from our own fancy, and our religion, in so far as they form part of it, is a delusion. But they stand for realities, and that is why the Christian mind demands them. It knows that there is another world which is as certain as this one, and it seeks to grasp the certainty. Whatever may have been the origin of those apocalyptic ideas, or whatever may be their intrinsic value, they serve to vitalise the objects of faith. By means of them we can throw ardour into our quest, setting a goal before us which we can actually see. The old explorers shaped their voyages by rude charts, constructed for the most part out of travellers' tales or vague astronomical guesses. As maps they were worthless, but at least they gave the confidence that there was something to be discovered. The mariners could feel, as they sailed the pathless ocean, that they were seeking a land which somewhere existed, although they could not learn its true outline and character until they reached it. The apocalyptic beliefs were of a similar nature. They had grown out of guesses and surmises, and those who trusted them too literally were often led astray. Yet they gave the assurance that there was something to reward the seeker. What it might be was not yet apparent, but it was there. As in a glass darkly the unseen was made visible.

CHAPTER VII

THE MORALISTS

IT HAS often been asserted that in the years which followed Jesus' death his own teaching was almost forgotten. He was now worshipped as a heavenly being who had appeared on earth for man's salvation, and his message was expounded in a doctrinal system which was entirely foreign to his own intention. He had been, above all else, a prophet of righteousness. He had proclaimed the Kingdom of God and had taught how men might enter it by obedience to God's will. His ethical message was transformed by his followers into a mystical theology.

This view does not correspond with the facts, and can be traced back to two radical misunderstandings. On the one hand, it betrays a false conception of Jesus' teaching. No one can deny that by far the greater number of his sayings are concerned with the moral life in its manifold aspects, but he never makes morality an end in itself. The primary interest of Jesus is in the Kingdom of God, the higher spiritual order in which the divine purpose will reach fulfilment. For Jesus, no less than for the mystical thinkers who succeeded him, religion consisted in fellowship with God, and the one purpose of his ethic was to ensure this fellowship. On the other hand, it is not true that the ethical side of the message was neglected by the early church. The work of Jesus was indeed explained theologically, but always with a practical purpose. Jesus never ceased to be regarded as the teacher and the grand example of a new way of righteousness. Everything else was made secondary to the life in which a genuine faith in him would manifest itself. The proof of this may be found in the very fact that our Gospels exist. They bear witness to the continued interest in the actual life of Jesus, and to the scrupulous care with which his sayings were preserved. From the outset his teaching was fundamental to the new religion. Whatever might be their doctrines, all Christians were instructed in "the things which Jesus both did and taught." * It is certain that our Gospels were not written to satisfy a mere curiosity. They were the text-books of the early church, and every believer was expected to know them, and so to ground himself in his faith. They came to be called emphatically the "Gospels," because the record contained in them was nothing else than the Christian message in its primary and authoritative form.

It is evident when we examine the New Testament writings that the chief interest of the church continued to be ethical. Paul is commonly made responsible for the supposed perversion of Christianity into a doctrinal system, but his Epistles are in no sense theological tracts. They are letters, such as a man writes to his friends. They are among the most human of all letters, and have no other purpose than to advise and encourage little groups of believers who were trying to follow the Christian life amidst heathen surroundings. A great part of each Epistle is occupied solely with practical directions, covering the whole range of moral duties, down even to trivial details. In those sections which deal with theological issues the practical end is still carefully kept in view. We are made to feel that men are to think rightly about their religion so that it may have its outcome in right action. It may safely be said that Paul never wrote anything for the mere sake of speculation. His interest is always in the Christian life. He is not primarily a theologian but a great moral teacher, who

* Acts 1:1.

bases his ethic, as Jesus himself had done, on a new conception of the nature of God and of the purpose and meaning of man's life in this world.

So far, indeed, from being thrust into the background the ethical teaching becomes ever more prominent in the later period, so much so that it tended to obscure the spiritual import of the gospel. This is particularly evident in writings connected directly with the Gentile mission. There was much in the precepts of Jesus which was already familiar to Jewish converts, trained as they were in the morality of the Law. Many of the Gospel sayings are borrowed almost word for word from the Rabbis. Jesus had indeed put new motives at the heart of the traditional ethic, but to the Jewish mind it would still be intelligible. For Gentiles the demands of Jesus were all new and startling. They involved a reversal of the accustomed standards and often appeared to be contrary to nature and reason. Men were called on to regard humility as a virtue, to submit patiently to injuries, to honour the weak and outcast, to refuse wealth and success and abstain from pleasures, to put their religious convictions before their duty to the state. Even to the better type of Gentile all this was strange. It was possible in some measure to understand the Christian beliefs and to feel their attraction, but the behaviour of Christian men appeared foolish and abnormal. More often than not it aroused a bitter resentment. The Christians were bent on destroying virtues which were associated with heroes of the past, and which seemed to be indispensable to human dignity and well-being. In view of this Pagan attitude it was necessary for the Christian teacher to instruct his converts in the new way of living, and to convince them that it was the best. We usually think of the missionaries as concerned solely with the diffusion of their new doctrines, but this was the least part of their activity. Theoretical knowledge came easily to people of Greek culture, and the

Christian doctrines were no stranger than those of other cults; on the whole they were much more reasonable. In a discussion of ideas the Gentile was in his element, but when it came to the Christian ethic he was puzzled and dissatisfied. Why should a man forgive his enemies? Why should he deny himself pleasant society and bestow his care on persons who had no claim upon him, except that they were sick or unfortunate? The Christian ethic had to be explained and justified, and could not become a second nature without long discipline. The moral life was the chief pre-occupation of all missionaries, as it was of Paul himself. An ever larger place was given to ethical instruction, and there was a real danger that the purely religious message might fall out of sight. In the course of the second century Christians had come to speak of their religion as "the new law,"—the moral code which had superseded that of Moses and other legislators but was essentially of the same character.

Among the Gentiles the Christian ethic was affected by Hellenistic ideas, though in a far less degree than the doctrines. Modes of thinking vary with different races, and to make them intelligible to Gentiles the Christian beliefs had to be re-stated, often in terms which would have meant little to the first disciples. Moral demands did not stand in need of such interpretation. Kindness, sincerity, unselfishness have the same meaning to men of all times and nationalities, however they may be neglected in practice. In the teaching of Jesus there is much that cannot be rightly understood until we put into our own language what he expressed by means of Jewish apocalyptic, but the precepts of the Sermon on the Mount can safely be left as he spoke them. They explain themselves, and by changing his language you only spoil them. The parable of the Good Samaritan has the same charm for ourselves as for the people who first heard it. So when Christianity was carried to the West its ethic was left unaltered. Whenever Paul passes from theological argument to practical counsel we feel ourselves back again in the atmosphere of the Gospels. Paul is aware that the principles which Jesus had laid down in Galilee are equally valid for his readers in Rome and Corinth.

At the same time these principles had to be adapted to new conditions. It was found necessary, for one thing, to lay more emphasis on some of Jesus' demands than on others. In so far as the ethic of Paul appears to differ from that of the Gospels, it is chiefly because he keeps in mind those special evils which prevailed in Gentile society. He has much to say, for instance, on the matter of sensual vices. Thanks to the discipline of the Law the standards of ordinary morality were higher in Palestine than anywhere else in the ancient world, and Jesus had taken them for granted. Paul, however, cannot address his Gentile converts without warning them against the sins of the flesh, while he says little of that spiritual pride which was the inevitable outcome of the legal system, and for which Jesus continually rebukes the Pharisees. In like manner Paul has to deal repeatedly with the partisan temper which in all ages had been the curse of Greek political life, and which now manifested itself, under various forms, in his churches. He also condemns the "covetousness" which was a product of Pagan culture,—the ambition of each individual to assert himself and get more of everything than his neighbours. In various passages of the Epistles we come on lists of virtues and vices, and these, it has been shown, correspond closely with similar lists in the writings of Pagan moralists. They supply a vivid picture of the environment in which the Christian ethic had to make its way, and it is not surprising that many of the instructions in the later New Testament books are more concerned with morality in general than with the specific demands of Christianity. Before they could make anything of the teaching of Jesus, the Gentiles had to learn the elementary rules of all decent living.

Again, in the Pagan world morality had to be connected with a new set of motives. With the Jews it was possible to bring into play those religious sentiments which had been formed by the Law, but the Gentiles had not undergone this training. Paul indeed impresses on them that while they were "without the Law" they had yet a natural sense of right, a law written in the heart, but he is obliged to add that this inner law had become so dimmed that it more often misled than guided. For want of a right moral instinct the need for certain modes of action had to be enforced on the reason, with the result that motives are urged which are often little better than prudential. In the later New Testament period morality tends to be separated from religion, and this has often been set down to lack of insight into the nature of Christianity. This may be partly true, but it has also to be remembered that the majority of Gentile Christians were ethically immature. They had no underlying religious sentiment. They had to be incited, like children, by the promise of reward, by a spirit of emulation, by appeals to their sense of propriety and fair-play. Paul is careful to ground all right action on Christian principles, and it is this which gives permanent value to his ethic; but he is plainly aware that something else is needed to make his counsels effectual, and falls back, ever and again, on such considerations as were usual among moralists of the time. For himself those inferior motives have no force, but he knows that without them he will miss his mark with his half-Pagan readers.

To some extent in its substance, as in its expression, the Christian ethic was modified by Gentile influence. Pagan virtues were added to those which were strictly Christian, and were included henceforth in the conception of the moral life. The Stoic teaching, more especially, was laid under contribution. Even in Paul we meet with ethical ideas which appear to have their origin more in Stoic than in Christian morality. Much is made, for instance, of the idea of conscience; the Christian is required to be "self-sufficient," independent of external things; † the new life is described as a "reasonable service," ‡ that is, a worship in which the human is brought into accordance with the divine reason. This recourse to Stoic terms and conceptions is much more pronounced in the later writings, where there is something like a deliberate effort to combine the Christian ethic with that of the philosophical moralists. The result was a composite ethic in which the Christian and the Pagan elements are often hard to distinguish, but which was adopted henceforth by the church. It is not a little significant that Augustine, in the fourth century, was first turned definitely towards the Christian life by reading one of the moral treatises of Cicero. He read it, no doubt, in the light of Christian ideas, impressed on him in childhood, and found more in it than was actually there; but he was not troubled, either at the time or afterwards, by any reflection that Cicero was a Pagan. The Christian and the philosophical ethic had now blended together. All teachers who pointed towards a nobler kind of living could be acknowledged as in some manner Christian. This, it may be granted, was a legitimate attitude, and led to the enrichment at many points of the Christian morality. Not a few of the Pagan virtues had a splendour of their own, and while not distinctively Christian were fully in accord with the thought of Jesus. It meant much for the Christian religion that it learned to place a value on courage, on the sense of honour, on patriotism, on such types of character as waken our admiration in Plutarch's *Lives*. Had it not been for this sanction bestowed on Pagan ideals some of the finest chapters of Christian heroism would never have been written. None the less, the effect of the Pagan influence was to bring a confusion into ethical thinking from which it suffers to this day.

† Phil. 4:11.   ‡ Rom. 12:1.

It was the aim of Jesus to put a new motive into all moral action. He took the maxims of wise men and Rabbis and radically transformed them by breathing into them his own conception of man's relation to God. In later ethic the sense of a distinctive quality in the Christian life was often obliterated. No line was drawn between the action of the Christian and that of the ordinary moral man.

Not only so, but morality tended more and more to become an interest by itself. With Jesus it was the means whereby men entered into the Kingdom, conforming their wills to the will of God, so that even now they were God's children. Jesus was not primarily an ethical teacher. His purpose was to bring men into a new relation to God, and this he did by creating in them the higher will. God is righteous, and by trying to live righteously we attain to fellowship with God; this, and not the right action itself, must always be our object. Paul is likewise conscious of a vital bond between ethic and religion. He thinks of the Christian virtues as the "fruits" which grow out of the new life. He declares that those who possess the Spirit will not fulfil the lusts of the flesh,[¶] for their whole nature has been regenerated, and they act, without knowing it, on the higher impulse. He can say "whatever is not of faith is sin,"[§]—that is, an act may be right in itself, but when it is divorced from the religious motive it is worthless. Paul does not deny that the heathen are capable of high virtues; he makes use of Stoic precepts and ideals, and sometimes compares his converts unfavourably with their Pagan neighbours.[†] But he is careful to attribute even those heathen excellences to an unconscious religious motive. The Gentiles, who are ignorant of the Law, have yet the law of God written in their hearts. In so far as they are guided by this inner light their actions have a moral value.

In later Christianity this sense of a bond between religion and

¶ Eph. 5:9; Gal. 5:16. § Rom. 14:23. † I Cor. 5:1.

ethic grew ever weaker, and the church took up the attitude which had now become the normal one in the Gentile world. A time had been when the gods were regarded as the arbiters and guardians of morality, and every act of injustice or unbridled ambition or flagrant vice was an offence which they were bound to punish. This belief that religion and ethic are inseparable is the governing motive in Greek tragedy, although in Euripides we can already discern a weakening of it. Philosophy took its stand on the principle that action was right or wrong according as it answers to certain requirements which must be correctly known. From the time of Aristotle onward ethic was a science, like mathematics or medicine. The chief thing necessary for virtuous conduct was a right understanding of man's nature, and of the conditions and limitations under which he must act. The old religious sanctions were deliberately set aside. Morality was an interest by itself, subject to its own special laws, which it was the task of the philosopher to investigate.

In the period after Paul this attitude was adopted, more or less consciously, in Christian thought. A new rule of life was held to be obligatory on the Christian man, but it was separated from his religion, and was defended, on its own merits, as the best and most reasonable. There were many earnest Gentiles who were indifferent to the Christian message, but were strongly attracted to the ethic which went along with it. Might it not be possible to accept the ethic without the religion, or with only a formal acquiescence in the religion? A situation had arisen in that age very similar to that which we are facing in our own. With the decay of old traditions and institutions the world was falling into a moral chaos, and it was evident that without some ethical basis no human society could hold together. Philosophy had come to the rescue, and had laid down principles by which men might guide themselves in their social and individual life. But there were many philosophies, all at variance with one another, and at best they could only offer theories, which could be thrown aside whenever they ceased to be convenient. Some ethic was needed which was open to no dispute, and had power to enforce its demands. This was manifestly the great practical need of the age. The world was perishing for want of moral direction, and the guides it followed were all doubtful about the road.

Earnest Gentiles were powerfully impressed by the Christian ethic. It was known that the Christians held strange beliefs, and practised a peculiar kind of worship; but whatever might be said against them they had found a new method of conducting their lives. By means of it they were able to put moral sentiments into action and to follow them out consistently. In their mode of life they quite evidently had a satisfaction to which the adherents of no other sect could pretend. Most Pagans, it is true, were repelled by the Christian ethic, and denounced it as foolish and dangerous, but there were always those who could appreciate it more justly. They could see that the Christians, with all their eccentricities, were merciful, upright, helpful to each other, patient and courageous under persecution. There was much, surely, in this behaviour which other men would do well to imitate. It might be that this new community was in possession of a wisdom which the philosophers had missed. We cannot wonder, therefore, that Gentiles were frequently drawn into the church, not so much by its religious message as by its ethic. For the sake of the ethic they accepted the message, not perhaps with much ardour or conviction, but still with a sense that it was necessary. The grand defect of all the other moral codes was their lack of any firm basis. They represented the opinions of wise men, to whom deference was certainly due, but they could not claim to be in any sense authoritative. The Christians rested their ethic on a divine sanction, and this was why they held to it without doubt or question, even when they were tempted in their own interests to put it aside. It was an ethic with this binding quality that the world was needing, and Gentiles who were attracted by the Christian mode of life accepted the message also. Their belief might be only superficial, but it gave them the necessary confidence for living by the Christian rule. The Gentile churches were largely made up of such people. They did not question the faith of the church. They felt that it was indispensable since apart from it the new morality would have no sure basis. But their interest was in the ethic, not in the religion.

In this manner there grew up a Christianity which may be described as essentially a moralism, but we must be careful not to employ this term too loosely. Morality, as such, has no connection with the faith in a higher world. It is concerned with man's life as it actually is, and seeks to determine how it can best be ordered, under the given conditions. This realistic morality may be lofty and exacting,—so much so that with teachers like Confucius and Marcus Aurelius it almost assumes the character of a religion; but it is something different. It is based on a mere calculation, which leaves out of account all forces which cannot be defined and measured. It requires nothing more than that a man should adjust himself wisely to the order of things which he knows. This might appear to be its superiority. All that may be fanciful and illusory is left out of account, and men are asked simply to take life as it is and use it to the best purpose. But the weakness of all such moral systems is this,—that they have no security. The moral life is not anchored to anything beyond itself, and is compelled to fall back on sanctions which are manifestly unstable. Sometimes it relies on old-established custom; sometimes on a general consensus of opinion. Plato cannot but ask himself, as he examines the common morality, how much of it would remain if each man had a magic ring which made him invisible, whenever he pleased, to his fellow-men.[‡] It was the aim of Plato, and this is equally true of all the great moralists, to discover an ethic which will stand on its own feet. The Roman poet does reverence to the man who is constant to his inward sense of right, and will remain unshaken although the whole world should fall in ruin.[¶] But even for this genuine moral principle there is no security. It depends, in the last resort, on the man's own judgment, and the best of men may grow doubtful of themselves, or change their conceptions of what is right and wrong. No man can be certain of his morality unless he can feel that there is something behind it which he cannot dispute. The standard by which you act is not your own, nor that of the people before you or around you, but has been set by some one outside of this world altogether, and you have no choice but to submit to it. This is where morality cannot but join hands with religion.

So in Christian moralism there is always something other than ethic, although this may not be at first sight apparent. In the history of the church there have been periods when the religious springs seem almost to have dried up, and nothing was left of Christianity but a code of morals, not conspicuously better than many others. One thinks of the eighteenth century before the Wesleyan revival. The church, as Wesley found it, had become little else than a school of moral instruction. Preachers had ceased to speak of the gospel, and confined themselves to dreary commendations of what they called "virtue." Anything beyond this aim of respectable living was dismissed as fanaticism, which could only disturb and confuse the sensible Christian. Something of the same kind may be observed at the present day. The church has grown aware that in the past it has unduly neglected the more practical interests, and these are now tending to claim a dispro-

[‡] Plato, *Republic,* II, 3.　　　　[¶] Horace, *Odes,* III, 3.

portionate place. Instead of the gospel we have the social gospel, in which religion too often becomes a handmaid to politics or economics. No one can deny that the ethical emphasis is necessary, but the Christian mind is conscious that when it is pressed exclusively something is lacking. So at the close of the New Testament period the religion of the Apostles was displaced by a moralism, and this is the pervading note in the writings which have come down to us from the second century. As we read them, and compare them with the Gospels and Epistles, we cannot but ask ourselves, "what has become of Christianity?" The interest appears to have shifted wholly from the problems of faith to those of everyday living, and these are discussed with almost no reference to the principles laid down in the New Testament. For the most part, indeed, these later writers derive their arguments from that Pagan philosophy which they formally condemn.

None the less, there is an essential difference between the Christian and the Pagan moralism. By the very fact that it allies itself with Christianity, ethical teaching has taken on a new character. It may express itself in the same language as the ordinary ethic and make only the same requirements, but it has undergone a radical change. This is true of all those varieties of Christian moralism which have seemed, from time to time, to displace religion. There may be nothing on the surface to distinguish them from the common morality of their day, but in their whole basis they are different. For an ethic which is in any way connected with Christian faith is religious in spite of itself. It is permeated with a new conception of the meaning of man's life and of his relation to God. It possesses the religious quality of linking man's action in this world with his sense of another. The teaching of Jesus himself is for the most part purely ethical, and presents an ethic which is sometimes little different from that of the current Judaism. It can be argued, and this has often been done, that

Jesus did little more than repeat in a more impressive form the precepts known to us in the Rabbinical writings. Such criticism, however, leaves out of account the one vital factor. Jesus had arrived at a new outlook on life, and brought everything into the light of it, so that all he seemed to borrow became new. Long before Copernicus the motions of the stars had been closely observed, and it was possible to make accurate calendars and predict eclipses. The old observations still hold good, and it might be maintained that our modern astronomy is nothing but the old one over again. Yet everything has been transformed by the discovery that the earth goes round the sun. This has given a new significance to all the facts that were previously known, and has created a different science. Jesus effected a similar change in the sphere of ethics. In so far as morality has become Christian it has become different, however it may retain the ancient forms.

An ethic which allies itself with Christianity is thus, in a true sense, religious. It may often seem as if the religion were nothing but an ornamental border around a mere moral code. The suggestion is sometimes made in our day that the religion may now be discarded and the Christian ethic preserved by itself, as a practical rule of living. But when this is done the ethic soon goes the way of the religion which it has supplanted. Its whole meaning and power depend on its connection with an attitude of mind which is not moral but religious. Men may not be fully conscious that they still have this attitude of mind. They may ostentatiously cut themselves adrift from any definite creed and call themselves Pagans. But so long as they practise the Christian morality they hold, without knowing it, to the Christian beliefs, and without those beliefs they would see the world in a different fashion, and any ethic they might have would not be the Christian one. When Christianity was first offered to the Gentiles they were attracted by its moral teaching, and sometimes adopted the morality without much understanding of the religious message. Yet all the time it was the message which had attracted them. Here was an ethic which was also something more. It rested on beliefs which gave it authority and stability. It enabled men to order their lives in this world with an abiding sense that they also belonged to another. Under the Gentile influence Christianity appeared at times to become nothing more than a superior ethic. It drew into itself elements which were derived from Pagan morality more than from any Christian source. All this, however, was only on the surface. While it seemed to have little but a formal connection with Christian beliefs the ethic had been changed by them in its very substance. In this Christian quality which was now inherent in it lay the secret of its appeal.

No clear line, therefore, can be drawn between Christian moralism and Christian religion, and much harm has been done, at various times, by making this distinction. Paul had to protest against the common belief that certain gifts were peculiarly "spiritual," while others, of a more practical nature, were on a lower plane. The church has never rid itself of this delusion that the moral and the spiritual activities are different in kind, and ever and again great Christian movements have been disparaged because they did not bear the accredited stamp of religion. Even in our estimate of the New Testament writings we are much too apt to apply this false standard. Luther spoke contemptuously of the Epistle of James as "that Epistle of straw." Many good Christians have been doubtful even of the Synoptic Gospels, which are full of ethical teaching, and are therefore less "spiritual" than the Gospel of John. There may be reason for such judgments in so far as morality, taken by itself, is not religion; but they overlook the fact that in the Christian ethic there is always the further element. Man's life in this world is related to the faith in God, to the consciousness of a higher order. Ethic has become religion in action.

There is a sense, therefore, in which all the New Testament teaching may be described as a moralism. Its purpose is always the practical one of making religion effective in the conduct of life. Jesus closes the Sermon on the Mount with a warning, "He that knoweth these things and doeth them not is like a foolish man who built his house upon the sand." [§] Paul is a theologian and a mystic, but in his moral fervour he is a true successor to the Hebrew prophets. But while the prophets were great ethical teachers their primary interest had been in the sovereignty of God. There is an obvious difference between their writings and such books as Proverbs and Ecclesiasticus, which have no other aim than instruction in the moral life. In the New Testament we encounter a similar contrast. Along with the books which present Christianity as a religion there are others in which it is predominantly an ethic. They date, almost certainly, from the later period, and their character may be partly due to the exhaustion of that first ardour in which the believers had held immediate fellowship with the unseen Lord. This, however, cannot be the whole explanation, for the church which braved the storm of persecution in the second century was no less devoted than the church which had seen visions in the first. We are to think, rather, of a change of direction in Christian thought, consequent on the progress of the Gentile mission. What the Gentiles had long been seeking for was a faith which would afford them moral guidance. This was a matter of life and death to them. Old religious sanctions had broken down, and the new ones offered by philosophy had been tried and found wanting. Might it not be that Christianity could supply what was needed? Here was an ethic to which man's best instincts could respond, and which was also a religion, with that

[§] Matt. 7:26.

quality of command which was absent from the philosophical systems. It was on this side that Christianity appealed to thoughtful Gentiles. They embraced it as a religion but what they prized above all else was its ethical teaching, which they set themselves to clarify and develop, with the help of many suggestions from their own thinkers. They carried out this task, it must never be forgotten, in a spirit of intense earnestness. The word "moralism" as we commonly use it implies something superficial and almost frivolous. It makes us think of a church, like that of Wesley's time, which had lost hold of the great realities and cared only for the dull respectabilities of life. But to a world like that of the second century, visibly dying from moral ignorance as a man chokes from want of air, morality meant everything. It was felt that no grander service could be rendered to Christianity than to concentrate on its moral teaching and bring it within the reach of all. Thus there arose that ethical movement which is represented in some of the New Testament writings. They might seem to be unfruitful on the religious side, and for this reason have often been viewed with suspicion. Their right to a place in the New Testament has at times been questioned. But if they were left out we should know nothing of early Christianity in one of its characteristic aspects, and the New Testament, to that extent, would be defective.

The most remarkable of these writings is that Epistle of James which Luther dismissed so scornfully, on no other ground than a theological prejudice. No one who reads it with an open mind can fail to see in it a noble and inspiring book, perhaps the finest of its kind ever written. From beginning to end it consists wholly of moral exhortation. The author appears to think of the church as little more than an ordinary society, devoted to the pursuit of high moral aims. He says nothing of the specific Christian message, and hardly even mentions the name of Christ. As to the origin and date of the Epistle there has been much dispute. Traditionally it is ascribed to James the Lord's brother, the leader of the church in Jerusalem. If this were indeed its authorship it would rank as one of the earliest of New Testament writings, and perhaps the very earliest; and there are some things in the book that might seem to bear out the tradition. From all that we know of James he was a man of stern moral principle, more interested in the practical issues of the gospel than in its religious purport. The Epistle has many affinities with that Jewish code of righteousness of which James was the typical exponent, and parallels with the Rabbinical teaching and the Wisdom literature can be discovered in every part of the short writing. Yet its Hellenistic origin cannot well be questioned. Ever and again its thought echoes that of the Stoic moralists. Phrases occur from time to time which clearly belong to Greek philosophy, and could never have been employed by one whose training had been purely Jewish. Regarded as a whole it may at once be classified with homilies like the so-called Second Epistle of Clement, which are undoubtedly Hellenistic. It represents, in fact, that ethical Christianity which was becoming more and more prevalent in the Gentile church.

The author is indebted to previous moralists, Jewish and Gentile, and this was inevitable. A work of ethical instruction does not lay claim to originality, for its very purpose is to gather up and enforce the lessons which have proved most valuable in the experience of the past. Sometimes, as in the Annals of Confucius and the Book of Proverbs, the work is nothing but a collection of wise maxims already current. The teacher takes for granted that the necessary rules of life have disclosed themselves in the actual process of living, and is content to sift them out and put them on record. In the Epistle of James, however, we have much more than a patchwork of approved counsels. The writer is himself a man of strong personality, with pronounced views of his own, and he puts the force of his convictions into all that he borrows. To this day his Epistle maintains its place as one of the most vital of all ethical treatises. In its whole outlook it is curiously modern, and contains some passages which might have been written by a social reformer of to-day. At the same time it belongs not to purely ethical but to Christian literature. The virtues on which it lays stress are always the Christian ones,—patience, humility, sincerity in word and deed, practical kindness. Its affinities with the Sermon on the Mount have often been noted, and consist not merely of coincidences here and there in topic and phrase. The writer has learned to think in the manner of Jesus. While he does not deal explicitly with religion he takes the religious attitude to life. He has a profound sense of man's responsibility to God and of the eternal issues which are involved in common duties. The Christian message is everywhere pre-supposed, and gives depth and significance to the moral teaching. It is not a little remarkable that this Epistle, so often regarded as the least spiritual of the New Testament writings, is in some ways the most akin to the First Epistle of John. Both of these writings, in their different ways, express the same faith and outlook. They present moral principles as understood by the Christian mind.

It cannot be denied, however, that morality, in the Epistle of James, becomes too much an interest by itself. The writer thinks of Christianity as primarily a new ethic. It has indeed brought a higher knowledge of God, but this is intended for the quickening and direction of the moral life. In one famous passage the writer appears to attack Paul's conception of faith as the central motive of the gospel.* He declares, in so many words, that it is conduct alone which matters, and that men only deceive themselves when

* Jas. 2:14–26.

they rely on faith. His argument, however, would seem to be directed not against Paul himself but against some form of teaching in which Paul's doctrine had been abused and distorted, as it has been many times since. It would be clear to any intelligent reader of Paul's own Epistles that what he meant by faith was not a dogma or a sentimentalism, doing duty for practical religion. It would be clear, too, that the "works" which Paul condemned were not moral activities but the ritual performances enjoined by the Law. None the less the passage is significant as marking the cleavage which had now begun between religion and ethic. For this writer the faith which saves was no longer the inward surrender of man's will to the will of God. It consisted, rather, in action conformable to the Christian rule of life. "Show me thy faith by thy works." "Faith without works is dead," "True religion is to visit the fatherless and widows in their affliction, and to keep thyself unspotted from the world." † All this is beautifully said, and would have been fully endorsed by Paul. He is constantly impressing on his readers, in even more emphatic language, those practical truths which make up the message of James. But he never fails to add that all Christian action must be the fruit of the Spirit, and has no value unless it expresses Christian faith.

The Epistle not merely identifies Christianity with right living, but defines it as a "law" to which the followers of Christ are now subject. Here we have one of the characteristic marks of that ethical religion which was now growing up in the Gentile church. As Paul had clearly perceived, the aim of Jesus was to break away from the whole idea of law, which had proved so deadening in the Jewish religion of his time, and to substitute for it that of a new will, an inward instead of an outward constraint. When Christianity was conceived as a new law this idea tended to dis-

† Jas. 2:18; 2:26; 1:27.

appear. Right action was now severed from its religious springs, and became much the same as it had been in Judaism,—a mechanical obedience to a number of stated rules. The legal conceptions which Paul had fought so hard to overthrow were all brought back in a new form. It is indeed contended that between the new law and the old there is an essential difference. The Christian rule is described as a "law of liberty," ‡ and this is sometimes understood to mean that law has been replaced by moral freedom. But nothing more is implied than that the Christian law is more comprehensive than any other, and that men may decide for themselves how they will obey it. An officer has more freedom than a private soldier, and to some extent makes the rules instead of trying to obey them to the letter. Yet he is subject to the same military discipline, and is bound to observe it even more strictly. So the conduct of the Christian, no less than of the Jew or Pagan, is regulated by law and will be judged by law. The sole difference is that while previously there had been many specific rules, irksome to remember and obey, there is now the one commandment "love thy neighbour as thyself." This "royal law" includes all the others, and leaves us free to use our own judgment as to how it should be practised in each particular instance. To this extent it is a "law of liberty," but does not cease, on that account, to be a law. As a law of liberty it is, indeed, far more exacting than any set code. It applies not to some specified acts but to all alike, and as the Jew was guilty of breaking the whole law if he offended at any one point, so the Christian lies open to judgment if he does not, in all times and circumstances, fulfil the law of love. The writer of James thus enlarges the idea of law in such a manner as to bring the whole of life within its scope. Freedom has been given us in order to lay on us a far stricter obligation.

‡ Jas. 1:25; 2:12.

We can thus observe, at a crucial point, how the ethical teaching of the later time differs from that of the Gospels. The author of this epistle is at one with Jesus in making love the one grand motive of right action. This simplification of the old legal system was a tremendous advance, and ensured that all ethical thought in the future should develop along Christian lines. Men were to take the central principle of Jesus' teaching and make this their standard in the handling of all ethical questions. But the principle was understood as a commandment, explicitly laid down. Jesus himself had ordered it, and it therefore had a divine authority. None the less it was an enactment, and as such must be accepted and obeyed. This was not how it had been conceived by Jesus. When he spoke of the "great commandment," inclusive of all others, he had meant that the old system of rules was now ended, and the moral life had been placed on a different basis. Men were to enter into a new relation to God, so that their wills might become one with the higher will. Love, as he regarded it, was not a law but a frame of mind, a disposition which would come of its own accord when men knew themselves to be children of God. With James, love is a law, imposed on us from without. It has to be examined, like any other law, and its range and applications clearly defined. How does it bear, for instance, on the possession of wealth? The writer of the Epistle enters fully into this question, and concludes by denouncing all rich men. He finds that when the law of love is applied to them they must be denied all mercy. This is a strange contradiction, but something of the kind is inevitable when the Christian ethic is changed into a code of law. It needs at every point to be qualified and safe-guarded. Love itself is no longer spontaneous and unreserved, but is an obligation laid on us, with penalties attached if it is not performed in the right way. In this type of Christianity the ethic is separated from the roots that nourish it, and becomes an interest that has to be cultivated for its own sake. As a result the man who aims at Christian living is like one who is pre-occupied with his health. Always thinking about it, and neglecting the business and the natural joy of life in order to preserve it, he misses the very thing he is seeking for. The Epistle of James is the work of a sincere and lofty soul. One feels that this man has grown weary of the empty sentiment which for many in his time had taken the place of religion. He protests against it, and tries to impress on his readers that Christianity is worth nothing if it does not manifest itself in moral action. In his zeal for active righteousness he condemns everything that seems to him mere thought and feeling. And this is the weakness of his Epistle. By his one-sided emphasis on action he fails to supply the necessary impulse to action. He has indeed left us one of the most inspiring of all ethical books, but the reason is that in spite of himself he is much more than a moralist. With all his insistence on ethic he appeals to us in the name of religion. He enables us to realise, as he does himself, that by justice to our fellow-men we offer service to God. He does not weave an "epistle of straw," in which religion is debased into morality. He takes the best morality he knows, and makes it one in substance with the Christian religion.

An ethical position of a somewhat different kind is represented by the Epistles to Timothy and Titus, the so-called Pastoral Epistles. These letters are written in the name of Paul, and are based, most probably, on fragments of Paul's correspondence which had fallen into the hands of a disciple and admirer of the great Apostle. He believes that in his elaboration of these brief notes by Paul he is continuing the Pauline tradition, and in some respects he does so. He gives new currency to Pauline terms and ideas, and does his best to reproduce the Pauline gospel as he has understood it. But he understands it imperfectly, and this is nowhere so apparent as in his ethical attitude. The Christian life, as Paul knew it, is a unity in which faith and action are inseparably bound together. By faith the believer surrenders himself to Christ; his moral activity proceeds from the new will which has thus taken possession of him. Paul's enemies contended, as they have often done since, that by his doctrine of faith he had destroyed the moral law, but he justly answered that he had established it. He had taught how men might obtain the inward power, apart from which their best moral effort would always be futile. Faith and morality were ultimately the same thing. The writer of the Pastoral Epistles has failed to grasp this Pauline conception. He thinks of faith and morality as both necessary, but as separate from each other. The Christian life is divided, so to speak, into two parts. A Christian man is one who believes in the gospel, and who is intent, at the same time, on living a good life. In so far as the two things are connected, faith is like the foundation, which gives stability to the house; but when once the foundation is laid it can be taken for granted, and all care can now be directed to the building and furnishing of the house. This is still the popular conception of the Christian life. To be a Christian you require to hold certain beliefs, and this soundness in the faith is indispensable. You must also take care to act in accordance with the principles laid down in the Gospels. These two obligations of faith and conduct must go together, but little attempt is made to relate them to one another. They are simply the two component parts which make up the Christian life, and which must both be present. There are people whose faith is doubtful, although their conduct is irreproachable; there are others who are strict in the matter of belief, but break down when it comes to practice. Both of these classes are open to suspicion, and the true Christian is he who combines the right belief with the right mode of action. Broadly speaking this is the position adopted in the Pastoral Epistles. Faith and ethic, although they have no inherent connection, are assumed to go together, and both are required of the Christian. The author employs a special word to denote their combination, "godliness" (*eusebeia*). His object is to form in his readers the "godly" character, in which Christian morality is conjoined with Christian belief.

From this it follows that the ethic of these Epistles is not one which has grown spontaneously out of the new message, but one which has been attached to it by deliberate effort. Its Christian nature is strongly insisted on, but the more it is examined the more it is seen to be a compound of various elements. The principles of Jesus are no doubt primary, but they are supplemented by others, taken over from Jewish and Pagan ethic. The Christian man must be merciful and unselfish, but he must also be mindful of his personal dignity; he must cultivate a wise moderation, and have due regard to material as well as spiritual needs. The ideal which is thus set before us is an admirable one, but it is not that of a saint, modelled on the pattern of Jesus. In the view of this teacher a Christian man is one who has paid heed to many good examples and has taken what is best from each of them, and who thus proceeds to build up a virtuous life on the basis of his faith. It must be granted that an ethic of this kind is unsatisfying. No one can read the Pastoral Epistles without a sense of something arid in their thinking, something that is common-place and superficial when we remember the Gospels and the writings of Paul. With all its pleasing features there is little glow or inspiration in the picture here given us of the Christian as a good citizen and parent, diligent in all duties, genial and benevolent, practising all virtues but always on his guard against pushing any of them too far.

Nevertheless the writer is firm in his conviction that Christian faith must be the basis. He believes that God has now revealed himself in Christ, and that this has given a new meaning and a new certainty to all moral demands. His ethic may have much in common with that of the Pagan moralists, but it stands on a different ground. The Christian is one who has knowledge of a higher world, who looks for the return of Christ in glory, who is conscious of a heavenly calling and of an eternal life which is to be the reward of right action. It is wrong, therefore, to describe the ethic of these Epistles as nothing but the higher ethic of the time, linked on to the Christian beliefs. These beliefs are essential to it. They may not be the root out of which it grows, but they are like the solid rock beneath it. Pagan morality at its best was never secure of itself. It was based on theories which might or might not be true, and which every thinker was free to modify at his pleasure. The "godly man" of these Epistles, although his judgments might seem to differ little from those of the conscientious Pagan, was in no doubt about them. He knew whom he believed, and could build up his moral life in the full confidence that it would stand. Not only so, but as a Christian he had a sense of purpose in all his action. There was much that was noble in the Pagan morality, but those who practised it best were the most bitterly conscious that it aimed at nothing. Why should they labour to do right? In the last resort there was no answer, except that virtue was praiseworthy and should be practised for its own sake. Few could engage with much ardour in this thankless task of doing right because it ought to be done. The Christian was able to feel that his moral action was well-pleasing to God. He could perform even his common duties with an abiding sense that they were bound up in some way with eternal issues. This is the constant undertone of the Pastoral Epistles, and we cannot do justice to them without bearing it in mind.

They offer a moral teaching which is conditioned by a Christian faith.

The ethical interest is linked up with an ecclesiastical one. This, indeed, appears to be the chief object for which the Epistles were written,—to strengthen the church for its work of moral leadership by improving its government and discipline. For this writer the church has little of the mystical significance which it had for Paul. He is content to regard it as a community which has been formed by holy men for the preservation of Christian belief and the practice of a new rule of living. If this society is to fulfil its purpose it must be wisely administered by men who were well grounded in the faith, and who set a virtuous example. All its members must be enabled to feel that the church will assist and encourage them in their effort towards a better life. It may fairly be said that the programme which the church has kept before it ever since was first drawn up in the Pastoral Epistles. Its task has been chiefly that of moral education,—not so much the maintenance of an inward fellowship with Christ as the training in his way of life. Christianity is the new law, and the church is like the school in which men learn what it requires of them, and how they can apply the lesson in their personal and social duties.

The Epistle of James and the Pastoral Epistles are typical of that interpretation of the gospel which appealed more widely, perhaps, than any other to the later New Testament age. It presented the new message with a strong emphasis on its ethical side, at the risk of obscuring or subordinating its deeper import. To these Christian moralists the church owed more than it has sometimes realised. The world in which they appeared was infected with terrible evils, which Paul hardly exaggerated in his great indictment in the opening chapters of Romans. He indeed admits in those very chapters that the Gentiles had an inner law to guide them, and we know, from signal examples, that amidst the general corruption there were not a few who ordered their lives by the highest standards. As we consider the teaching of Seneca, Epictetus, Marcus Aurelius, we are sometimes tempted to believe that Paganism, out of its own resources, might have developed a morality little inferior to that of the church. This, however, is a mistaken, and not altogether an honest view. It is the simple historical fact that Pagan society, in spite of splendid exceptions, was steadily deteriorating, and this, when we look to radical causes, was inevitable. For one thing the Pagan ethic, at many points so admirable, was grounded in principles which were essentially wrong. It glorified brute force; it made egoism a virtue; it regarded sins of the body as venial and indifferent. Errors of such a kind were bound to vitiate all moral judgments, and the evils became ever more apparent as society advanced out of a state of war into one of peaceful intercourse. Thoughtful men in the first century were fully aware that disaster was threatening, although they failed to discern the true causes. Again, the Pagan ethic, even when it was sound, had no means of asserting itself. It depended on traditions which were always growing weaker, or on philosophical doctrines which were all in conflict and might at any time be changed or abandoned. The conception of Christianity as a new law was indeed inadequate, but it answered to a need which had become desperately urgent. A law implies a force behind it which makes it effectual. Men are required to feel that here is something which they are compelled to do, whether they will or not; and without this same feeling an ethical code is useless. The moral law must be armed with the same constraining power as ordinary law, and it was this which made the Christian ethic different from any other. It had behind it the authority of the Christian religion. The religion might be understood imperfectly, but it impressed on men the confidence that God had declared his will through Christ, and that these were his demands. To offend against the new law was to challenge the majesty of God.

The moral emphasis was thus necessary if the new religion was to make its way in the Gentile world. Whatever might be unintelligible in its message it offered a clear moral guidance, and this, above all else, was what men were seeking. And by accepting it as an ethic they were able to appreciate, as they could not otherwise have done, its meaning as a religion. Jesus had proclaimed the Kingdom of God, and this conception might seem to be utterly remote from man's common interests. In the first century, as now, there were many who acknowledged the charm of the gospel but could see in it nothing but beautiful ideals which had no bearing on the grim realities of life. It was the task of the moralists to make the teaching concrete. Out of the ideals they formed a rule of conduct, a code of definite directions for the performance of daily duties. The message that seemed to be intended only for rare saints and mystics was thus brought within the reach of ordinary men. This has always been the service which moralists have rendered to our religion. The church has looked on them doubtfully, as if they were seeking to displace the spiritual gospel, when their aim has been to interpret it. They have made it intelligible to the mass of men, for whom all other accounts of it are written in a strange language.

Yet there is always a danger that Christianity will lose its substance when it is reduced to an ethic, leavened with some vague religious sentiment. This became ever more apparent as time went on. Not only was the religious message thrust into the background, but the ethic itself, when separated from it, ceased to be effectual. The power of Christianity consists in its new revelation of God, and of the eternal life offered to men through

Christ. It is this which gives value to the moral teaching, and a Christian code of morals, when it is nothing more, will quickly fall to the same level as any other. Paul makes it his chief complaint against the Jewish Law that while insisting on the higher demands it provides no means of obeying them, and this is no less the weakness of the Christian law when it is divorced from faith and the regenerating Spirit.

Christian morality was saved because it continued to attach itself, however loosely, to the Christian message. The church not only trained its members in the new ethic but engaged them in worship, made them familiar with the record of Jesus, taught them to believe in him as Lord and Redeemer. Their morality was never left hanging in the air. They were kept mindful that in their endeavour to follow the Christian rule they were seeking after God, they were looking beyond this world to a life everlasting. The author of the Pastoral Epistles is a moralist, and might seem at times to regard the gospel from no other point of view, but his interest is all the time a religious one. "Denying ungodliness and worldly lusts, we must live soberly, righteously and piously in this present world, looking for that blessed hope, and the glorious appearance of the great God and of our Saviour Jesus Christ." ¶ This must always be the inspiring principle of the Christian ethic. While it remains Christian it can never be merely a moralism. At the heart of it there is the religious message, vitalising the ethical demand.

¶ Tit. 2:12, 13.

CHAPTER VIII

WESTERN CHRISTIANITY

FROM THE time of Paul onward the church was identified with the West. Its teachers were still, for the most part, of Jewish race, but they were Jews of the Dispersion, who had grown up under Gentile influences. There is probably no book in the New Testament which had its origin in Palestine. The writers employ the Greek language because they were born to it, and addressed themselves to readers who knew no other. It was customary, until the beginning of this century, to think of the New Testament as a Jewish book which had accidentally come down to us in Greek, but we have now learned to reverse this judgment. The New Testament is a Greek book which has a Jewish background, but is related at every point to Western thought and culture.

The term "Western," however, is a misleading one when it is applied to the world of the first century. In that age the West had become, to a large extent, Orientalised. Within the universal empire all national divisions were fast disappearing, and the races of Syria, Egypt, Asia Minor had flowed over into the cities of Europe, bringing with them their customs and beliefs. It was chiefly among those foreign elements in the Western population that Christianity made its way, and long after it had firmly rooted itself the cultivated Greek or Roman still thought of it as one of the barbarous creeds, peculiar to the invading Orientals. This, indeed, was the chief underlying motive of the persecutions, which began near the end of the first century and increased in violence during the second and third. The decay of the empire had now set in, and was attributed by statesmen and writers to the encroachment of Eastern ideas on the virile temper of the West. Measures were taken to counteract the Oriental influence, which had assumed its most dangerous form in Christianity. The persecutions were directed not so much against a religion as against an alien type of culture.

None the less, as the Gentile mission progressed the new religion took on more and more of a Western character, and as we approach the third century the transformation becomes fully apparent. Christian teachers have learned to think in terms of Greek philosophy; they have begun to use the Latin language as well as the Greek; their cast of mind and their outlook on life can be plainly recognised as Western. The change must have been a gradual one, and signs of it may reasonably be looked for in the New Testament. They are not to be found, however, in places where they might most naturally be expected. Paul wrote his longest letter to the church at Rome, the representative church of the West, but there is little to distinguish it from his other letters. He takes for granted, and no doubt correctly, that the people for whom he writes were in general sympathy with his own point of view, and were Orientals now resident in the great Western city. Several New Testament books, such as the Gospel of Mark and the First Epistle of Peter, were actually written in Rome, but their outlook is purely Jewish. The author of I Peter describes the Christians as "strangers and sojourners," and he might have applied these terms in a literal as well as a religious sense.* He himself and the people among whom he worked were settled in the West, but they were exiles, amidst surroundings which were not properly their own.

There is one writing, however, which appears to stand on a different footing. It has come down to us under the title of the

* I Pet. 1:1; 2:11.

Epistle to the Hebrews, but this is a later guess, and almost certainly a mistaken one, founded on the writer's pre-occupation with the religious ceremonies of Judaism. In the Epistle itself there is nothing to suggest that he addresses some group of "Hebrews,"—conservative Jews who had refused to fall in with the larger Christian movement. On the contrary, he shows himself strangely ignorant of the true nature of Judaism. He knows it only through his reading of the Old Testament, and seems to be unaware that the Law had long displaced the ritual of the Temple. One has only to contrast his argument with that of Paul in the Epistle to Galatians. Paul has to deal in that Epistle with the position of Jewish Christians, and he has good reason to know it thoroughly. He never mentions the high-priest and the sacrifices but fastens entirely on the question of the Law, which was the one stumbling-block. As an answer to Jewish difficulties the laboured argument of Hebrews would have been utterly beside the mark, and for this and many other reasons the old assumption as to its purpose is now pretty well abandoned by competent scholars. The opinion, however, still persists that this Epistle lies outside of the main current of Christian thought, and is the work of some teacher who held views peculiar to himself and to a small, forgotten circle. A place is assigned it among the quiet backwaters of early Christianity, so that little attention is paid to it in any study of the general development. This is unfortunate, for there is reason to believe that the Epistle, so far from reflecting the views of some eccentric sect, is in the fullest sense representative. It is valuable for its own sake, as one of the noblest of the New Testament writings, but it is valuable above all because it marks a new departure, which was to have far-reaching consequences.

The truth is that this so-called Hebrew Epistle is the least Hebrew book in the New Testament. This is apparent in its very language, which is a finished, literary Greek, indicating an effort on the part of the church to break loose from its foreign associations and ally itself with the higher culture of the time. The Epistle is intimately Greek, not only in its style, but in its fundamental thinking. The writer is steeped in the idealism which had coloured all Greek philosophy since Plato. He works ostensibly with apocalyptic conceptions of a heavenly world, where God is enthroned in the true Temple, but behind this imagery it is not hard to discern the Platonic idea of a sphere of reality, over against the changes and shadows which are all that our senses can apprehend. Of the man who wrote the Epistle we know nothing, and all attempts to identify him with one person or another whose name is recorded will always be futile. From the earliest times the church was evidently as much puzzled about him as we are now. We cannot even tell whether he was a Jew or a Gentile, but this does not much matter, for he wrote in a time when the distinction had ceased to mean anything. Christianity now stood out as a new religion which transcended all racial divisions. Judaism had significance only in so far as it pointed to the new revelation which had brought it to an end.

Whoever the writer was he belonged to the Roman church, and this fact is more illuminating than anything that might be told us about his race or name. The Epistle closes with the words "they of Italy salute you,"—which may imply either that it was written from Rome, or that it was sent to the Roman church by one of its teachers who was travelling abroad, and who couples with his own greetings those of other Roman Christians. The latter interpretation is much the more probable, and is supported by various allusions in the body of the Epistle. It is written to a church of old standing, proud of its illustrious past. This church is distinguished for its liberality, has offered counsel and example to other churches, has witnessed the labours of holy men on whom it looks back with veneration. All this applies in a pre-eminent degree to the church of Rome. There is also one peculiar feature of the Epistle which can best be explained on the theory of its Roman origin. It joins together, with hardly any attempt at fusion, the most primitive Christian ideas with those which were not developed until the later part of the first century. On the one hand, it has a number of striking affinities with the speech of Stephen in the book of Acts; on the other hand, it pre-supposes the Alexandrian doctrines which appear in the Fourth Gospel. It seems to be almost unaffected by the Pauline teaching, which bridges the interval between the earlier and the later types of thought. This is intelligible if the Christianity of the Epistle is that of Rome, which had never been evangelised by Paul. When he wrote to the Roman church, less than thirty years after the Crucifixion, it was already large and flourishing and must have been in existence for a considerable time. Most probably it had owed its foundation to some of those followers of Stephen who were dispersed after his death, and had returned to their previous homes. Rome would thus receive Christianity directly from Jerusalem. In course of time it would produce its own teachers, imbued with that Western culture which had its capital in Rome, but they would build on the primitive assumptions. The result would be such a type of doctrine as we find in Hebrews,—philosophical and at the same time primitive. An advanced theology had come into being, but it had not grown naturally out of the early apocalyptic beliefs as they had been interpreted by Paul, but had simply been overlaid on them.

The author was thus a teacher in the Roman church, and his work is best explained when we regard it not as an Epistle in the strict sense, but as a discourse or lecture which is to be delivered in his name. Except for a few personal notices at the end it has none of the characteristics of a letter, while on the other hand it is eloquent and skilfully arranged, and combines argument with fervid appeal, after the manner of a spoken address. Several times the author explicitly describes himself as in the act of speaking,[†] and from a purely literary point of view his work may be justly ranked among the finest examples of Greek oratory. The question of its form has an important bearing on its scope and purpose. It is customary to speak of the "theology of Hebrews," as if the writer had set himself to expound in this one short document his whole system of doctrine. Some of his omissions have naturally caused much perplexity. Why, for instance, does he discuss the death of Christ without any reference to the Resurrection? Why does he allow no place to the Sacraments? He leaves out so many things which are clearly of primary value that he has sometimes been taken as the spokesman of a peculiar sect, which taught a Christianity entirely different from that of the church at large. But it was not his intention to cover the whole field of Christian belief. He is making a speech on one particular subject which he considers of primary importance, and as far as possible he keeps other things out of sight, so as to concentrate the minds of his hearers on this one theme. He expressly tells us, in a remarkable passage, that he will say nothing of "the principles of the doctrine of Christ," [‡]—the fundamental verities on which all Christians are agreed. He wishes to confine himself to one aspect of the faith, a strange and difficult one which has hitherto been neglected, although practical issues of the highest consequence are, to his mind, involved in it.

The main object of the Epistle is practical. At first sight we seem to have before us a purely theological discussion, but the author himself describes it as a "word of exhortation," that is, a hortatory discourse.[¶] This, when it is examined more closely, is

† Heb. 8:1; 9:5; 11:32.   ‡ Heb. 6:1.   ¶ Heb. 13:22.

indeed its character. Ever and again the argument is interrupted by a passage in which its meaning for the Christian life is earnestly pressed home. Towards the close the theological scaffolding is removed altogether, and there emerges from it a magnificent practical appeal. To understand this appeal we need to remember that the Epistle was written for Christians of the third generation. This is stated, in so many words, by the writer himself.[§] The church was now largely composed of those who had been born into it, and who had accepted its teaching as a matter of course. As a result, the primitive fervour had died down, and those who believed the message had ceased to realise its newness and wonder. While assenting to it they had fallen into a mood of indifference, which was changing, under stress of adverse conditions, into something like distaste. A generation had arisen which had not been called on, like the one before it, to face a savage persecution and "resist unto blood." It was exposed instead to ridicule, slander, loss of property, nagging discomforts which irritated without uplifting. Many had grown half ashamed of a religion which involved so many social drawbacks, and apparently gave so little in return. The aim of the Epistle is to inspire the Christians with a noble pride in their calling, and to revive the ardour which had cooled down. This the writer seeks to do by demonstrating that the Christian religion is the highest and the final one. Those who believe in it possess the reality of all that had previously been known only in shadow and symbol.

In this endeavour to present Christianity as the absolute religion the author adopts the method of contrasting it with Judaism, which was not only the loftiest of the old forms of worship, but was the only one which had been ordained by God Himself. Through the angels He had given His Law to Moses, prescribing the means whereby His people might have access to Him.

§ Heb. 2:3.

The Jewish ritual thus bore a divine character, but was intended merely to prefigure the true approach to God. It is shown that in Christianity the purpose of God, as suggested in Judaism, has reached its fulfilment. Through Christ we have received not merely the types and shadows but "the very image of the things." *

The writer thus centres his attention on the Jewish worship, as it was practised in the tabernacle fashioned by Moses, "after the pattern shown him on the mount." † He had been granted the vision of a heavenly sanctuary, and had made an earthly one, which, on the material plane, had resembled it, so that from the visible holy place something can be learned of that which exists in heaven. The Mosaic ritual is therefore examined in order to discover from its hidden suggestions how God ought truly to be worshipped. Little is said of the legal system as a whole. It is regarded as nothing but a sheath or a protective wall, guarding those ritual ordinances which were the substance of the old religion. The ritual itself, in most of its provisions, was only an inner sheath or wall. Everything else was subsidiary to the institution of the priesthood, which mediated between God and man. Even the priesthood had value only as a protection around the high-priest, in whose person the old religion had its centre. This one man had been singled out, by a hereditary right, to make approach to God on behalf of the nation he represented. But even with the high-priest we have not yet reached the absolute core of the Jewish religion. All his other activities converged on his entrance once a year into the holy of holies, to stand in the presence of God, and offer the blood of the sacrifice which atoned for sin. As all else in the religion existed for the high-priest, so he existed for that one supreme act. For a few moments, year by year, he entered the inner shrine and stood, in the name of

* Heb. 10: 1.   † Heb. 8: 5.

his people, before God. To make this one act possible was the whole purpose of the ancient religion.

We thus arrive at what the writer himself calls the "crown," the central theme of his Epistle.[‡] Christ is the great High-Priest, who has performed in very truth what was only foreshadowed in the old ritual. To be sure he was not a priest by any hereditary right, but this only proves the finality of his priesthood. He exercised his office in virtue of a quality inherent in himself. Like Melchizedek in the book of Genesis, he owed nothing to human antecedents, but was a priest by divine appointment. While at all points one with men he was Son of God, and could thus mediate between God and man. And this priesthood of Christ, like that which had prefigured it, was summed up in one culminating act. Christ had offered a sacrifice, not of some passive animal but of himself, and with the blood of this sacrifice of surpassing worth he had entered, not into a material holy place, but into the eternal sanctuary in heaven. For the writer of Hebrews the death of Christ was only the necessary prelude to that entrance through the veil into the presence of God. This was the priestly act for which he came into the world, and though it was performed once for all, it was perpetual in its effect. The levitical high-priest was only permitted to stand for a moment in an earthly holy place; Christ had passed into the heavenly sanctuary where God dwells in very deed, and there sat down to remain for ever. In him his people have a Mediator who is one of themselves, and who yet abides with God, making intercession on their behalf.

The Epistle reaches its climax in the great eleventh chapter in praise of Faith, which is too often read by itself but cannot be rightly understood apart from the whole argument, theological and practical, which has led up to it. For this writer faith has a different meaning from that given to it by Paul. It is not that

‡ Heb. 8: 1.

self-surrender to God which is evoked by the Cross, but is rather the instinct in us which testifies to the reality of things unseen. It corresponds, in some degree, to what Paul calls hope, except that it has more of an intellectual quality, arriving by intuition at truth which is not capable of logical demonstration. The writer expressly defines it as the "proof of things not seen," the insight by which we are made certain of what is hidden from our senses. His aim is to awaken this faculty which is lying inactive. He has shown that the old religion gave only the symbols of something beyond, and now he exhorts his readers to lay hold by faith of that higher reality which has at last been revealed.

It is thus apparent that his thought, in its essence, is philosophical. He works with the language and the assumptions of Jewish apocalyptic, and it may be that he believed literally in a heavenly temple which was the dwelling-place of God. But by the apocalyptic imagery he seeks to impress on us the conception of Plato and Philo, that over against this material world there is an unchanging one, and that things seen are only the shows of things invisible. Christ has passed into that higher world, and through him we are enabled to apprehend it. It is no longer in the realm of imagination or surmise, for Christ, who made himself one with us, has now ascended to it and we can feel that in him we also have our part in the eternal. Christianity for this writer is the religion of faith, and faith is the power of spiritual apprehension. A means has been offered us whereby we can live, even on this earth, as citizens of the higher world. We can rise above the shows of things, and grasp the realities.

Such, in brief, is the interpretation which this writer gives to the Christian message, and it is undoubtedly a lofty and impressive one. But it must be admitted that the Epistle does not stand, religiously, on the same level as the other New Testament writings. This is obscurely felt even by casual readers, and perhaps we have here to find the ultimate reason why Hebrews, in spite of all its splendid eloquence and fervid Christian spirit, was for a long time denied a place in the New Testament canon. It suffers, as a Christian book, from two obvious and radical defects.

On the one hand, it connects the Christian message with ideas of a purely ritual nature. Christ is regarded as á Priest, and his work is explained on the analogy of old ceremonial. It is highly significant that this is the only New Testament writing in which the death of Christ is compared to a sacrifice. This, it might be supposed, was the line of thought which would suggest itself most naturally to worshippers of that time, familiar with the rite of sacrifice as it was practised in all known religions. Yet it is avoided by the New Testament teachers, one cannot but think deliberately. They were conscious that it externalised the meaning of the Cross,—that it associated the new religion with an alien order of ideas. Jesus had himself discarded the whole system which has been built up around the temple worship. He had lifted religion to a different plane altogether, and had made it consist in an inward fellowship with God and an active obedience to God's will. The author of Hebrews falls back on ritual conceptions. His object is to prove that Christianity is superior to all previous religions, but he appears to miss the very element in it which makes it superior.

On the other hand, he takes his stand on authority. All through his Epistle he argues from the word of scripture, from tradition, from the approved beliefs of the church. Reference has been made to the significant passage in which he exhorts his readers to pass on to a higher knowledge, "leaving the principles of the gospel of Christ." The assumption is that the fundamental beliefs must be accepted without question or enquiry. Grounding himself on these, the Christian is to go forward to a new and larger faith. Such an attitude may be contrasted with that of Paul, who is always concerned with the "principles," the elementary truths which are also the essential ones and must constantly be re-examined and established more surely. This is why Paul's thinking, beneath all its old-world forms of expression, has an enduring value. Its aim is always to reach down to fundamental principles, and since it thus deals with the realities of religion it has never ceased to be living. The Epistle to the Hebrews has too much of the character of an academical exercise. Assuming certain things to be true, the author seeks to deduce from them, by ingenious methods, other things which must also be true. He may be considered as in some respects the first of the scholastics, whose logic is convincing when once you have granted their premises. But it is just those primary assumptions of which we require to be convinced. When they are simply taken as they are, and all testing of them is forbidden, the logic has proved nothing.

It might seem, therefore, as if the Epistle were hopelessly out of date, like so many other doctrinal treatises which were in their time unanswerable, but which rested on suppositions that have long since been discredited. Very strangely, however, this Epistle, of all the New Testament writings, is in many ways the most modern. It is not the deepest or the most valuable, but it anticipates, more than any other, ideas and sentiments which we commonly think of as peculiar to our own time.

This is true, in a remarkable degree, of the writer's attitude to other religions. The church has usually taken it to be self-evident that Christianity is the true religion, while all the others are false. This is the position normally adopted in the New Testament, and it was never seriously questioned during the centuries that followed. The Epistle to Hebrews, however, takes a different ground. It presents the new religion as the "perfecting" or fulfilment of those which preceded it. They were not false but only incomplete. They had offered the truth "darkly and in fragments," [¶] and now God has revealed it fully in his Son. At the time when the Epistle was written our doctrine of historical development was still undreamed of, but for this writer the idea of symbolism serves much the same purpose. To past ages God had given in types and forecasts what he has now perfected. This attitude to alien religions is that which is now forcing itself on thoughtful men, and is giving a new direction to missionary effort. No sincere religion has ever been false. In every form of worship there is something which points forward, however obscurely, to the message of Christ. He came not to destroy but to fulfil, bringing to its consummation the whole religious struggle of mankind. It was the writer to the Hebrews who first gave any clear expression to this view of the nature of Christianity.

Again, he is modern in his fearless assertion that everything must stand by its own intrinsic worth. He looks for a day of testing, when "things that are made," things which are hollow and fictitious, will be shaken, and those only which cannot be shaken will remain. [§] This thought recurs, under various forms, throughout the Epistle, and perhaps most conspicuously in those chapters on Melchizedek, which would be singled out by most readers as the most utterly antiquated in the New Testament. They are really among the most modern. Their purpose, when we probe beneath the ancient mode of expression, is to affirm that true priesthood must be inherent in the man by whom it is exercised. No hereditary claim, no forms of solemn investiture, can make a genuine priest. He must be of the order of Melchizedek, mediating between God and man because in his own person he bears the priestly character. This is the idea which, in its manifold applications, is now in process of transforming all

[¶] Heb. 1:1.   [§] Heb. 12:27.

society. In previous times everything was based on artificial values of race and rank and class. We are now demanding that the tools must go to those who can use them, that every man must be judged by what he is in himself. In like manner we are impatient of institutions which have nothing to rest on but some credit or privilege which they acquired in the past. We ask "what are they doing now? Is there anything in them that makes them worth preserving?" The church itself is compelled to face this challenge. It has come down to us with a halo of antiquity, and professes to represent the cause of God on earth. What can it show, in actual deed and character, to justify its profession? This is the question which we are now learning to put to everything, even to things which have always been accounted most sacred, with the result that a new world is arising before our eyes. In every department of life there is a growing sense that something was wrong with the old order, and that it must give way to a different one. What form it will take we cannot yet tell, and our counsellors are all at variance. It was this better order, in which all things should be estimated at their true value, that the writer of Hebrews had in his mind. He called it "the order of Melchizedek," and this is the order towards which the world is aspiring, more and more consciously, at the present day.

Again, the Epistle is modern in its recognition of the earthly life of Jesus as the true basis of the Christian religion. It is the only New Testament writing, outside of the Gospels themselves, in which this significance is given to the life. The author is never weary of reminding his readers how Jesus had made himself one with men, and had known their infirmities, and had set them the great example of courage and patience and faith. He rests his whole argument on the idea that Christ was the true High-Priest because he had shared our human life and known it from the inside, while at the same time he was of the nature of God. For the most part the references to the Gospel history are of a general kind, although one definite fact, that the Crucifixion took place "without the gate" is only known to us from Hebrews.* Another allusion would seem to imply some information of which we learn nothing in the Gospels. We are told that in his Agony, when he prayed "with strong crying and tears" to be saved from death, the prayer of Jesus was answered, but he refused the offered deliverance, so that he might submit himself utterly to the Father's will.† But apart from any special allusions the writer is everywhere conscious of a religious value in the earthly life. Paul was content to see in it nothing but the interval between two redemptive acts,—Jesus' entrance into our world and his atoning death. For Paul he is the glorified Lord, of whom he can say, "even if I have known him after the flesh I know him so no more." For the writer of Hebrews the life on earth was an essential element in the redeeming work of Christ. By his participation in the human lot he gained that sympathy with men and that insight into their needs, which fitted him to be their High-Priest and Mediator. This also is an aspect of the teaching of Hebrews which has only come to its own in modern times. During far the greater part of Christian history faith rested on dogma. Christ was indeed central to his religion, but he was viewed in the light of certain speculations as to his nature. These constituted the Christian beliefs, and it was often doubtful whether they related to an actual personality or to a theological abstraction. It is only in the last century that the church has re-discovered the historical Jesus and given him a cardinal place in its religious thinking. We consider this, not unjustly, to be one of the great achievements of modern Christianity. It has secured for our religion a solid basis and a practical import which were too much wanting in former times. But it must not be forgotten that the new atti-

*Heb. 13:12.   †Heb. 5:7.

tude was anticipated by the writer of Hebrews. He also perceived that the Christian message was inseparable from Jesus himself, not only as he appeared to the mind of faith but as he had actually been while he lived and taught among men.

This emphasis may partly be accounted for by that sense of intrinsic values which is one of the marked features of the Epistle. The writer insists that everything must be judged, not by some worth imputed to it, but by that which it really possesses, and he does not hesitate to apply this standard to Christ himself. We know him by his recorded life; what was there in that life which justifies our faith in him as Lord and Saviour? But the historical interest may have been due, more directly, to the Roman origin of the Epistle. Rome had received the gospel, not through the agency of Paul, but at an earlier date, from missionaries who had come straight from Jerusalem. The tradition that Peter, in his own person, was the Apostle of the Roman church may be considered doubtful, but the men who brought the message to Rome had been, like Peter, in immediate contact with Jesus, and their knowledge of him was concrete and human. Mark, our primary Gospel, was almost certainly of Roman origin, and represents the kind of teaching which was doubtless familiar to the Roman Christians. In course of time this teaching would be supplemented by philosophical doctrines, but it would continue to be fundamental. Roman Christianity might be compared to an ancient city which has grown by constant additions into a great modern capital. It now includes vast areas of building, in many styles of architecture, but still at the centre of it are the old walls, enclosing the parent city. Care is taken that whatever may be changed or added, this should be preserved. For many centuries Roman Christianity continued to be a strange composite. It was hospitable to all new doctrines but still maintained beliefs and customs which had come down from the earlier days. It was under such conditions that the author of Hebrews had thought out his new interpretation of the Christian message.

In many respects the Epistle stands by itself in the New Testament, and perhaps its unique character is best explained from its connection with a church which had grown up independently, and stood for a new departure in the Christian mission. The Epistle reflects not only peculiar doctrines but a changed attitude of mind. Even when it seems to be in harmony with other writings we can always detect something in the thought which makes a difference. This is often set down to the presence of speculative ideas, due mainly to Alexandrian influence, which had come to affect the Christian outlook. But the Fourth Gospel also accepts the Alexandrian teaching, more fully and explicitly than the Epistle to Hebrews, and no two writings could be more unlike. There is hardly a verse in the Gospel which would not be felt out of place if it had wandered by some chance into the Epistle. How has this difference arisen? Much can no doubt be accounted for by the strongly contrasted temperaments of the two writers, but apart from this, they belonged intellectually to different climates. With the Roman mission Christianity had thrown in its lot with the Western World, and was adjusting itself to the Western habit of mind.

Here we may find the ultimate explanation of that quality in the thought of Hebrews which impresses us as modern. The other New Testament writers are Orientals, and their teaching, even when it rests on Greek philosophy, continues to bear the impress of the East. This writer belongs to the West; we recognise in him one of ourselves. To be sure he speaks to us out of an ancient time, when the forms of thought were different from ours, and employs the language of apocalyptic allegory and of speculations which are now dead. Yet essentially he looks on the world with our own eyes. His problems are similar to ours, and he falls back instinctively on the same solutions. As a religious thinker he cannot compare for depth and power with Paul or the Fourth Evangelist, but in his presentation of the gospel there is something which makes an instant appeal to us. Take, for example, his great chapter in praise of Faith. Perhaps in the whole Bible there is nothing to which we respond with such heart-felt emotion. Familiar as it is to everybody we can never listen to it without a thrill. And the reason is that it gives splendid utterance to what has always been the deepest and sincerest mood of the Western mind. Eastern thought is mystical where Western thought is idealistic. In the West there have indeed been many great saints, but the type of devotion which drives men into solitude, to spend their lives in inward communion with God, has always been exotic, and is growing ever more rare. The Western man is practical and energetic, so much absorbed in present interests that his outlook is often called materialistic. Nothing could be more unjust, for he is alive, almost in a dangerous degree, to ideas of freedom, loyalty, patriotism, self-sacrifice. The upheavals of our time have been chiefly due to this idealism, exploited and perverted to their own ends by unscrupulous demagogues. It is something different from religion but has its roots in the same conviction that man belongs to a higher world, and that only the invisible things are real. The gospel is interpreted by the writer of Hebrews in terms of this Western idealism.

The Epistle may thus be regarded as the first manifesto of Western, and more especially of Latin Christianity, and from this point of view is profoundly interesting and suggestive. Again and again, as we read it attentively, we can discern at least the outline of conceptions which were to govern the history of the following centuries, and to shape the society in which we are living to-day. The Epistle is like a photograph taken in his childhood of a friend whom we know well. He has grown so different that we could never have recognised the picture, and yet, when we examine it closely, we can make out the familiar features. The child has been father to the man.

We cannot but note, in the first place, that reliance on authority which is characteristic of the Epistle. The writer sets out from certain things which must be taken for granted. He is eager for new light, and writes with the express purpose of imparting a difficult doctrine which had hitherto been neglected. But he deduces the new truth from texts of scripture. He takes care to explain that it is simply additional to the old beliefs and will leave them undisturbed. This has always been the attitude of Roman Christianity. It inherited from Rome the conviction that amidst all flux of opinion there must be standards which were not to be questioned. Respect for authority was in the very blood of Rome, and to this she owed her greatness. The ideal of the Greek cities was individual freedom. All institutions and beliefs were open to constant revision, and every citizen was allowed full play for his own personality. Hence the charm and variety of Greek history, and the marvellous flowering of every kind of genius, but the penalty in the end was national suicide. Rome was content to build on the sense of discipline inherent in its people. Amidst all changes there was an unwavering reverence for law and custom, for duly appointed officers, for stated principles and traditions. The fundamental things were not to be criticised, but must remain always as they were. This Roman attitude communicated itself to the Roman church, which in course of time became dominant in the West as the Roman state had been, and for the same reason. Maintaining the principle of authority it enforced order and cohesion, and stood immovable while all other powers shifted and crumbled. Protestantism broke off from Rome, but was faithful, on the whole, to the same pattern. It placed authority, not in a sovereign church but in the Bible, in stated assemblies, in doctrines generally accepted. Perhaps there has been no Protestant church, however free in matters of opinion, which has not finally identified itself with some kind of orthodoxy. The last word is left with an authority, which is not subject to question, but must simply be accepted and obeyed. Much can be said for this deference to authority. Our very word "religion," which comes to us significantly from the language of Rome, implies a force that binds.[‡] Men cannot be permitted to believe and act just as they please. There must be standards imposed on all, truths that must never be challenged. What we want in religion is a sure basis on which to rest our lives. In all other things we ask for liberty, but there must be something we can hold to, in every tide of opinion, as ultimate fact.

Yet the hand of authority is always obstructive, and most of all when it interferes in our relation to God. A religion based on authority is, indeed, a contradiction in terms, for religion consists in nothing else than in the appeal from all earthly judgments to that of God. Paul declares proudly that his gospel was not from man, neither was he taught it, but it was given him by revelation of Jesus Christ. This inner assurance is of the very essence of Christianity, and in the Western type of religion it is too often lacking. The truth is enforced on men from without. They are required to accept it for the very reason that it has approved itself to some one else, whose right they are forbidden to question. This reverence for authority may be said to enter Christianity with the Epistle to Hebrews. It is one of the grandest and most impressive of Christian writings, but it lacks the immediacy of conviction of which we are everywhere conscious in the Gospels and the Pauline Epistles. Authority has taken the place of the Spirit. In this

[‡] It is derived, apparently, from *ligare*—to bind, with a prefix which intensifies the meaning.

work of a Roman teacher we begin to breathe the atmosphere of the later church of Rome.

Again, the Epistle is Western in the strong practical interest which pervades its thinking. The author is a theologian, but where he seems most concerned with abstract ideas his mind is chiefly set on their application. He turns in a moment from the loftiest speculations to the lessons that may be drawn from them in the actual business of life. Here, also, we can perceive the Roman temper, which was above all things practical. For centuries the Romans took nothing to do with ideas for their own sake, and when they changed their attitude it was only through contact with Greece. Even then they set no value on knowledge as an end in itself. They rejected thought as futile unless it could be made an instrument for action. The one philosophy which attracted them was Stoicism, because it supplied principles by which they could frame a system of law and which they could apply directly to the conduct of life. In like manner the genius of the Roman church was practical, and has always borne this character. It has often been observed that while Rome was for ages the religious centre of the world, it never originated any theology. At the most it only appropriated the ideas of thinkers elsewhere, and made them effective in the ritual and government and instruction of the church. The writer of Hebrews stands at the beginning of this Roman tradition. His purpose is not so much to discover a deeper meaning in the Christian message as to give it a practical direction. With all his interest in doctrine he is quite untouched by the mysticism which is the constant background in the thought of Paul. He is not a mystic but an idealist, intent on conceptions which will inspire noble action. With the inward springs of religion he does not concern himself. The desire for personal fellowship with God is not only foreign to him but is incompatible with his whole religious attitude. He thinks of God as "the Majesty in the heavens," [¶] before whom we can only bow down in worship, and we cannot even offer him this homage without the aid of a Mediator. Since this is our relation to God the idea of union with Him becomes almost blasphemous. Christ himself is removed to a distance. He was indeed made one with men that he might become their High-Priest, but he is "holy, harmless, undefiled, separate from sinners." [§] We can only look up to him as the supreme pattern, whom, with all our striving, we can never hope to approach. He remains in heaven seated at God's right hand, and we think of him, not as our comrade, but as the Victor who has now won his crown. Not the fellowship with Christ but faith is for this writer the great energising power. He finds his examples of it in the Old Testament heroes who subdued kingdoms, wrought righteousness, out of weakness were made strong. Christ himself is the author and finisher of faith, the Captain of all those who endure and struggle that they may attain. Everywhere in the Epistle emphasis is laid on action. The writer is a theologian, who points the way to a higher knowledge, but he never allows us to forget that knowledge is of no value unless it has its outcome in more strenuous living.

Here we can recognise the Roman bent of mind. As the Romans had taken up the Stoic philosophy because of its utility for law and morals, so they were now drawn to the Christian religion. With its mystical doctrines they had little sympathy, but they could appreciate its worth as an incomparable motive to action. "Strengthen the feeble knees and lift up the hands that hang down"; [*] this is the call which rings through the Epistle to Hebrews, and it sounds the key-note for the whole subsequent history of the Western church. In the East theology was occupied with metaphysical discussion; in the West it became an instrument for moral training and church organisation. The great religious teachers of the

[¶] Heb. 1 : 3.   [§] Heb. 7 : 26.   [*] Heb. 12 : 12.

West have been at the same time men of action, whose names are inseparable from the social and political movements of their times. It has to be admitted that in this zeal for practical results the deeper import of the Christian message has often been lost, and along with it much of the energising power. When all is said, the faith which can move mountains must have its roots in the faith which has known God as an inward presence. We cannot but wonder, as we read the Epistle to Hebrews, whether those Christians who had fallen into indifference were much aroused and fortified by the elaborate argument, in which the "principles of the doctrine of Christ" were purposely left out of sight. The power of faith has never been described so magnificently as in the eleventh chapter of Hebrews, but nothing is told us of how we may possess this faith which can accomplish so much. The proof that Christ was a High-Priest of another order than the levitical is indeed convincing, but it appeals only to the intellect and leaves us cold. By his insistence on action to the neglect of the inward Christian life the writer to the Hebrews has in great measure defeated his own ends. None the less, his lofty idealism brought a new and enriching element into Christianity. It served to interpret the gospel in a manner congenial to the Western mind. From the time that this Epistle was written, faith has been understood in terms of action. A religion which might have lost itself in mere contemplation has joined hands with all practical interests and has afforded them guidance and inspiration.

In a more definite way the Epistle foreshadows the course of Western religion. Its dominant theme is the priesthood of Christ. All other aspects of his work are made subordinate to the one conception that he is the High-Priest through whom we have access to God. It must never be forgotten that the Epistle makes no pretence to offer a complete theology, and confines itself to a single doctrine, on which, for the time being, the writer concentrates his whole attention. Yet the fact remains that the doctrine which attracts him beyond all others is this one of the priesthood of Christ. Elsewhere in the New Testament the idea of Christ as a Priest is entirely absent, or is only incidental and figurative. For this writer it contains the very key to everything in the Christian message. He indeed maintains that Christ was a Priest in a new and unique sense, and on this fact he grounds the supremacy of the Christian religion. Nevertheless it is taken for granted that God cannot be approached except through priestly mediation. With all his genuine Christian devotion the writer never escapes from the sacerdotal mode of thought. He makes no claim for Christianity except that it is priestly religion in its full perfection, and in the light of subsequent history we cannot but see in this interpretation the first step on a dangerous road. Jesus had himself protested against the Temple worship and all that was involved in it. He had inaugurated a spiritual religion in place of a sacerdotal one, and his earlier followers were conscious that this had been his purpose. It might appear as if the writer to the Hebrews, even more emphatically than the others, asserts the spiritual character of the new religion. It depends, he says, on no outward rites, performed by an official priesthood in a material building, but on the intercession of one who has passed, out of the visible sphere, into the very presence of God. But in this account of the work of Christ he merely takes the old conceptions and lifts them to a higher plane. He does not find in it something different in kind from anything that had gone before. He merely thinks of Christ as unfolding what was signified in the priestly forms of worship, so that they help to illuminate for us the meaning of our Christian faith. As a consequence of this mode of thought the ideas which Jesus had discarded were brought back into his religion. The writer to the Hebrews had aimed at something very different. He had sought to prove that old forms of worship had lost their value, now that we have the realities instead of the types. But in order to make this clear he fell back on ritual ideas and described the work of Christ as one of priesthood, exercised in a higher sanctuary. When this doctrine of priestly mediation was thus placed at the centre of Christian teaching it came to affect all thought and worship. Christ was the High-Priest, and the church, as the body of Christ, must represent his function of mediating between God and man. Its ministers must be regarded as priests. Its ordinances must be brought into line with those of the Temple. In this manner the new religion was assimilated in ever greater measure to the older cults which it had displaced. They all turned on the belief that God must be approached through priestly mediators, and while the church declared that this belief had now been transcended it acknowledged that it was still valid. The process had begun by which Christianity was changed into a sacerdotal religion.

It would indeed be unjust to lay the whole responsibility for this change on the writer to the Hebrews. In its Pagan environment the church had already been affected, in a hundred insidious ways, by Pagan influences. The author of Hebrews was well aware of the danger, and does his utmost to counteract it. He shows that the old forms of worship were now things of the past, and had fulfilled their purpose in pointing forward to the work of Christ. Nevertheless he opened the way, more than any other teacher, to ideas which were inherently Pagan. The effect of his doctrine was to supply a rational, and to all appearance a genuinely Christian basis to a sentiment that was alien to Christianity. He conceived of Christ as a priestly mediator, and the aim of the church from this time onward was to give fuller embodiment to this doctrine of the mediation of Christ. Behind this doctrine there is a truth which is profoundly Christian, but when it is conceived in terms of priesthood it changed the whole character of the gospel. A ritual and sacerdotal religion established itself as Christianity, and was identified most of all with the Church of Rome. Through this church it was diffused, in the course of centuries, over the Western world.

The conception of priesthood is closely related to another, which pervades the Epistles to the Hebrews, and was developed, ever more fully, in the West. The writer thinks of God as revealing his truth by means of symbols, visible types which are the shadows of unseen realities. On the ground of this conviction he examines the ancient ritual, and seeks to discover its hidden significance. It was enacted in a material building, by priests of a given descent, and to the outward eye consisted of mere ceremonial gestures. These, however, had been ordained by God, and were like the earthly mirrors of his mind and purpose. The writer holds that as Christians we apprehend what was reflected in the mirrors. Instead of the symbols we have the things they signified. It might have been expected that by this line of thought he would arrive at conclusions similar to those of the Fourth Gospel. The religion of visible symbol has had its day, and through Christ men can enter into inward communion with God. "Neither in this mountain nor yet at Jerusalem shall ye worship the Father; but the hour cometh, and now is, when the true worshipper shall worship the Father in spirit and in truth." †
Instead of this, however, he allows no place to a purely mystical devotion. Worship, as he conceives it, is the same in kind as it has ever been except that the old sacrificial system has lost its meaning, since the act which it pre-figured has been accomplished. So far, indeed, from discarding the idea of symbolism he gives it a vastly wider range and significance. All outward

† Jn. 4:23.

things, as he sees them, have become types through which we can reach forward to the truth which lies beyond them. Christ has passed through the veil, and by him we can lay hold of the higher realities, but this does not mean that the earthly things are now superfluous. On the contrary, they are fraught with a meaning which was formerly unsuspected. They have become, as it were, transparent, so that through them we can discern the eternal. This is the conception which underlies that conception of faith, on which the whole Epistle may be said to centre. Christ is the perfecter of faith, not in the sense that he has made us independent of everything that belongs to this present world. He has rather enhanced the value of the visible things, since they now speak to us of that which is unseen. We can throw ourselves with a fresh courage into the earthly struggle as we realise the mighty issues which are involved in it. We can look on the passing scene with our minds intent on something behind it which does not change. In the great chapter on faith this idea finds clear expression. Those heroes who lived by faith were no mere visionaries. They did their part manfully in this world, working for what might appear some very limited and material end,—the possession of a new land, the victory over an oppressor, the building of a temple; but they did those things in the assurance that the earthly object was the pledge and sign of some other that was everlasting. "They looked for a city which hath foundations, whose builder and maker is God." ‡

The symbolism of Hebrews cannot be rightly understood when we look only at its application, often frigid and pedantic, to the ancient Jewish ritual. It determines the writer's whole view of the world. His mind is naturally symbolical, and in all created things he sees more than meets the eye. He believes that over against this world there is another, and that everything around us bears

‡ Heb. 11:10.

witness to that higher realm of being. Faith, as he conceives it, is nothing else than the faculty which apprehends the spiritual through the material. His Epistle may seem to demonstrate that the age of types and foreshadowings has come to an end, but its real intention is to give them a new value. It teaches us how we may live by faith, discerning in all the visible things some gleam of that other world which has now been revealed to us through Christ.

Religion in the West took hold of this symbolism of Hebrews, and embodied it in the Christian system of worship. It is necessary, indeed, to keep the Epistle in our minds if we are to do justice to that form of religion which became dominant in the Western church. As we leave the first century we cannot but feel that everything is being externalised; and this was formerly explained by the theory that the church was now in process of corruption by worldly ambitions and false teaching. Modern scholars have rejected this view, but they still assume that the new religion was yielding gradually to Pagan influences. It had lost its original character and was transforming itself into a semi-Pagan cult, which appealed to the senses by means of buildings, relics, pictures, lights, incense, vestments. The whole mystery of salvation was now bound up with magical formulae and sacramental rites. Now it may be granted that the Pagan influence accounts for much, but when we read the Epistle to the Hebrews we become aware of a genuine religious motive in the later development. Spiritual things were not materialised, but the other way about. Material things were invested with a spiritual value. In the light of the Christian revelation the natural world was consecrated and became a ladder whereby the soul could ascend to God.

It must never be forgotten that the chief danger in the early period was in too much abstraction. The Hellenistic peoples had inherited the Greek belief that knowledge is the true end of life. They tried to absorb themselves in inward contemplation, and held that no one could aspire to fellowship with God unless he mortified the flesh and broke loose, as far as possible, from earthly interests and duties. The Christian ideas were understood metaphysically, with the result that they lost all contact with reality. Nothing was left of the gospel but those bloodless creeds which were formulated by the various Councils, and which could be little more, for ordinary men, than strings of meaningless words. It can be fairly argued that the image-worship which was so bitterly denounced by the Byzantine church was the thing that saved Christianity. By means of those sacred objects, which they could grasp with their bodily senses, men recovered something which was denied them in their formal profession of faith. Their religion was kept in contact with actuality. They were enabled to feel that as God had manifested himself in the flesh, so in tangible things he still offers some assurance of his presence. This in all times since has been the function of symbolism, and in one form or another it will never cease to be a necessary element in our religion. Without it the higher world is entirely separated from this one, and the religious mood becomes unreal. Not only so, but the world around us is deprived of meaning. Nothing is left in it but dead material things,—a heap of mere empty shells. By means of symbolism the dead things are touched with life; they become vehicles of what is real and spiritual. In bread and wine we discern the Lord's body. A building of stone and lime is changed into the house of God and the gate of heaven. A relic that can be seen and handled imparts to us the feeling of contact with the divine. This reverence for material things is not to be condemned as idolatry. It serves rather to bring home to us the great religious truth that we live in God's world, and that everything in it, if only we had eyes to see, is full of his glory.

The symbolism of Hebrews may seem to be alien to the teaching of Jesus. It rests on the Platonic conception of a world of higher reality, which is known to us by its reflections in the things we see, and when we meet with this conception in a New Testament writing we are reminded forcibly that the Christian message, transplanted to the West, took on itself a new character. Yet on deeper consideration we cannot but feel that the symbolism of the Epistle brings out an essential aspect of Jesus' own religion. While he proclaimed the Kingdom of God he did not shut his eyes to the world around him. Without a parable, we are told, he said nothing unto them,¶ and he adopted this mode of teaching not merely to explain his thought to those who heard him but because the truth presented itself in this manner to his own mind. In all common things he read the suggestion of something deeper. He spoke in parables because the whole world was for him a parable, a manifestation in visible form of that divine order which would be realised in the Kingdom. If we speak of the symbolism of Hebrews we may apply the same term to the Gospels, and it was all-important that this element of the Gospel teaching should be preserved. More than any other it was in danger of being forgotten. In the mistaken effort to make it more spiritual the message of Jesus has ever and again been emptied of substance. Mystical thinkers have sought to lift it into a rarified atmosphere of pure ideas in which ordinary men and women can hardly breathe. Symbolism in all ages has indeed lent itself to many abuses. The symbol is confounded with the thing it stands for, and out of a spiritual worship there grows up a new idolatry. Again and again this has proved the ruin of some lofty form of religion. Yet it means everything that the higher world to which we aspire should be related in our minds to the world we see. Our life is spent among material things,

¶ Mk. 4:34.

and with the help of these we must reach forward to the truth beyond.

Christianity in the West became a religion of symbol. Its message was associated with acts and objects which to the devout mind were full of significance, although too often they came to be valued for themselves. The conviction that we have access to God through earthly symbols has sunk deep into the Western mind, and perhaps has done more than anything else to vitalise religion. It has inspired all that is greatest in art and music and poetry. In our own time it has been the driving force behind the effort towards social reform. We have ceased to think of the Kingdom of God as a vague ideal, utterly remote from the earthly scene in which we toil and suffer. We believe that although on earth it can never be realised, we can yet make the actual society a type of the heavenly order. It may be said, too, that in modern science the symbolic idea is gradually coming to its own. Not so long ago the scientific enquiry appeared to lead nowhere but to a crass materialism. The belief in a spiritual world was thrown aside as delusion, and all effort was directed to explaining every mystery from the operation of physical laws. This materialism is now dissolving through deeper investigation of the material things themselves. The world, as we learn to know it better, becomes the revelation of some power which cannot be weighed and measured. Those forces which were once conceived as ultimate are seen to be mysteriously linked with others which involve mind and spiritual purpose. God is reflected in the things he has made, and through knowledge of them he comes more clearly within our vision. It is not too much to say that behind all the great movements which have shaped and are still shaping our Western religion there is the symbolism of this Epistle to the Hebrews.

CHAPTER IX

THE JOHANNINE TEACHING

FOR MORE than a century after the death of Paul Christianity had its centre at Ephesus. This city, encircled by others which were hardly less famous, had always been the home of intellectual movements. Homer, according to tradition, was born at Ephesus. It had certainly witnessed the beginning of Greek philosophy. As the seat of the great temple of Artemis it was the religious capital of Asia Minor. In the first century, owing to its situation on the confines of East and West, it had become the meeting-place of the two main types of ancient culture, and they fused together in ever new varieties of art and thought. Paul quickly realised, when he set foot in Ephesus, that "a great and effectual door was opened" to his mission.* He worked in this city for three years, the culminating years of his marvellous career, and left behind him the most vigorous and progressive of his churches.

It is not surprising that this Ephesian church, as it developed, took on a character of its own. The Pauline teaching was never submerged, but it was affected by all the currents of thought which mingled with each other in the eager life of the city. Paul himself, according to the book of Acts, gave warning to the elders of Ephesus that men would arise among them, after his departure, who would pervert his gospel.† It is the historical fact that Gnostic heresy, in so far as it had any definite beginning, found its cradle at Ephesus. But while Christianity was exposed to danger in this city of miscellaneous creeds, the effort was

* I Cor. 16:9.   † Acts 20:29.

made to preserve it, and to establish it on a surer basis. This effort is chiefly associated with the great teacher who has left us the Fourth Gospel and the First Epistle of John. He now stands out as a solitary figure, but it is hardly probable that he stood quite alone. The supreme thinkers and artists, Plato, Shakspeare, Michelangelo, have always been the topmost peaks of a mountain range, and it was doubtless the same with the Fourth Evangelist. He only perfected the work which many were attempting, but he so moulded it and stamped it with his individual genius, that it was the work of this one man.

For more than a century criticism has been occupied with the problem of the Fourth Gospel, and cannot yet pretend to have solved it. If there has been any advance it has been mostly of a negative kind. Judgments were confidently made a generation ago which have now been qualified, or withdrawn altogether. Responsible scholars are content for the present with a guarded attitude. Perhaps none of them would maintain the traditional view that the Gospel was written by the Apostle John, in his old age at Ephesus, but the theory has gained ground that somewhere behind it there is a primitive document of the highest value. Opinion has shifted, too, with regard to the date of the Gospel. So recently as fifty years ago it was often dismissed as a writing so late in origin that it had no legitimate claim to be included in the New Testament; but evidence has accumulated that it belongs to the very beginning of the second century, or perhaps to the closing decade of the first. The question of date, indeed, has been almost set at rest by the manuscript discoveries of the past few years. It can now be affirmed with certainty that there never was a New Testament in which the Gospel of John did not hold a principal place. By a chance which seems almost ironical the oldest piece of New Testament writing which has thus far come to light is a fragment containing two verses of the Fourth Gospel.

This precious relic can be assigned to about 140 A.D. and is positive proof that within the first half of the second century the Gospel not only existed but had become one of the standard Christian books. In point of time there can have been no great interval between the Gospels of Matthew and Luke and that of John.

Not only its early date but its historical value is now generally acknowledged. Formerly it was considered by many to be little more than a romance, faithful to history only at the few points where the author had obviously borrowed from the Synoptists. Lives of Christ were written, towards the end of the last century, in which the testimony of the Fourth Gospel was not even mentioned. Scholars would now admit that in some particulars this Gospel is nearer to the facts than any of the others. In the reaction from the old view there is, indeed, a danger that its historical value may be over-rated. At all events, its title to rank as a Gospel, a record of the life of Jesus, is not seriously called in question.

Every one, however, is conscious of a difference between this record and the other three. It was remarked by Clement of Alexandria, in the earliest criticism of the subject which we now possess, that after the other evangelists had dealt with the facts of Jesus' life, John wrote a "spiritual Gospel." This view has been generally accepted, and is expressed in modern language by describing the Fourth Gospel as interpretation rather than history. The suggestion is that it belongs to that class of literature in which historical narrative is used as a vehicle of philosophical theory or moral instruction. Plato wrote dialogues in which Socrates is the leading character, and undoubtedly he brings into them many authentic episodes in his master's career, but his object plainly is to interpret the thought of Socrates in the light of his own reflection. In like manner, it is held, John interprets Jesus. There is no intention to deceive, and it need not be doubted that most of the things narrated in the Gospel did actually happen; but the writer is interested not so much in the facts as in the meaning he reads into them. If the Gospel has been mistaken for a literal account of the history of Jesus the fault does not lie with John himself but with his later readers, who have failed to appreciate the real purpose of his work.

Now it may be granted that the Fourth Gospel is something more than a historical narrative, but it is certainly written in that form. Books were in circulation under the names of Mark, Matthew and Luke which purported to deal with Jesus' words and actions, and this Gospel was offered to the church as a similar record. A generation later men allowed their fancy to play freely around the life of Jesus, and a number of Gospels appeared which we now call apocryphal. They were written in a fantastic strain, and the authors cannot have intended that their fancies should be taken literally. The object, as every one could see, was to advocate some doctrine, or to stimulate some mood of Christian piety. This, however, was a later development. John's Gospel, as we can now recognise, belongs to the same general period as the Synoptic records; it cannot be separated from them by much more than a dozen or twenty years. The old tradition as to its authorship may be set aside, but it is justified to this extent, that in the time when John's Gospel was issued the church was still in touch with the Apostolic age. Jesus had not yet receded into a dim past, and a book concerning him was expected to contain facts, which men still living had heard of from eye-witnesses.

That the Gospel is in this sense historical cannot well be doubted. However he has obtained his information, whether from oral tradition or from some primitive document, the author has preserved the facts at a number of points where his accuracy can be tested. He tells us that the Crucifixion took place, not on the day of Passover, as the Synoptic writers assume, but on the day before; and this is almost certainly correct. All through his account of the Passion he shows a knowledge of details which to the others had become obscure. He is the one writer, for instance, who appreciates the part taken by Annas, the former high-priest, in the conspiracy against Jesus.[‡] He can describe the trial before Pilate with the place and circumstances vividly before his eyes.[¶] In one remarkable passage he is at pains to tell us that the incident of the spear-thrust had been vouched for, to his knowledge, by a trustworthy witness.[§] An author who had collected this detailed information, and was anxious to make the most of it, must have had some historical aim. He cannot be set down as a mere romancer, intent on his private theories and manipulating the facts to suit them. For that part, with all the latitude which he allows himself, he is careful to adhere to the broad lines of the Gospel story as we know it from the other evangelists. He separates the career of Jesus into the same parts,—a time of preparation, a period of teaching, a journey to the Passover at Jerusalem, a week which ended with the trial and Crucifixion. He introduces the same characters, and takes particular care in noting times, places, names, accompanying circumstances. Evidently he is proud that he is able to supply this detailed knowledge, which in itself is unimportant. Amidst all digressions we are never allowed to forget that we are following an actual history, and this is no mere device, contrived to give an air of verisimilitude to an imaginative work. The writer has a real, and one may fairly say an absorbing interest in the historical facts.

Even more than the other evangelists he seeks to present Jesus as a human personality. Nothing, indeed, could be further from the truth than the statement so often made that the Jesus of the Fourth Gospel is colourless, a theological symbol rather than a

[‡] Jn. 18: 13, 14.   [¶] Jn. 19: 13.   [§] Jn. 19: 35.

man. With marvellous skill he is made to live before us in his love, compassion, friendship, in his courage, and humility, and sovereign dignity. The Gospel is full of incidents, more often suggested than described, which have printed themselves ineffaceably on the world's memory. We are made to see Jesus as he sat weary beside the well, as he wept over Lazarus, as he healed and comforted the blind man, as he washed his disciples' feet, and poured out his heart to them after the Supper. More than any other book the Gospel has provided subjects for great painters, and this is no accident. It aims at conveying a life-like impression of Jesus as he lived on earth, and a work which gives us this impression, and was plainly written with this end in view, may surely be regarded as historical. Christian sentiment has not erred when in all ages it has turned to the Fourth Gospel for the most satisfying of all the portraits of Jesus.

What, then, is the difference of which we are at once conscious when we turn from the other Gospels to the Fourth? It cannot be defined by a vague statement that John offers an interpretation rather than a history. If this view be accepted the Synoptic Gospels must also be called interpretations. As we are now beginning to realise they are not mere chronicles of fact but are meant to impress on their readers the significance of Jesus as the Messiah, appointed by God to bring in the Kingdom. To be sure the Synoptists interpret the history by primitive apocalyptic ideas, John by the ideas of Hellenistic thought; but in all these Gospels alike the facts are viewed through a medium of later reflection. Nevertheless the chief interest in all of them is historical. John, no less than the others, is concerned with the facts about Jesus, but he differs from them in this,—that instead of a single he gives us a twofold history, a history enacted on two planes which cannot be held separate. Jesus lived for a brief time as a man on earth; he lives for ever as an invisible presence. For John these two existences are equally real. The Jesus who dwelt as a man in Palestine is one with him whom we now know by faith. The earthly life prefigured that which was to follow it, and the invisible life explains the earthly one, which men had failed at the time to understand. John aims at blending the two histories, so that they may illuminate each other.

It cannot be doubted that in thus framing his Gospel John had in mind the peculiar conditions of his own age. He has often been regarded as a timeless thinker, who had broken loose from the world he lived in and dwelt on a mountain-top of pure contemplation. In a passage of his *Autobiography,* J. S. Mill has told of the aversion he had always felt to the Gospel of John. With his hard, realistic intelligence he could not endure a writer who lived, apparently, in a cloudland of his own, where facts had lost all meaning. There might be a majestic severity in his thought, but the reason was that it took no account of disturbing realities, and was empty and futile. This is the impression which the Gospel is apt to make on unsympathetic readers, but it is radically mistaken. The Evangelist was no recluse but an active church leader, intent on finding a solution to urgent problems. The more we examine his work the more we see that it is intimately related to the time and environment in which it was written. This is obviously true of the three Epistles of John, and beneath the placid surface of the Gospel we can trace the same practical interests as are dealt with in these Epistles. From one point of view the Gospel is a controversial work, hardly less so than the most polemical of Paul's Epistles.

The most critical period in the whole history of the church was that which began with the closing years of the first century. It was then that the state became openly hostile, and the church was involved in a prolonged struggle for its very existence; but this danger from without was accompanied with another from within, which was recognised by all thoughtful Christians as far more serious. The church was in the position of a ship which has dropped the pilot and is passing out of sight of land into the open sea. The primitive age was now definitely over. Not only the original disciples but their immediate successors had disappeared from the scene. No one was alive who could profess any contact with Jesus, even at second hand. The hope of his glorious return had proved illusory. Christianity had finally broken with Judaism, and was obliged to seek its future as a new religion in an alien world. The church was thus faced with the necessity of making a new beginning. All its institutions and its ways of thinking had to be re-adjusted, and it had now no guidance on which it could rely. We cannot wonder that in those difficult days opinion was much divided, and that the younger teachers, thrown on their own resources, were often in doubt as to their message and the manner in which they should proclaim it. Broadly speaking they wavered between two attitudes of mind in their effort to reconcile the old tradition with the new time.

On the one hand, there were those who refused to acknowledge that anything had changed. They held to the apocalyptic beliefs, just as they had been understood by the first disciples, and still looked for the visible return of Christ and the end of the present world. They clung to the memory of the earthly Jesus, and would admit nothing into their thinking which seemed at variance with what he had himself said and done. His revelation had been given once for all during that brief time when he had been manifest, and the whole task of his disciples was to perpetuate what he had taught, and to follow in his steps. Religion thus became a matter of pious reminiscence. Jesus had appeared at a given time, which was receding ever further into the distance. All habits and conditions were changing; the needs of

men were becoming different; their thought was advancing and
was expressing itself in new language. Nevertheless they were
required to hold stedfastly to the past, and venture on no step
forward. It has always been the trouble, as it has been the
strength, of Christianity that it began as an historical religion,
and so lends itself to a blind conservatism. In the nature of things
we leave the past behind us, and it can never be restored; but
Christianity anchors itself to the past, and too often the charge
has been justified that it cramps the free movement of the human
mind. What passes for religion is sometimes little more than an
obstinate cleaving to ideas which have served their day. It was
so with many Christians in that period when the church was
entering on its third generation. They were conscious of forces
which were driving them forward, and for that very reason they
refused to move. As Christians they felt themselves bound in
loyalty to the past. God had made his revelation in Palestine,
during the reign of Tiberius Caesar, and since then had withdrawn into silence. There was a real danger that the memory
of Jesus might become a postive hindrance to his religion. It
was cherished only as a memory, which could not but grow ever
fainter and more uncertain.

On the other hand, there was an effort to detach the religion
from the historical events which seemed to identify it with the
world of change. This was the motive behind the Docetic heresy
which exercised such a strange attraction in the later New Testament period. The Docetists held, as we have seen, that the
earthly appearance of Jesus had been an illusion, and that while
he seemed to live as a man among men he had all the time been
a divine being, outside of all human limitations. By means of this
doctrine the Christian could feel himself released from all that
was merely temporal in his religion. The Christ whom he worshipped had dwelt always in the eternal world. He had stood

apart from the flux of things, and was pure spirit, like God himself. It is not difficult to see how this teaching, with all its absurdities, made a strong appeal to Christians of a philosophical cast of mind. They were convinced of the spiritual value of their religion, but as commonly taught it seemed to be only an historical cult, devoted to a bygone hero. When the earthly life was dissolved into mere appearance, the grosser elements of the faith seemed to fall away, leaving nothing but what was spiritual. It was not perceived that the effect of this doctrine was to empty the gospel of all power and meaning. If the humanity of Christ was unreal, he became a mere abstraction. He could never have saved the world, since he had never truly entered it. Men could not love and serve him and unite their lives with his life, for he had come and gone like a ghost, and all endeavour to take hold of him was a clutching at thin air. Christian teachers were not slow to perceive that this was the fatal defect of the Docetic theory, and their criticisms have a permanent value. Docetism, in its original form, was crude and grotesque, and could not long maintain itself, but it was the forerunner of many similar attempts, some of them of very modern date, to secure an enduring worth for Christianity by cutting it loose from historical fact. We are told that it matters little whether Jesus ever lived, or whether anything we know about him is literally true. We can still hold to the teaching which has come down to us under his name, to the conceptions of God and of man's duty of which he is the symbol. The historical Christ may be a phantasm but faith can rest securely on the essential Christ. Such teaching must always end in depriving our religion of all substance. It leaves us with a baseless speculation in place of a reality.

The First Epistle of John was directed against the Docetic heresy, and there can be little question that the Fourth Gospel has the same underlying purpose. In a narrative of the life of

Jesus the writer can make no express mention of a doctrine which did not arise until long afterwards, but it is constantly in his mind. His Gospel opens with the great assertion, "The Word was made flesh," uniting itself with an actual human life, and on the ground of this thesis the whole work is written. Christ was a man, who sojourned with men as one of them. All that he did and suffered was real, and was woven inextricably into the texture of this world's history. It was doubtless with the purpose of affirming the true humanity of Jesus that John set himself to write a Gospel. He might have presented his teaching in some abstract form, as he does in the First Epistle, but instead of a theological or devotional treatise he gives us an historical record, embodying his thought about Jesus in a concrete picture of his life. We are made to feel that the truth has force and significance only as we apprehend it in a living Personality. The whole Gospel is thus an implicit protest against the Docetic view; and when this is borne in mind there can be little doubt that it is meant to be genuine history. If it were fictitious the writer would defeat his purpose. He is contending with those who had denied the reality of the facts, and by supplying his own imaginations in place of facts he would cut the ground from under his feet. The heretics would have had the right to argue that he held their own position. They believed that Christ was the eternal Word, and had only seemed to live a human life. In this Gospel also he appeared as the Word, and his history was a mere invention. Between the new view and that of the Docetists there would be no difference except that John had gone a step farther than his opponents. They were willing to grant that the things recorded of Jesus had at least appeared to happen. In this Gospel they were set aside altogether, and a life was assumed which had not even an apparent existence. Not a shred was now left of the reality of the earthly Jesus. It is easy to see that if John had written a Gospel out of his own imagination he would justly have laid himself open to this criticism. If his answer to the heretics was to carry any weight at all he needed to present an actual history. This was essential to his purpose, and he was fully aware of it. He takes care to impress on his readers that what he tells them is true. He connects his story at every point with definite times and places, with men and women whose characters are strongly marked, with human joys and sorrows and friendships. We are made to realise that the life of Jesus was the same in its nature and circumstances as that of every man. So in his refutation of Docetism John insists on the historical facts, and the whole value of his record is made to hinge on its veracity. Christ was indeed the Word, but the Word became flesh.

The Evangelist, however, while he answers those who denied the reality of the life, is equally opposed to those others who saw nothing in Jesus but a man who had once lived on earth. The revelation, as they knew it, consisted wholly in the recorded words of Jesus, in the things which he was reported to have done and suffered. He stood out before them as an ideal figure of the past, and they made it their one endeavour to recall and imitate him. As against this narrow conception the Evangelist dwells on the abiding significance of the life. Jesus became one with men, and was subject to human weakness and limitation, but he was still the Word made flesh. While sojourning with men he had shared in the divine nature. His earthly life had an import and potentiality which reached out beyond it. Although confined to a few years, and spent wholly in Galilee and Judaea, it foreshadowed a life which would endure for ever, and manifest itself to all men. The revelation which Jesus brought was not to cease when his earthly voice was silent. The power which resided in him did not depend on his visible presence, but was still active in that fellowship with him of which his people were conscious. For this Evangelist the earthly career of Jesus was only the prelude to another which was still in process. It was not merely the prelude but the pledge. In our knowledge that Christ once lived on earth we have the assurance that he continues with us. We can ponder on the record of his life, and by the light of it we can recognise him as he is now, and make out the meaning of what he still says and does.

In writing his Gospel, therefore, John seeks to present an authentic history, but a history which has two aspects. Jesus lived once, and gave us his revelation in certain words and actions, but he is living still and makes the same revelation, although he now moves invisibly, and speaks in new language. These two histories are blended in the Gospel. Each incident, when we examine it, has a double significance,—a literal and a spiritual one. This does not mean that the facts are resolved into allegory, or that interpretation takes the place of fact. Both histories are understood to be real. Jesus lived that life in Palestine; he lives just as truly here in the present. These have been the two modes of his activity, and they cannot be separated from one another.

It is necessary to lay emphasis on this double character of the history, for here we discover the nerve of John's reply to the Docetic teachers. They maintained that what was real in Christianity was the faith in a divine presence of which we can be sure, however we regard the memories of Jesus' historical life. They felt that their religion gained in certainty when it was lifted above the accidents and contradictions which must always attend an historical tradition. John sees, however, that the religion and the life must stand or fall together. The aim of the Docetists was to secure the validity of Christian faith, and they did so by insisting that it needed nothing outside of itself. Christ is the eternal Word, and his earthly history does not affect that commu-

nion with him of which the believer is conscious. This, at least,
is real, and gives us all that is essential in the Christian message.
The Evangelist is concerned, no less than the Docetists, with the
validity of faith. He realises, like them, that we can believe in
Christ only when we know him as not merely an historical memory but as a fact in inward experience. How can we tell, however, that the presence revealed to us in the life of faith is no
other than that of Christ? We can only do so through our knowledge of what he was when he lived on earth. Comparing those
things which he is doing now with the things recorded of him,
we can assure ourselves that the same Person is still working.
And if the historical life of Christ was imaginary, may it not be
equally so with this other? When we speak of a presence which
abides with us, we may be mistaking for a reality what is nothing but a creation of our own minds. All that we possess may
be some empty sentiment to which we give the name of Christian
faith. It is necessary, therefore, that the historical life and the
inward fellowship should go together. So far from confirming
our faith by making it independent of the history, we deprive it
of the one sanction on which it can rest. There may indeed be
a voice in the heart which we call the voice of Christ, guiding
and uplifting us, but there are many sounds which come to us
in the dark and which we imagine to be voices. To make sure
that we truly hear a voice we must learn something of the person who utters it, and this we do by our knowledge of the actual
life of Jesus. If that was real, then our sense of a living divine
presence is real also.

It has often been remarked that when John speaks of the
Spirit he hardly distinguishes it from Christ himself. He passes
almost in the same sentence from "I will come to you" to "the
Spirit will come to you." From this it has been inferred that
Christ had ceased, for his mind, to have any definite personality,

and was vaguely identified with the higher influence which breaks in from time to time on the devout soul. This, we are told, is the conception which underlies his Gospel. He thinks not so much of a human being as of a divine principle which he personifies and calls by the name of Jesus. But the truth is just the other way. He was so sure of the historical Person that he transfers all his attributes to the Spirit. What has often been regarded as a confusion in his thinking is almost certainly intentional. He seeks to impress upon us that as Christians we have to do with no mysterious influence which we cannot name, but with the presence of Christ himself, the same now as when he lived on earth.

The whole Gospel may be said to turn on one peculiar idea which marks the identity of the two manifestations of Christ. According to the primitive belief he had departed from earth but was shortly to return in the clouds of heaven, as the glorified Lord and Messiah. It was the failure of this hope which had perplexed and discouraged the church, and had caused many to abandon their faith. John, however, takes up the primitive belief, and transforms it into one of the boldest and most fruitful of all his conceptions. He maintains that the hope of Christ's coming has not failed. The Lord has indeed returned, not in the manner which the first disciples had expected, but far more truly and gloriously. He had departed only for a moment, and had then come back as an inward presence to abide with his people for ever. They know him more intimately than when he appeared in the flesh, for he is no longer divided from them by earthly barriers, but can enter into their very hearts. Their fellowship with him is not subject, as it once was, to many interruptions, for they abide in him as in an atmosphere which surrounds them always, and he imparts to them his inmost secrets, which he could not, when he was first with them, express in words.

From this point of view the Evangelist interprets the death of Christ, which is no less central for his thinking than for that of Paul, though for a different reason. He allows room for all the doctrines current in the church,—for instance, that the death had a sacrificial value and took away the sins of the world; that it was the crowning evidence of Jesus' love to his friends, and the pattern of that love which Christians should bear towards one another; that it was the formative principle of the church, the magnet which attracts out of the world those whom God has chosen. But its primary meaning, as John understands it is this,—that by his death Christ broke through the limits which his earthly life had imposed on him. The Word was made flesh, but now threw off the flesh with all its hindrances. Christ, who was once a man, became through his death a universal Spirit, present everywhere and for ever to his people, so near to them that he could dwell in their very hearts. His death on the Cross had been at the same time that return to glory for which his disciples had been vainly gazing into heaven. The Word had become flesh in order to share in our humanity, but having achieved that oneness with us had carried it now into a new state of being. The divine presence of which we are conscious in the experience of faith is no other than that of Christ himself who once dwelt visibly with men on earth.

The Gospel turns on this conception, and hence derives its unique character as a genuine history but a history on two planes, Christ lived once; he is living still. His earthly life anticipated his enduring, omnipresent life, and the two lives must be viewed together. Because it thus moves continually on two levels the Gospel is often regarded as an allegorical work, but a judgment of this kind is entirely misleading. The Evangelist never loses his hold on the history. His aim is to recount the actions of one who passed through the world at a given time and left an inspiring memory, like other great men. But between him and all others there was this difference, that not only his memory survived but his living personality. He continued to act and speak as he had done before, but on a far grander scale, since he was no longer held in by material conditions. His earthly life could not be re-counted without some suggestion of this other life which was involved in it, and from this point of view John writes his Gospel. He has been accused of distorting the history, and adding to it much that was his own invention; and it has to be admitted that he ascribes to Jesus words that were not actually spoken, and that his record of events cannot sometimes be taken as a literal chron-icle. But to say that he consciously invents is to misrepresent his method and purpose. He is dealing with a life which is as real to him in its new form as when it was visibly manifest, and he seeks to describe it in both its aspects, and to make us feel that they are inseparable. He may be compared to a painter who throws into his landscape the effects of depth and solidity. This, it may be objected, is to delude the eye, which looks only on the level surface of a canvas; but the painter, instead of deceiving, is trying to put the scene before us as it really is. The more he can create the delusion, the nearer he approaches to the truth. In this manner the Evangelist portrays the life of Jesus. Record-ing the facts, he seeks also to convey the impression of what was within and beyond them, for without this we cannot rightly see the facts themselves.

The Gospel, then, rests on the belief that Christ, who once lived on earth, has passed through death into a new life, and so remains in abiding fellowship with his people. This belief has come to the Evangelist through his personal experience. He

knows, in his life as a Christian, that Christ is not a figure in the past who is growing ever more remote, but is with him now as a living presence. But he feels it necessary to discover a rational ground for this certainty of faith. He is a Hellenist, writing for his fellow-Christians in the Gentile world. Although he speaks of the Jews disparagingly, as a nation now rejected by God, he was probably himself a Jew, and again and again betrays his Jewish sympathies, declaring proudly that "salvation is of the Jews." *
He is careful to distinguish between the unbelieving nation and those who like Nathanael and Nicodemus, were "Israelites indeed." † But while a Jew he was one of those liberal and intellectual Jews of the Dispersion who had gone for their training, not to the Rabbinical schools but to Greek philosophy. Whether he was directly acquainted with the work of Philo it is difficult to say. In some of his main conceptions he is at one with Philo, and constantly makes use of terms and phrases which can be found in the Philonic writings.‡ All this, however may have come to him by indirect channels, and the differences between his thought and that of Philo are no less marked than the agreements. This is especially noticeable in his fundamental doctrine of the Logos, which for his mind is not so much the divine Reason as an energy which proceeds from God, and is possessed, moreover, of a personality, which became incarnate in Christ. But whatever he may have known of the Alexandrian teaching he was a Hellenist, and the Hellenistic mode of thought was natural to him. Attempts have been made to detach the Prologue of his Gospel from the work as a whole, and to show that it was prefixed by an afterthought, to commend this Christian writing to a philosophical public; but such a theory cannot for a moment be accepted.

* Jn. 4:22.
† Jn. 1:47.
‡ His indebtedness to Philo is discussed most fully by J. Grill: *Untersuchungen über die Entstchung des vierten Evangeliums.*

The term "Logos" does not indeed recur after the Prologue, and could not rightly do so when the pre-existent Logos had become man in Christ. But the Gospel in its whole extent is saturated with the ideas set forth in the opening verses, and cannot be read intelligently apart from them. They have no other purpose than to supply the key to everything that follows.

The Evangelist, then, is a Hellenist, who cannot but think in the Hellenistic way. He does not try, by a deliberate effort, to put himself at a philosophical point of view and so re-interpret the gospel. He has the Hellenistic mind, to which a philosophical outlook is natural, and as he takes hold of the Christian ideas they pass through a medium which colours them. Most likely he was unaware that his position was substantially different from that of the church before him. Attention has often been called, in recent years, to the contradictions which are encountered at every turn in the Fourth Gospel. Primitive conceptions of the Messiah, the Resurrection, the Parousia, intrude on the writer's own thinking, and cannot be reconciled with it. The theory has thus gained ground that what we possess is a work in which several authors, differing widely in their theology, have all had a hand. But this apparently composite character of the Gospel may rather be taken as evidence that the writer had never consciously broken with the traditional teaching. Like a man to whom two languages are equally familiar he slips at times out of one idiom into another without knowing. To us, as we compare him with those who went before, he appears an innovator, but this was far from his own intention. He simply looks at the Gospel history with Hellenistic eyes and sees the same objects as his predecessors, but sees them differently.

What is really new in the Gospel is the effort to combine the recorded history with that which had followed it. Jesus had lived and died, but through death he had passed into a larger life, and is present always and everywhere to those who believe in him. He is the same now as he was on earth, and in the light of his earthly life we can know him as he still manifests himself in the communion of faith. How was it possible that the earthly history could thus renew itself and continue for ever? To answer this question John falls back on the philosophical doctrine of the Logos which had already found its way into Christian thought, and which he adopts without explanation, as one with which his readers would be already familiar. God is himself transcendent, but within the being of God there is a second divine principle which goes forth from him, and by which he effects his work of creation and revelation. A man projects himself in his word, which has a life apart from him, and which yet carries with it his personality. When we speak of Shakespeare we think at once of a man, who is remote from our knowledge, and of a body of writings which we still possess. These two are altogether distinct, but the man expressed himself in his word; through the word we apprehend what was most intimate in the soul of the man. So the Word was with God and was divine. It became flesh in Christ, but although he was a man like others, he shared in the nature of God, and in their vision of him men beheld God's glory. They now see him no more, but since he is one with the eternal Word he lives on, and abides with us, and in fellowship with him we lay hold of God.

John thus explains the Person of Christ by means of his Logos theory, and in like manner he explains his gift to men. "In him was life," and he came that we might participate in this life. For the Greek mind, as we have seen already, man's primal calamity was to be born man. Whatever may be his virtue or his wisdom he belongs to the earthly order, and is therefore subject to error and weakness and mortality. His one desire is to escape from his human bondage and share in the divine nature, which alone can

make him free and blessed. How can this miracle be wrought in
him? Only in one way. He must enter into union with a divine
being, whose life will be transfused into his own, and so change
it from its original quality. This was the meaning of the secret
rites performed in the Mysteries; and this, as John sees it, was
the purpose of Christ's coming. He was the Logos which had
been from the beginning with God. He had appeared on earth
and had made himself one with man, so that men might receive
that divine life which dwelt in him. One thinks of the theory,
advanced by some men of science towards the end of last century, that the germ of life was first brought to this planet in a
meteor which fell from some remote world. The mysterious po-
tency could never have arisen out of any force or substance
which exists on earth, and could only have come as a gift from
somewhere beyond. John held a theory not dissimilar to this one.
The higher life had nothing in common with anything that we
know in our own world, and by no possibility could it have sprung
up of itself. It was the life of God, and man could only receive
it by God's direct gift. Christ, as the Logos, was one in nature
with God, and had entered this world, and allied himself with
our humanity. In him was life, and by fellowship with him we
obtain life. To use John's own analogy he is the Vine and we the
branches, which draw into them the life of the vine.

The Logos doctrine is wonderfully fitted to the Evangelist's
purpose. By means of it he is able to secure a rational basis for
his religious belief. He can explain how God had manifested
himself in Christ, how Christ had brought a new life, and had
continued to dwell with men and to bring them into union with
himself and with God. Ever since the Gospel was written the
church has rested its theology on the Logos doctrine, and has not
done so from mere deference to a tradition. The doctrine has survived because it has proved necessary to any philosophical ac-

count of the Christian faith. All thinkers find themselves compelled in the end to fall back upon it, however they may disguise it under modern forms. If Christ has brought a divine revelation he must in some sense have been the Word, the self-expression of God. Nevertheless the doctrine is beset with grave difficulties, which are fully apparent in the Fourth Gospel itself. For one thing, it tends to change the Christian religion into a metaphysic. All stress is laid on the abstract being of God, and his love, mercy, forgiveness,—those very attributes of God which Christ came to reveal—fall out of sight. Christ himself, viewed simply as the Logos, loses his humanity and becomes the colourless medium of the divine essence. For centuries the church was distracted by dreary controversies as to whether the Son was of one substance with the Father, and as to the precise manner in which two natures were blended in one Person. The whole mind of Christian men was occupied with these fruitless speculations, which were supposed to deal with the inmost mysteries of religion, and the only result was to empty religion of its true meaning. Eastern Christianity in the seventh century went down before Islam with scarcely any resistance; and the ultimate reason was that Islam was more of a religion than the abstract creed into which the Christian message had evaporated. Even in the Fourth Gospel we cannot but feel at times that the religious interest is submerged in the metaphysical. For chapters together Jesus is made to confined himself to vague assertions of his divine nature, and we long for one of those Synoptic sayings or parables which convince us, without his telling, that his nature is indeed divine. Throughout the Gospel, as every one has felt, there is a dearth of ethical teaching. The Evangelist is certainly alive to the moral demands of Christianity, and in the First Epistle he dwells on them almost exclusively. Here and there in the Gospel itself his feeling for the Christian ethic finds exquisite utterance. Yet for the most part he is compelled by the exigencies of his metaphysic to avoid any practical teaching. His one anxiety is to proclaim a new life which is of different quality from that of the flesh.

Here we can perceive the inadequacy of a religion which is founded on Logos speculation. Its whole aim is to demonstrate that through Christ we exchange the earthly for the divine nature, but in the end it offers us, under the name of the spiritual life, one that is semi-physical. The new life is made to consist, not in love and goodness and holiness, but in some kind of ethereal substance, which passes from the higher state of being into the human. A different life-principle is infused into man's nature, and this can be effected only by some magical process. Men are born again by water and the Spirit,—the Spirit finding entrance through the material water of baptism. They must eat the flesh of Christ and drink his blood, for the new life is an essence which resided in the Person of Christ, and is given us in the sacramental elements which represent his body. John is indeed far removed from the later materialistic doctrines which made everything depend on the efficacy of outward rites. He can say, "It is the Spirit that quickeneth, the flesh profiteth nothing." ¶ Nevertheless he is haunted by the thought that the Christian salvation is in some way bound up with physical means, and in view of his philosophical assumptions he cannot think otherwise. Life is an essence quite apart, in itself, from all moral qualities in which it is manifested. It cannot be attained by faith alone, or by following in the way of Christ. The mysterious substance in which it resides must be transferred from him who possesses it to those in whom it is wanting, and this can only be done by some direct contact, as when one candle is lighted from another. Spirit, as interpreted by Logos theory, becomes little else than an ether or energy which is still material.

¶ Jn. 6:63.

John seeks to explain the Christian message metaphysically, and it cannot be so explained. His Logos conception, taken over from an ancient philosophy, is open to many criticisms, even from a metaphysical point of view. For these reasons it has sometimes been concluded that his whole interpretaion falls to the ground. No one can deny that by means of it he gives expression to some profound religious truths, but his interest, we are told, was more intellectual than religious. As an interpreter of the Christian message he has failed. This view, however, is based on a complete misunderstanding of the nature of his Gospel. Its author was indeed known pre-eminently, from a very early time, as "John the Theologian," and this title is still prefixed to his work in our copies of the New Testament. But it is used in its original sense of one conversant with divine things, and applies not so much to the doctrines taught as to the spiritual insight which lies behind them. John himself was probably unconscious that he was a theologian. As a Hellenist he thought naturally in terms of certain ideas which he took for granted. Earlier teachers had conceived of the work of Jesus apocalyptically, for this was the tradition in which they had been trained. John thinks of it metaphysically, and so tries to make it more intelligible to himself and to his Hellenistic readers. As we now study his Gospel it seems to be involved in a theology which has been laboriously worked out, and ingeniously applied to the Christian facts; but the author himself was unconscious of any such effort. He understood the message, and could not do otherwise, through the medium of those ideas which belonged to the whole texture of his thinking. To-day we are scientifically minded. Our religious faith is combined with a belief in the new physics and astronomy, in the theory of evolution, in the results of social and psychological enquiry. This is the pattern of the world given us in our modern culture, and our religion is adjusted to it, and does not thereby lose its intrinsic quality as religion. The Evangelist lived in an age which was philosophically minded. He accepted, as a matter of course, that view of the world which commended itself to all intelligent men, and his religious thinking fitted itself into that context. All the time his primary concern was with his religion, not with its forms of expression.

One cannot but feel that much of the modern discussion of the Fourth Gospel begins at the wrong end, and for this reason goes hopelessly wrong in its conclusions. It is taken for granted that John first of all thought out a system of theology. By diligent reading of Philo and study of current theory and speculation he formed for himself a doctrine of God and his relation to the world. Then he took the Christian message and tried to adapt it to this philosophical frame-work. He could not do so without a great deal of re-adjustment. The whole Gospel history had to be taken to pieces and reconstructed; the ethical conception of the Christian life had to be changed into a mystical or metaphysical one. But he persevered in his effort, and finally produced a work in which his Christian faith was more or less harmonised with his theology. Is it not possible that this account of the Gospel ought to be reversed? John starts from his Christian beliefs and his Christian experiences. This, indeed, can hardly be doubted by any one who reads the First Epistle of John, where the emphasis is always laid on immediate religious knowledge. "That which we have heard and seen and our hands have handled of the word of life declare we unto you, that ye also may have fellowship with us." [§] Throughout the Gospel there is the same underlying emphasis. Instead of argument we have the ever-recurring affirmation, "we know," "we believe." This is the Evangelist's starting-point. He is conscious of a new life that has sprung up in him through his faith in Christ, and he cannot doubt that it has been planted

§ I Jn. 1:3.

in him by God. By his theology he seeks only to find some explanation for the religious fact.

The motive of the Gospel is summed up explicitly in the concluding words: "These things were written that ye may believe that Jesus is the Christ, the Son of God, and that believing ye might have life through his name." * The writer's one intention is to bring home to men the significance of Christ, and so enable them to receive his gift. The Gospel is marked everywhere by a profound sincerity. It is written in the simplest possible language, and keeps ringing the changes on a few cardinal ideas. This has sometimes been set down, with a strange perversity, to intellectual barrenness. The writer, we are told, has very little to say, and wearies us by his monotonous insistence on the same thoughts, hardly troubling, for the most part, to repeat them in different words. But the natural explanation is surely that he is intensely in earnest. These are the truths he lives by, and he cannot dwell on them too much. May we not say, too, that this is the true explanation of that mode of thought which we now call theological? Here is a man who believes with his whole heart in the Christian message. He cannot but try to understand it in the manner that is most real to him and to harmonise it with his view of the world. This has been the instinct of the sincerest Christians in all ages. They cannot merely repeat ancient phrases and subscribe to creeds which have obviously become outworn. They try to apprehend each belief in its essential meaning, and put it into their own language, and integrate it with the life and thought of their time. The truth does not rightly come home to them, they cannot honestly live by it, until they have thus expressed it in the forms most real to themselves. This is the position of the Fourth Evangelist. He has no quarrel with the traditional faith, and does not wish to change it into something different. Neither does he

* Jn. 20:31.

make any deliberate effort to conform it to the Hellenistic modes of thinking. But he is himself a Hellenist, and apocalyptic ideas were not congenial to him as they were to Palestinian Jews. He replaces them with others which come nearer to his own convictions. The theology of the Gospel must be explained in the last resort from the writer's feeling for reality. He had a faith which had grown out of his own heartfelt experience, and when he gave it utterance he could not employ conventional forms which had ceased to be vital to him. He described the things that meant most to him in terms of his own habitual thought, which was that of a Hellenist of Asia Minor. We misunderstand him altogether when we think of him as chiefly concerned with his metaphysic, and as forcing his beliefs into this artificial frame. His whole effort is to state the Christian message in such a way that he could honestly believe it. There might be nothing wrong with the old presentation, but he could only accept it on the word of others. What was the meaning of the message when he looked at it with his own eyes?

In his doctrine of the Spirit he declares, almost in so many words, that this was his position. Christ had told his disciples that although he must depart he would send them the Spirit, which would be like his other self. It would take his life as it had been, and keep his people mindful of it, and disclose the meaning of things they had been unable, at the time, to understand. Not only so, but it would bring new revelations. Jesus, while on earth, had delivered his message only in part, but the Spirit would continue to speak for him and would teach men, as time went on, to apprehend the truth more fully and in new ways. John believes that he is himself an instrument of the Spirit, and in this conviction he writes his Gospel. He is aware that in some respects he may appear to speak differently from those before him, but this is only because he follows the guidance of the Spirit as it is active now.

The earlier teachers had been of their own age; he belongs to another, and is working among Christians of a different culture. The message is the same as it has always been, but the Spirit now reveals it in other aspects and by other modes of knowledge. Nothing was further from John's intention than to lay down doctrines which were henceforth to be accepted as final. He was the vehicle by which the Spirit conveyed the truth in his own particular time. His task was to discover what Christ meant for men now, and so to utter his thought with perfect sincerity. If he could have known that a time was coming when much of his theology would appear doubtful, and when his Logos doctrine would be more of a problem than a help, he would not have been greatly disturbed, or have tried to revise his thinking. He would have said, "The Spirit leads to all truth, and in every age it leads by a new road. For the thought of men in the future I am not responsible; they must wait on the Spirit, as I have done, and follow its guidance. The paths are many, and are always diverging, but the truth they lead to remains the same."

So the Gospel is not to be regarded as a theological tract, written in the interest of a given theory. The theory is incidental and the writer is always concerned with a fact, or rather with two great facts, both of which he desires to affirm more clearly and to link together.

On the one hand, he is occupied with the actual life of Jesus, which heretical teachers had dissolved into myth and illusion. This life had been recorded in previous Gospels, but he was plainly dissatisfied with them, or he would not have felt the need of writing another. They had confined themselves to what had literally happened, and had failed to suggest the inward and permanent significance of this outward history. John deals with the events, and insists no less than the other evangelists on their historical character, but he seeks to penetrate through the surface to their deeper import. To his mind, as he himself indicates, they were of the nature of "parables," [†] and he so recounts them as to bring out the truth conveyed by them. In like manner he seeks to impress on us the true nature of Jesus' personality. To casual onlookers he was a man like others. To his own disciples he was a revered Master, a Prophet sent by God, perhaps the very Messiah. But what was he in his ultimate being? Why had he appeared on earth? John introduces into his story a "Beloved Disciple,"—one who stood nearer to Jesus than the rest, and was able to enter into sympathy with his deeper mind. It may be that this disciple is vaguely identified with one of the Twelve, or perhaps he is only an ideal figure. The Evangelist feels that among the actual associates of Jesus there was none who rightly understood him, and asks himself how he would have appeared to one who had the necessary gift of insight. The whole Gospel, it may be said, is the story of Jesus as seen by this Beloved Disciple. The Word was made flesh; Jesus once sojourned with men and the facts recorded of him are true. But they have value only when we apprehend them as that disciple did. We require to see that in all his words and actions Jesus manifested the glory of God. Appearing on this earth he brought us the vision of that higher world, to which all the time he belonged. John does not wilfully distort the life of Jesus, or obscure its human reality. His one object is to make it still more real by insisting on the divine significance which was the essential element in the facts.

On the other hand, he always keeps before him the continuing life of Jesus. Here also he starts from a fact, just as real to him as the earthly history. He believes that Christ had departed only to return to those who loved him, and this belief is not derived from any theory that being one with the eternal Logos he must live on for ever. The Evangelist had known for himself the

[†] Jn. 16:29.

presence of Christ; he had heard him speaking and had seen him do mightier works than in his lifetime. We can make little of the Fourth Gospel unless we find in it the transcript of a personal experience. Here is a man who does not depend on any tradition or doctrine but who speaks of what his hands have handled, and who tries to make real to others what was intensely real to himself. It is this knowledge of Christ in the present which convinces him that the past history must also be true. The facts which he has found in the record are all of a piece with the facts he directly knows.

The aim of the Gospel is thus to bring the two histories together, and to show how they are related. To understand the earthly life of Jesus it must be compared with that which is still manifest. To understand what Christ is in the present we must go back to what he was on earth. John lived at a time when many strange constructions were placed on the Christian message. Then, as now, there were many voices, each of which professed to be that of Christ, and in this confusion of voices it seemed impossible to distinguish the true one. John points his readers to one sure criterion. They can look back on the recorded life, and by this knowledge of what Christ was they can recognise him as he still lives invisibly. It cannot be affirmed too strongly that John does not treat the historical facts as mere raw material, which he modifies at his pleasure in the interest of certain doctrines. The truth of the history is vital to his purpose, for he thinks of one indivisible life of Christ. All that he knows in the present has its guarantee in the past, and the inward fellowship with Christ is real because Christ once lived in the flesh. It may be granted that the Fourth Gospel is much more than a history. It is not written, like the Gospel of Luke, that its readers may know the facts more fully and accurately,[‡] but that they may believe in

§ Lk. 1 : 4.

Christ and believing may have life through his name. But this life-giving faith is imparted by a record of the facts, viewed in the light of their inner significance.

Everything else in the Gospel is subordinate to the religious interest. The writer indeed employs the language of theology, and of a theology which we now associate with a bygone phase of thought. Christ is identified with the Logos of Greek specula-tion. The life he bestows is conceived metaphysically, as a prin-ciple inherent in the divine nature, over against the earthly. It might appear as if the Evangelist moved in a world of abstrac-tions, which have little to do with the realities of the Christian message. Yet the motive is everywhere a religious one. However he expresses himself John is filled with the one desire that men should receive that life which was in Christ. He feels profoundly that life can only proceed from life, and that men can obtain it only as they apprehend Christ as a living Person. "In him was life,"—not merely in the things he taught but in himself, as he appeared on earth, full of grace and truth. How can we know him still as an actual presence, so that the life he possesses may become ours? This, for John, is the supreme question of Chris-tianity. He seeks to answer it in his twofold history of a life once lived but ever repeating itself in the experience of faith.

To the religious aim all the rest is secondary. John was a Hel-lenistic teacher, and his theology was only his mode of giving utterance, in the language of his own age and culture, to the truth which had come to him religiously. His theology may be left en-tirely out of sight, and his Gospel will still disclose its essential meaning. Millions have so read it in all ages. They have never suspected the many critical problems involved in it. They have not been aware that it contained any philosophical doctrine. All that they found in it was a sublime picture of Jesus as he once lived, and as he lives still in the fellowship of those who love him. It is perhaps those simple readers who have understood the Gospel best, for they have been content to read it as the writer himself intended. He had little interest in theological doctrine for its own sake. His one aim was to explain to himself the life of Jesus, and he therefore looked at it with his own eyes, in the light of those conceptions which were most natural to a thinker of his place and time. We can now recognise that his vision was coloured by the medium through which he looked, but what he saw he has recorded faithfully. He has imparted to all Christians his own knowledge of that enduring life of Christ, which is one with his life on earth.

CHAPTER X

THE RISE OF A COMMON RELIGION

IF SOME impartial observer towards the end of the first century had been asked to forecast the future of Christianity, he would probably have said that it could not survive as a separate religion. He would have pointed out that the Christians, although their number was always growing, had broken up into various sects, which in course of time would drift ever further apart. Some of them would merge eventually in the older cults which had come in from the East; some would join hands with one or other of the philosophical schools; some would lapse back into Judaism. For Christianity as such there could be no future. It was not allied with any stable nationality; it rested on a few visionary beliefs which could not be reduced to any definite statement. Many of the Christian ideas were no doubt valuable, and would permanently enrich the world's thinking; but the religion in itself was only one of the short-lived fanaticisms which rise up suddenly out of nothing, and then fall to pieces of their own accord.

The Christians themselves were haunted by the fear of dissolution. Paul has occasion, in almost all his letters, to warn his churches against their fatal tendency to divide. He tries, by every means he can think of, to promote a sense of brotherhood, and to remove at the very outset every misunderstanding which might lead to dissension. He keeps a watchful eye even on private quarrels, knowing that some graver conflict may grow out of them. In the later New Testament writings this fear of division becomes ever more apparent. Heresies are condemned, not so

much because they are erroneous as because they draw the
brethren into opposing camps. In the culminating chapter of the
Fourth Gospel Jesus makes intercession for those who will hereafter believe on him, and prays above all else "that they may be
one." * He has no anxiety about the continuance of his church,
but will it preserve its unity? We are made to understand that
here lies the future danger.

Such fears were amply justified, and for a long time there was
a very real possibility that in the strife of parties the religion itself
might be lost. Yet it may be fairly argued that too much emphasis is laid in the New Testament on the need for unity. The writers fail to realise, as we can now do, that the divisions which they
deplore were the best evidence of the vitality of the message. Men
could not agree as to its meaning because it was so many-sided.
Their ideas about it were always changing because it was infinitely
fruitful, and could not but unfold itself and grow, in spite of all
efforts to keep it fixed. What seemed at the time to be the chief
weakness of the religion was in reality its strength. As we compare the various writings of the New Testament we can see that
any unifying of the faith in those early days would have been
nothing less than a disaster, but fortunately there was not yet an
official church which could enforce its authority. The various
teachers were left to themselves, each of them free to think out
the gospel in his own way, even if it might be a mistaken one.
To this freedom we owe the New Testament, which pleads so
eloquently for Christian unity and is yet the standing example of
that diversity without which our religion cannot truly be itself.

Throughout the first century the movement was all towards
division, and it might seem, disintegration; then this movement
was reversed. Parties that were bitterly opposed began to approach one another; conflicting theologies gradually drew together; out of the antagonisms of the earlier period there emerged

* Jn. 17:21.

a uniform church. It is hard at first sight to account for this change of attitude, which cannot be set down to any specific cause. A number of forces were working together, some from within and some from without, and by their combined action produced the movement towards unity.

Much was due to the mere lapse of time, and the passing from the scene of men who had been storm-centres of controversy. A reaction always follows a period of conflict, and to this fact the world has owed its occasional brief intervals of peace. Old leaders disappear, and the passions they have aroused cannot be kept alive after they go. Their followers begin to wonder whether all the turmoil has been necessary. They realise that whatever happens they and their opponents will have to live together, and that each side must be willing to give up something. A state of war cannot go on perpetually. It was towards the end of the first century that the church arrived at this condition in which all parties were anxious for some mutual understanding.

Along with the healing effect of time there was a closing of the ranks under stress of persecution. By the success of its mission the church had brought on itself the jealousy of the Roman government, which knew nothing of the inner divisions and put all who called themselves Christians under the same ban. Whether they would or not they had now to hold together. Their differences became of little moment in the face of the common danger. This outward pressure did more to consolidate the church than all the pleadings of its teachers. Side-issues were forgotten, and Christians became aware, as never before, of the fundamental truths on which they were all agreed. The author of I Peter writes from Rome "to the elect sojourners in Pontus, Galatia, Cappadocia, Asia and Bithynia," [†] in order to encourage them and confirm them in the faith. They are far distant from him, and he knows nothing about them except that they are fellow-Christians, ex-

† I Pet. 1:1.

posed to the same peril as himself, This, however, is enough, and he exhorts them to remain stedfast to the common cause.

The outward danger was coincident with another, very different in character. Ever since the beginning of the Gentile mission the church had been infected with false doctrines. They were known to be working mischief, and it was the duty of all good teachers to refute and condemn them; but the heretics were still regarded as Christian brethren, who had received the Spirit, and with it the right to liberty. This tolerance gave place in the next generation to open hostility. The heretics were excluded from the church, and had themselves no desire to remain in it. On both sides it was recognised that the strange beliefs were no mere eccentricities, but marked a new type of religion, which was opposed to Christianity although it availed itself in some measure of Christian beliefs. For a considerable time there was a real danger that the Gnostic heresy might supplant the church, and provide a bridge whereby Gentile converts might insensibly return to Paganism. Some limit had therefore to be imposed on the freedom of the Spirit. It was no longer sufficient that converts should be admitted into the church on the vague confession, "Jesus is Lord." They were required to state definitely in what sense they understood the confession, and thus to mark themselves off from the false brethren. The Gnostic movement which had threatened to break up the church became, in this manner, the most potent means for securing its unity. In view of the insidious opposition all the lines of belief were more firmly drawn. The fear of disruption which had hung over the early teachers was now removed, and the church was ready to march forward as a single brotherhood.

It would be wrong, however, to think of the unity as due to nothing more than accidental causes. This is the view too often taken by church historians, and it has distorted our whole conception of the early development, and of the nature of the church itself. We can perceive, when we look more closely, that external forces served only to bring into action a unity which had always existed, although Christians themselves had been barely conscious of it. Not only so, but we can see that the divisions, which had apparently been rending the church to pieces, had all the time been working towards an opposite effect. Teachers had been left free to proclaim the gospel, each in the manner he thought best. They had come to it with their individual minds, with ideas impressed on them by their previous training and their personal experiences, with the result that they differed widely in their modes of interpretation. It seemed as if they were separating the church into parties, which would shortly destroy each other; but along their diverging paths they were making for a common centre, and a time came when they were able to clasp hands. This in the end is always the outcome of honest controversy. There is a truth somewhere, and all sincere men are trying to find it, and their several opinions, however much they may vary, are pointing in the same direction. So we are not to think of those differences in the early church as mere contradictions which were finally patched up by a series of compromises, in which the real issues were cunningly disguised. The uniformity which was at last achieved was a genuine recognition that all parties had been in the right. By their divisions they had affirmed the truth in all its different aspects, and to that extent had been helping each other. The unity of the church had never been in danger. All Christians had been at one in their central convictions, and had gradually been learning, through the conflict of opinion, what they really believed.

We have clear evidence, in the later New Testament books, of this movement through difference to a common faith. The writers tend more and more to adjust their particular views to others of a contrary tenor, and they do so, not by way of concession, but with a real perception that the varying opinions all have their place. Many theories have been put forward to account for the seeming contradictions in the Gospel of Matthew, the book of Acts, the Gospel and Epistles of John. It is held that each writer, while holding a position of his own, has clung to some fragments of bygone thinking, or that his work has been edited and interpolated, or that documents by different hands have been pieced together. Such theories must be allowed their due weight. The early writings were the property of the church, which employed them in its public worship, and felt itself at full liberty to correct them and adapt them to its purposes. The writers themselves were practical missionaries, whose object was much more to commend the Christian message than to work out some view of their own with logical consistency. But the more comprehensive character of the later writings has chiefly to be explained from a new disposition of mind. Christian teachers no longer desired to form parties. Whatever might be their theological bias they were willing to consider other men's views, and to include them, as far as possible, in their own. They had grown aware that the message was large enough to admit of many interpretations. They had also learned to see that amidst all varieties of doctrine there were some things which remained constant, and must therefore be of the very substance of the Christian faith. Believers might think differently of the nature of Christ, but they all knew him as the Saviour; they trusted the God whom he had revealed; they sought in their manner of life to follow him. All the strife and debate had served only to throw a stronger emphasis on these essential elements of the gospel.

It need not be supposed that the later teachers set themselves deliberately to reconcile varying types of belief for the sake of church unity. This view has found favour with many scholars, who have held that in the whole development after Paul's death there was something artificial, and not entirely honest. The church, we are told, was seeking to maintain itself amidst increasing difficulties, and everything else was subordinated to this one aim. It was no longer advisable to encourage freedom of opinion. If the church was to hold together it had to devise some formula on which all should agree, and this could only be done by a method of compromise. Writings were therefore produced in which a balance was struck between opposing doctrines. The aim of Christian thinking was not so much to arrive at the truth as to present the message in such a form that every party could feel satisfied. This effort, begun in the New Testament and continued during the centuries that followed, had its issue in a theology which was little more than an ingenious mechanism, so contrived that all the pieces were carefully fitted into each other. Such a reading of the history is a mere travesty of the facts. Unity was not achieved by artful compromises, made necessary by the pressure of outward forces. These forces indeed counted for much, but they only compelled men to see what already existed. In its deeper interests the church had always been one, and now it was made to realise that these interests were more important than any others. It learned to concentrate on what was vitally Christian, leaving the debatable matters to settle themselves. In the religious history of our own time we have a clear illustration of what happened in the early period. On all sides the sectarian barriers have been steadily breaking down. Churches that were separated last century by differences which appeared unsurmountable are coming to draw together, or have been already united. It is not that the controversial questions have now been answered, or that they have been slurred over by some doubtful compromise. The questions are still there, for any one who cares to trouble about them, but of their own accord they have fallen into the background. Everywhere the church is confronted with purely Pagan conceptions of life; it has grown conscious, as never before, of the nature and the incomparable value of the Christian demands. The battle is now for Christianity, not for some one variety of it as against another. So it is now perceived that the old religious leaders, whose names were once the war-cries of division, were serving under the same banner. They seemed to be working against each other, but were fellow-labourers, and the ideas they advocated are no longer sectional but are part of the common Christian inheritance. We would refuse to admit that in this modern movement towards unity there is any make-believe, or any unworthy concession to outward danger. The danger has only driven the church back on a faith and a brotherhood in which it has always been rooted. So in the early period the process which led to unity was a natural and unconscious one. Christian teachers did not try, of set purpose, to adjust their views to those of others; for of this there was no need. They were now concerned with no special doctrines but with the great Christian interests which were struggling to survive. Under these conditions it was possible for opposing parties to make room for opinions which hitherto they had warmly contested. Lines of partition within the church grew ever fainter, and different types of belief were interwoven. The one aim now was to find the solid ground on which all Christians could stand together.

In the later New Testament books we have a record of the several phases in the progress towards a common religion. Nothing at first was attempted but a union of two different modes of thought, without regard to seeming contradiction. Of this we have the most striking example in the Gospel of Matthew. It originated, most probably, in the church at Antioch, which was made up of Jews and Gentiles in almost equal numbers, and a place is given to both their modes of interpreting the message. The Jewish party held fast to the Law, the Gentiles discarded it, and Matthew accepts both positions as valid. Paul had held that those who adhered to the Law had fallen from grace, but this, as Matthew saw it, was obviously not true. He knew of those in both camps whom Christ would gladly acknowledge as his servants, and he addresses his Gospel to both alike. Sayings of Jesus are recorded which upheld the Law, along with others in which it is set aside. There is no attempt to harmonise those opposite groups of sayings. Both judgments are allowed to stand side by side,—to the perplexity of later commentators, who have never been able to determine whether this is a Jewish or a Gentile book. But it is not intended to be either. Christianity for Matthew does not consist in any given attitude to the Law. He is content to write a Gospel in which both views are fairly represented, and leaves his readers to decide between them, with the suggestion that either of them may be right, or both together. All that matters is to follow the teaching of Jesus, with or without the Law.

An advance on this method may be discerned in the book of Acts, and likewise in the Epistle to the Hebrews. In these writings there is no mere conjunction of the earlier type of belief with the later. The Gentile interpretation has now been frankly accepted, so much so that the question of the Law falls almost out of sight. But a place is still reserved for the older tradition. The writer to Hebrews, while he works with ideas derived from Greek philosophy, takes over the primitive hopes in their most literal form. He thinks of Christ not only as the Logos, but as the Messiah who will presently appear in glory, and gather his servants into a new Jerusalem. These, for the writer, are not merely popular beliefs in which he acquiesces but to which he has ceased to attach any serious meaning. Although he has passed into a different world of thought he remains faithful to the early tradition, and uses it to supply the chief motive for his practical appeal. Two modes of understanding the gospel are equally real to him; and instead of trying to reconcile them he lets them stand together in his mind. Such an attitude need not perplex us, for it is that of most thoughtful Christians at the present day. They are open to the new knowledge, and would define their Christianity in terms which would not have been intelligible to the founders of the churches in which they worship. Nevertheless they adhere, in all sincerity, to those churches. Far more than they ever realise they still hold the beliefs of their fathers, and in this there is no inconsistency, or if there is, it must be blamed on the nature of things. A truth by which you live cannot be summed up in a clear-cut formula, like one of mathematics. It may be stated in new terms, more satisfying than the old, but you always feel that in the old statement also there was something valuable, which must not be left out. At the risk of contradicting itself the mind holds to both together.

Unlike the writer to Hebrews, Luke seeks in the book of Acts to mediate between the Jewish and Gentile positions. His method is to remove, as far as possible, all traces of the conflict which had accompanied the early mission. He makes out that Paul and the other Apostles had worked together harmoniously, and that any misunderstandings which arose were entirely due to the malice of "false brethren." Luke must not be accused, as he has sometimes been, of wilfully misrepresenting the early history. He wrote, it must be remembered, after a considerable interval, when events had fallen into perspective, and old quarrels could be viewed in a softer light. He honestly admires all the great men whom he commemorates, and cannot admit that there was anything questionable in their relations to one another. Moreover he is no theologian, and has little interest in the points at issue between Paul and the earlier teachers; whether he understood them is more than doubtful. He responds with his whole heart to the message which has brought joy, courage, brotherhood, healing, liberty, but does not try to explain it in terms of doctrine. At the time he wrote, too, the church was in no mood to recall the old dissensions. The great period of missionary expansion had set in, and Christians were proud of their wonderful achievement, and wished to know more of the men who had made it possible. Paul and his fellow-workers may have had their differences, for this was only human nature; but how had they accomplished so much? What was the power which had sustained them? What were the aims and convictions which they all had in common? Luke sets himself to answer these questions, and if he had enlarged on the various disputes he would only have confused and repelled his readers. His aim is to concentrate their minds on the gospel itself. It is a divine message, which transcends all interpretations that may be placed on it from time to time, and though the Apostles differed they were all proclaiming the same faith. They had contributed, each in his own way, to the building up of the one church, which was now offering a new life to all mankind.

A further step is taken in the Fourth Gospel. Here, too, the writer is at no pains to be consistent, and introduces fragments of earlier doctrine which cannot be harmonised with his thought as a whole. Nevertheless he makes a real effort to merge all previous interpretations in a new and higher one. Previous teachers had been aiming, from their several points of view, at an ultimate truth; might it not be so presented that Christians of every party would recognise the object of their quest? It was not enough that the different types of faith should be simply conjoined. They needed to be melted down and fused into a new one, which should contain them all and yet be something more. John was the first to attempt a statement of Christianity on which all believers might agree, and in one sense his undertaking was successful. Instead of the old conceptions which were bound up with a national tradition he made use of others which in their nature were universal. Christ was the light of the world. He came that he might give life. We find in him the revelation of God. These primary ideas of the Fourth Gospel are independent of all stated creeds, and devout souls everywhere and in all times have fallen back on them for the ultimate expression of their faith. John set himself to write a catholic Gospel for a catholic church, and he achieved his purpose. Yet he failed in so far as he rested his teaching on the philosophy of a particular age. Nothing might seem to be more comprehensive than his doctrine of the Logos, which was one with God, and therefore manifested Him once for all. But this doctrine was intelligible to none but Hellenistic thinkers like John himself, and to this extent he substituted one partial type of Christianity for others of the same kind. It soon became evident, indeed, that even for the Hellenistic mind his theology was inadequate, and in the generations that followed it gave rise to the countless schisms and controversies which fill the history of the Greek church. In some respects the interests of Christian unity were better served by the earlier teachers who admitted all the contradictions of doctrine, than by this Evangelist who sought to remove them.

A movement thus set in towards a uniform Christianity, and its progress can be clearly traced in the later writings of the New Testament. During the second century it acquired an ever greater momentum, until the church which had once consisted of many scattered communities, differing at almost every point of doctrine and practice, became a single organisation, the most compact and elaborate in the world. Its ideal was perfect unity, and this ideal seemed, at times, to be attained. Yet the unity always proved to be delusive. Beneath the common religion, enforced by outward authority, there continued to be the impulse towards division, and the impulse was often strongest when the church appeared to be most harmonious. The New Testament is in this respect a prophetic book. We think of it as preserving for all times the example of primitive days, when all believers were of one mind, and no dubiety had yet arisen as to the meaning of the gospel. But as we examine it more closely we can see in the New Testament a forecast of what our religion was always to be. Within that century at the beginning the church passed through the experience which was to repeat itself, ever and again, in the course of its later history. The New Testament might almost be regarded as a Sibylline book, which the church may consult in every emergency, and so learn beforehand what the issue will be. In that first age the church was divided, as it is now, and the New Testament is in great measure the record of its divisions, and without them would never have come into being. It does not speak for an ideal, harmonious church, such as we dream of, but for a church that was constantly divided against itself, like that which we know.

The New Testament is not only prophetic of later divisions, but it foreshadows, in a remarkable way, how they would come about, and the character they would assume. In every age the church has been thrown into some struggle of which it had no previous warning. No one could have foreseen the barbarian invasions, the rise of Islam, the emergence of the new nations, the revival of learning, the birth of modern science, the social movements of our time. These all had far-reaching consequences for our religion, and produced types of faith which to all appearance were new. But human history keeps repeating itself, and the later events had all some kind of analogy in ancient times. The church of the first age had to face difficulties which were the same, in their intrinsic character, as those which it has encountered since, and their effect on religious thinking was not greatly different. In the New Testament we can discover some anticipation of almost all the later efforts to re-interpret the gospel. There were teachers who sought to reconcile their faith with the science and philosophy of the time; others who were mainly concerned with ethical and social problems; others who sought the truth by way of sacraments and mystical contemplation. The divisions in the early church followed much the same lines as in the later centuries and at the present day. Perhaps they have become more pronounced, and associated themselves with ideas and watch-words which were unknown in the ancient world; but the types of teaching which can be distinguished in the New Testament are those which are always re-appearing. They answer to differences in mind and outlook which have separated Christian thinkers in every age.

We can see further, as we study the New Testament, that the divisions were inherent in Christianity itself. Often they have been traced to accidental causes, but these served only to bring to the surface things that were already present in the religion. Paul and John, the authors of Hebrews and James and Revelation, all interpret the gospel differently, not because they read into it what was not there, but because they were able from their new points of view to see aspects of it which were hidden from the others. Their diverse interpretations are all valid, although they seem to be in mutual conflict. It has often been regarded as the fatal weakness of our religion that those who believe in it are so much at variance as to its import. They acknowledge the same Lord, but in their service of him they are always drifting apart. This is the reproach constantly thrown at them by the outside world, and the church itself bewails its unhappy divisions, as due to some disloyalty. The New Testament, as we have seen, is full of similar complaints. Then, as now, it was felt that Christianity was failing in its mission because those who professed it would not give up their differences and stand together as one. They proclaimed the truth in so many contrary ways that men were bewildered, and grew doubtful whether there was any truth. In one sense this has indeed been the weakness of Christianity. It has offered a confusion of voices instead of one clear call to which all men could respond. Yet the differences are inseparable from those attributes which mark it off from all other religions, and which make its greatness and its power.

For one thing, it is a universal religion,—the only one which has a message for all mankind. Because it is meant for all it cannot but be apprehended in an endless variety of ways. Men are all different, and cannot but see the truth with different eyes, and if Christianity were summed up in one uniform creed this would only mean that it was valid for one particular type of human beings. It has often been objected to our religion that while it proclaims human brotherhood its followers do not have that sense of identity which is produced by some other forms of faith. Islam, for instance, has more of a uniting force than Christianity, and has thereby resisted all efforts to overcome it. Those who accept that austerely simple religion can tell precisely what they believe, and are knit together like a single disciplined army, marching in step. Christians hold a faith so varied in its implications that they never can define it. They are always seeing it in some new light, and waste their energies in futile disputes with one another. This may be true, but it is also true that a religion like Islam has no variety of appeal. For people of a given race, at a certain stage of culture, it has a compelling force; to those outside of its own circle it has nothing to offer. So it is with all the non-Christian religions. In their varying degrees they are local and restricted. The unity they create is like that of patriotism, which must be exclusive before it can be really strong. Christianity is for all races and all types of mind. It makes men conscious, not of the things that separate them, but of those which they have in common, as spiritual beings. At the same time it awakens in them the sense of personality. Out of the mass of humanity it shapes individual men and women, who are known to God and must learn to serve him one by one. For this reason Christianity is the universal religion, but it also makes for apparent division. The unity at which it aims must be one of persons, each of them in full possession of his own mind and will.

Again, the divisions were the necessary consequence of the inherent richness of the Christian message. As we consider the various forms of teaching in the New Testament we cannot but feel that they were all inevitable. They were not forced into the original gospel but sprang out of it naturally. Different minds, striving to explain to themselves what Jesus had intended, could not but arrive at those diverse conceptions. At first sight nothing could appear more simple than the message of Jesus. It seems to be limited to a few almost self-evident truths, and in all times there have been those who rebelled against the complex theologies which have made it difficult. Again and again it has been summed up in a single formula. Jesus was a moralist, who sought to revive the ethical religion of the prophets. He was an enthusiast, fired with apocalyptic hopes. He was a social reformer, or a champion of the national cause. He was a mystic, absorbed wholly in his inward communion with God. Countless Lives of Jesus have been written in the last fifty years, and each writer has viewed the history in the light of some one conception, by which he tries to explain its whole significance. The effort is always to simplify what has been needlessly obscured by later tradition, but it has led to just the opposite result. The explanations are simple, and each of them as we read it may appear convincing, but they are all at variance. It may fairly be said that the modern attempt to get back from theology to objective fact has brought more confusion into Christian thinking than all the theologies. The fallacy of it lies in the assumption that there is somewhere a single key which will unlock the whole secret of Jesus. The truth is that he took hold of life on all its sides. His thought is made up of many elements, all of them blended so perfectly that they are lost in one another, as the mingling of all the colours results in white. Paul speaks of "the simplicity which is in Christ," but it must not be forgotten that he also speaks of the "fulness." This, indeed, is the thought to which he is always returning,—that in the gospel we have the sum of all wisdom and knowledge. "It pleased the Father that in him should all fulness dwell." ‡ Here we are to find the true reason why the message, from the first, was variously interpreted. Men perceived, as they began to reflect on it, that it had many meanings,—so many that they could not all be grasped together, and needed to be taken one by one, as if each part were the whole. We think of Jesus' teaching as simple, and that of the later theologians as complex, but the truth is the other way. Jesus was many-sided, and the aim of all subsequent thinkers was to elucidate what he taught. They found so much in him that they were obliged to take each element separately, and so presented the one gospel in many partial forms. This has always been the character of Christian thinking, and it cannot well be otherwise. There are many tracks through a forest, but the traveller must choose one of them, and he loses himself unless he keeps to this one and no other. Yet he must not claim that in so doing he has explored the whole forest. On either side of him there are vast regions, perhaps the best worth knowing, of which he has seen nothing. So the Christian religion is far greater than any one interpretation of it, though it is only by those limited apprehensions that it can be known at all.

Once more, the gospel contained in it a principle of growth. Its

‡ Col. 1 : 19, 20.

nature was such that it could not remain as it was at first, but was bound to unfold itself, and assume ever changing forms. This is the truth which the Fourth Evangelist seeks to convey by his doctrine of the Spirit. He conceives of Jesus, on the eve of his departure, as telling his disciples that instead of himself they will have with them the Spirit, which "will take the things that are mine and show them unto you." The future revelation will be the same as that which he gave in his lifetime, but it will come in a new manner and express itself in new ways, so that it will ever be fresh and living. John is doubtless thinking of how he had himself interpreted the message with the aid of Hellenistic ideas which were foreign to Jesus' own teaching. He is aware that many will object, as they read his work, "this is not the gospel as the older disciples taught it; you have re-cast and perverted it." He answers, "it is the same gospel, but it has renewed itself; Jesus is now speaking through the Spirit, in the language of this new age, in which his power is still working." The same idea is present in all the New Testament books, though it is not explicitly stated, as in the Fourth Gospel. Each of these teachers is addressing himself to a new time and a new circle of readers. His aim is to express the truth in such a manner as to give it meaning for the present. If it is to remain vital it must come to men in the form that is most real to them, in view of their actual circumstances and needs. This is how all true teachers have been dealing with it ever since. Often it has been maintained that if Christianity is indeed the absolute religion no change can be admissible. The doctrines we believe were laid down once for all, and must be preserved from age to age exactly as they were at first; otherwise there is no finality in our faith. But its finality consists in the very fact that it is capable of an endless renewal. While it remains in substance the same it clothes itself continually in new garments, so that it becomes a living part of every age. Its unchanging value depends on its capacity for infinite change. This must never be forgotten when we consider those divisions to which the church has ever been subject. We are wont to deplore them, and to long for the ideal church which will be perfectly united and built fixedly on the rock of faith. But what we call instability might be better described as growth and renewal. The message was never intended to be a merely static one. It has within it a principle of life, and life must preserve itself by throwing off old forms and vehicles as they become outworn. The divisions which have seemed from time to time to destroy the church are part of the life-process which keeps it secure.

Above all, where there was liberty there was sure to be division. Christians were set free from the old constraints. They could think of themselves as endowed with the Spirit, which directed them from within, and took the place of all other authority. Paul lays his finger on this, as the very mark of a Christian man,—that he is one whom Christ has made free. He is no longer in bondage to the Law, or to any custom or tradition, but determines his own action, under the guidance of the Spirit. "He that is spiritual judges all things, yet he himself is judged of no man." ¶ The church has never ventured to accept, in anything like its full extent, Paul's conception of Christian liberty. He was himself conscious that it was impracticable, and with all his insistence on the inward authority he took care to organise his churches under competent leadership, to lay down rules for moral behaviour, to remonstrate with men and women who presumed too much on their freedom. He recognised that although potentially they had entered on the new life his converts were still in the flesh, and must reckon with its frailties and errors. While ideally they were free, they must submit to restraints which were necessary under the conditions of this world.

¶ I Cor. 2 : 15.

There was one sphere, however, within which the believer might already exercise the full freedom of the Spirit. In his personal life he belonged to Christ, and had the right to approach Christ for himself, and to understand the new revelation as it had come to his own soul. This was not only his right but his duty. If he bound himself to some human leader, accepting as his own the faith of some other man, he had failed in his loyalty to Christ. His religion had worth only in so far as it was his genuine response to the manifestation of God in Christ. Too often we read the New Testament with the later standards of orthodoxy in our minds. Whenever a writer appears to deviate from certain beliefs we assume that he was ignorant of them, or had misconceived them, or had fallen under some misleading influence. But in that early period there were no set standards. Fidelity to the Christian message meant nothing else than that you had formed a conception of it of which you were fully persuaded in your own mind.* The primitive teachers did not travel by a beaten highway, with fences on either side which they were forbidden to cross. They were pioneers, making their own way over the waste, and guided only by the stars. Looking to those changeless verities of the faith they went by different paths, some of which are still in use, while some have now been abandoned. This difference of doctrine was involved in the very idea of Christian liberty.

There were dangers, however, in the primitive attitude which the church was not long in perceiving. For one thing, it was evident that some limit to division must be set if Christianity was to survive, and accomplish its task in the world. The tangle of separate streams had somehow to be brought into a common channel so as to form a river. There was the further danger that men might confuse their own imperfect judgments, and even their

* Rom. 14:5.

fancies and prejudices, with those impulses of the Spirit which they were honestly trying to follow. Paul is acquainted with instances in which actual blasphemies were uttered in what seemed to be a spiritual rapture,[†]—a phenomenon well known to modern psychology. The writer of the First Epistle of John finds it necessary to warn his readers not to believe every spirit, but to try the spirits whether they be of God.[‡] He offers various tests whereby the authentic voice might be distinguished from the false ones. So many abuses arose that in the later church the spiritual manifestations were discontinued, and the principle was laid down that the Spirit was only imparted to those whom the church had regularly ordained as teachers. In this way the belief which had once ensured religious freedom was turned to a contrary purpose. The Spirit was identified with the official church, which thus placed its authority on a basis that none could question. This, in its essentials, has been the position of the church ever since. It is taken for granted that our religion in the course of centuries has been moulded, under divine guidance, into its true and permanent form. Institutions, doctrines, ethics may be capable of improvement, but there is no place for radical change. The work of the Spirit is held to consist, not so much in new revelation, as in the maintenance of a faith which has now been settled. Unity is becoming more and more the conscious aim of the church. For multitudes of Christians it appears more important that they should be agreed than that they should assert their right to freedom.

Nevertheless this right belongs to the substance of the Christian faith. Jesus called on men to enter the Kingdom, in which they were to know God directly, and make his will their own. In becoming Christians they became free personalities, and the church exists for the very purpose of securing them in this liberty.

† I Cor. 12:3.   ‡ I Jn. 4:1.

Other communities require a full submission on the part of their members; the church is the community of the Kingdom, and has failed in its object when its own judgment in any matter is accepted as final. The task laid upon it is to bring men into such fellowship with God that they will look solely to his authority. It is true that the church unites men with one another, but it also keeps them divided, and this, it may be said, is its more important function. The natural human instinct is for all to herd together, every one sinking his own mind in some common mind which thinks and wills instead of him. Out of this mass of identical beings the church tries to make personalities. It aims at impressing on every one that he stands by himself, and is accountable for his own soul, and has access in his own right to God.

In its early days the church acknowledged this individual freedom. The ordinance of baptism by which men joined its communion was at the same time the definite act through which the Spirit was obtained. Henceforth the convert was to live and think under this divine direction. The New Testament is the sacred book of our religion because it comes to us from that time when thought was controlled only by the Spirit. It developed freely, under the power of an inner impulse, and assumed many diverse forms, some of which, when measured by later standards, may appear strange and mistaken. Yet they all had their spring in the vital message of Christianity. Believing in that message the early teachers thought it out with a free mind. They followed no leading but that of the Spirit, and spoke, each in his own language, as the Spirit gave them utterance. Amidst all this difference we may wonder sometimes what has become of the one message, but the difference is itself an essential part of the message. It serves to remind us that Christ called us to liberty. His gospel can mean little unless it comes as a personal revelation, which each man may interpret for himself.

So it was well that the early church allowed room for many divisions. Without them it would have been defeated even in its struggle for unity. If it had been confined from the outset to one presentation of the truth it would have excluded many things that were necessary, and sooner or later would have found itself cramped and fettered. Dissensions were bound to come, and within the limits of a single uniform creed there would have been no means of reconciling them. As it was, the gospel had been variously interpreted, and the church could feel that all sincere opinions might find their place in a larger and more comprehensive faith. This was never forgotten by the New Testament teachers even in the heat of their conflict. They were conscious that however they differed they all possessed the one Spirit, and were somehow working together.

The unity of the church was a dream even in those first days, when the believers were a small company, all of one race and nurtured in the same traditions. In the world-wide church of to-day no true unity is conceivable; and this is no matter for regret. So long as men are moving forward to some ever larger goal, there will be divisions. So long as men are free, they will follow the light within them and refuse to bow to any fixed authority. Division is involved in the very nature of our religion, and this is the truth brought home to us as we study the writings of the New Testament. They are all inspired by the one faith, but every teacher interprets it differently, as he has known it in his own soul. If the unity of the church means anything it must be grounded in Christian liberty. There will be endless differences as each one holds fearlessly to the truth that is in him, but out of this division will come the only unity which is worth our struggle.

INDEX